ENGLISH IN THE MIDDLE AGES

English in the Middle Ages

TIM WILLIAM MACHAN

OXFORD
UNIVERSITY PRESS

OXFORD
UNIVERSITY PRESS

Great Clarendon Street, Oxford ox2 6DP

Oxford University Press is a department of the University of Oxford.
It furthers the University's objective of excellence in research, scholarship,
and education by publishing worldwide in

Oxford New York

Auckland Cape Town Dar es Salaam Hong Kong Karachi
Kuala Lumpur Madrid Melbourne Mexico City Nairobi
New Delhi Shanghai Taipei Toronto

With offices in
Argentina Austria Brazil Chile Czech Republic France Greece
Guatemala Hungary Italy Japan South Korea Poland Portugal
Singapore Switzerland Thailand Turkey Ukraine Vietnam

Oxford is a registered trade mark of Oxford University Press
in the UK and in certain other countries

Published in the United States
by Oxford University Press Inc., New York

A catalogue record for this title
is available from the British Library

Library of Congress Cataloging in Publication Data
(Data applied for)
ISBN 0–19–926268–3
ISBN 0–19–928212–9 (Pbk.)   9780199282128

1 3 5 7 9 10 8 6 4 2

Printed in Great Britain
on acid-free paper by
Biddles Ltd., King's Lynn, Norfolk

For Christine, Charlie, and Tim

Contents

Preface

English in the Middle Ages explores the social meanings, functions, and status of the English language in the late-medieval period. Its concerns are thus medieval in focus and modern in scope, while it is literary in some of the remains it considers but linguistic in its consideration of them. Occupying a kind of grey area between linguistics and medieval studies, the sociolinguistic contextualization of Middle English became of interest to me precisely because my own research and teaching of the past decade have likewise involved both disciplines. During this time I have become acutely aware of the utility, even need, to transcend disciplinary boundaries for the richest appreciation of language in the Middle English period. The first chapter explicitly addresses this issue, but this entire book could be considered to do so implicitly, in the process, I hope, demonstrating the utility of its sociolinguistic methods for understanding medieval language and culture. I similarly have been concerned throughout with detailing the nuances and complexities of language use in the medieval period, and with showing how these nuances distinguish the pragmatics of medieval English from those of the post-medieval period. In this vein, though this is a book on medieval language, I have often drawn on modern examples to counterpoint and complement the sociolinguistic distinctiveness of medieval England.

Intellectually and methodologically, I have benefited greatly from seeing the concerns of linguistics and medieval studies in relation to each other and from hearing students' comments on these same interconnections. My first debt to acknowledge, then, is to the many students who have worked through this book's issues with me: if scholarship enriches the classroom, it is also enriched by it. I am likewise grateful to Marquette University for providing me with these teaching opportunities and also with funds to attend conferences and conduct research vital to the completion of this project.

Numerous scholars have assisted me in one way or another—
by fostering my interest in language, critiquing drafts of this book,
discussing its ideas, or simply inspiring me to go forward with it.
In particular, I would like to thank the following: Milton Bates,
Frederic G. Cassidy, A. N. Doane, A. S. G. Edwards, Edward Fin-
egan, John Fisher, Margaret Laing, Roger Lass, John C. McGal-
liard, A. J. Minnis, Päivi Pahta, Derek Pearsall, Charles Scott, and
Irma Taavitsainen. At Oxford University Press, John Davey and
Peter Ohlin have been helpful, patient, and encouraging.

As conventional as thanking one's family may be, my sentiments in doing so are vigorous, sincere, and inadequately expressed in the dedication. Without their support and joy, I cannot
imagine the time, environment, or inclination that make intellectual work either possible or satisfying.

For non-English works that are published with facing-page
translations, such as those in the Oxford Medieval Texts series,
I have (unless the notes suggest otherwise) quoted these translations. Any other foreign-language translations, such as those from
volumes contained in the Rolls Series, are my own, and I take full
responsibility for any errors in them or elsewhere in this book.

T.W.M.

October 2002

1

The Ecology of Middle English

A language is a population of variants moving through time,
and subject to selection.

Roger Lass[1]

Linguistic history and linguistic inquiry

Textbooks for courses on the development of English often focus on grammatical forms, giving chronological and contextual accounts of phonological innovation, lexical borrowing, and syntactic change. With the evidence of late Old English manuscripts, they demonstrate the levelling of inflectional morphology in the tenth and eleventh centuries, just as early modern rhymes and orthoepist discussions are used to document the phonological changes collectively known as the Great Vowel Shift. If a particular cause for a change or its precise beginning cannot always be determined, it is often possible, drawing on historical knowledge and the regularities of linguistic structure, variation, and transformation, to identify a change's general circumstances, its ordering in relation to other changes, and a general time scheme, sometimes as narrow as a half century, in which it transpired. The changes of the Great Vowel Shift well illustrate this principle. By one widespread if still contested analysis of rhymes and early modern metalinguistic commentary, these changes are judged to

---

[1] Roger Lass, *Historical Linguistics and Language Change* (Cambridge: Cambridge University Press, 1997), 377.

have begun with the rising of the mid-tense vowels /e/ and /o/, a rising that phonologically compelled the diphthongization of the high vowels /i/ and /u/ and allowed for the subsequent rising of low vowels; this shift is thought to be rooted in the sociolinguistic consequences of late-medieval immigration to London, particularly from East Anglia, that brought slightly different phonologies with slightly different social valuations into contact with one another; and traces of this change are understood to indicate that it was occurring already late in the fourteenth century, pervasive in the fifteenth and sixteenth, and completed in the seventeenth.[2]

Typically less prominent in histories of English is the fact that like syntax, phonology, morphology, and lexicon, beliefs about the status of a language—including its social meanings, its uses, and its speakers—have histories, too. They, too, come about in particular sociolinguistic contexts for particular reasons. The nineteenth-century identification of Finnish with Finnish independence is a case in point. In the face of increasing domination by Tsarist Russia, the use of Finnish worked to sustain the ethnic and cultural identity of the Finns precisely because the Finnish language, along with Finnish music, art, and other cultural traditions—emblemized by Elias Lönnrot's efforts to collect the poems of *Kalevala*—was cultivated as an ideological statement in and of itself, one that sought to articulate social and cultural independence in linguistic form. Social vision similarly underlay the nineteenth-century attempts of Ivar Aasen to formulate a Nynorsk, or new Norwegian. At a time of expanding nationalism across Europe and when Norway had emerged from hundreds of years of Danish rule only to remain a dependent of Sweden, Aasen saw in the northern, rural dialects of Norway traces of the Norwegian language that elsewhere had long since assumed characteristics of the Danish used by Norway's ruling class. From these dialects he constructed a language that aspired at once to be a linguistic

---

[2] See e.g. Jeremy J. Smith, *An Historical Study of English: Function, Form and Change* (London: Routledge, 1996), 79–111; and Roger Lass, 'Phonology and Morphology,' in Lass (ed.), *The Cambridge History of the English Language*, iii. *1476–1776* (Cambridge: Cambridge University Press, 1999), 72–85.

atavism and constitute a medium of nationalism, a medium that, even after Norway gained independence from Sweden in 1905, has continued to be the subject of grammatical adjustment and symbolic investment.[3]

Such examples suggest not only that the status of a language has a history but also that, like the history of linguistic forms, this is a history that is sometimes documented and that can be studied. Indeed, the development of sociolinguistics over the past forty years has provided much of the evidence for studying a language's roles in a linguistic repertoire and the means to approach them. Tape recorders, questionnaires, and census data offer concrete information about speakers and their beliefs, which in turn has served as the basis for studies of prestige in language variation, of group identification with a patois, and of responses to the cultural significances embedded in language shift. For English in particular, such analysis has refined thinking on the development and spread of standard written English, on the influential growth of Received Pronunciation, on the social implications of African American Vernacular English, and so forth.

Not coincidentally, all these examples from English and other languages date to the last few hundred years. It was print that led to significant increases in written material and (concomitantly) in literacy across Europe, increases that account for the substantive record on which studies of prestige or linguistic nationalism can be based. And these increases are recent to be sure: England's first press was established by William Caxton around 1476, and even rudimentary skills of reading and writing cannot be said to have been predominant in England and the United States until the nineteenth century. For structural linguistics, this relation between chronology and extant data means that studies of early periods must often rely on extrapolations from a relatively small record; but as long as there is a written document, there is some grammatical evidence, and the rigours of historical and comparative methodology provide well-attested principles by which such

---

[3] Einar Haugen, *Language Conflict and Language Planning: The Case of Modern Norwegian* (Cambridge, Mass.: Harvard University Press, 1966).

extrapolation can proceed. The history of a language's social meanings and functions is made more complicated, since it confronts not only the gaps in the historical record but also the fact that much of the linguistic self-consciousness that motivates individuals to write about sociolinguistic issues seems to be even more recent than the advent of print. If historians of Old English must content themselves with the limited poetry and prose that survive, for example, historians of Anglo-Saxon sociolinguistic practices in some cases have very little evidence at all. While it is reasonable to wonder whether women as opposed to men might have had distinctive Old English usages and beliefs, extant documents provide scant information to decide the matter, and throughout the medieval period the same is true for such topics as attitudes about the speech of children as opposed to that of adults or about the accents of native English speakers when conversing in Welsh or Cornish. Such topics may well have had sociolinguistic reality and speakers may well have had broadly shared opinions on them, but lacking the direct evidence that orthoepists such as John Hart or John Wallis provide for the Great Vowel Shift, analysis of them must remain tentative.

None the less, this is a book about linguistic beliefs and the status of a language, specifically about the status of English in the late-medieval period among those who used or encountered it, whether personally or institutionally. When Bede's Angles, Saxons, and Jutes invaded and conquered the British Isles in the fourth, fifth, and sixth centuries, they did so speaking varieties of a preliterate West Germanic language. These earliest preliterate Anglophones gave no clues that they conceived of themselves as anything but a loose confederation of groups sharing certain cultural traditions, just as they left little indication of the role (if any) that their language played in group definition, including whether they conceived of themselves as speaking the same language, what sociolinguistic functions varieties of the language served, and when they thought any speech or writing had special metalinguistic significance. Fifteen hundred years later, in the present, Anglophonic cultures are primarily textual ones, in which English figures significantly, though variously, in social structure and national self-definition. In modern Anglophonic cultures, indeed, there is often an administrative presumption and cultivation of linguistic and geographical boundaries as coincident; by means of such language rationalization, a common language and its identification with an ethnic or political group facilitate and help to constitute government or social policy.[4] If the structural history of English is one of continuous and gradual loss of inflections, regularization of syntactic ordering, and lexical borrowing from contact languages, then, its conceptual history is one of continuous and gradual transition from the largely unsystematized orality of the Anglo-Saxon period to the primary and well-documented textuality and linguistic rationalization of the modern one. This is the history that produced and institutionalized modern, socially powerful meanings of English.

Increasingly, the most important moment of transition in this conceptual history has been situated in the Middle English period. In Margery Kempe's early fifteenth-century critiques of English society and religion, for example, the English language has been seen to have political significance in and of itself, as a language that both embodies a resistant English community and articulates that community's radical orientation towards orthodox social and religious authority.[5] English has been attributed with similar sociolinguistic significance for both late-medieval mysticism and the heterodox Lollard movement. Here, it is sometimes understood to have helped constitute a distinctive and disruptive vernacular theology whose suppression by the 1407–9 Constitutions of Arundel was linguistic as well as theological: biblical translation was thereby proscribed, as was possession of other English translations dating to John Wyclif's lifetime.[6] An emergent status for English

---

[4] David D. Laitin, *Language Repertoires and State Construction in Africa* (Cambridge: Cambridge University Press, 1992), 3–23.

[5] Lynn Staley, *Margery Kempe's Dissenting Fictions* (University Park, Pa.: Pennsylvania State University Press, 1994). Also see her edition, *The Book of Margery Kempe* (Kalamazoo, Mich.: TEAMS, 1996).

[6] Nicholas Watson, 'Censorship and Cultural Change in Late-Medieval England: Vernacular Theology, the Oxford Translation Debate, and Arundel's Constitutions of 1409,' *Speculum*, 70 (1995), 822–64, and 'Conceptions of the Word: The Mother Tongue and the Incarnation of God,' *New Medieval Literatures*, 1 (1997), 85–124. For

as a community-defining language has likewise been implicated in late-medieval concerns with literary authority. In this case, Middle English works and their prefaces, when approached with postmodern theories of authorship, cultural practice, and social power, have been understood to advance collectively the cause of the idea of vernacular language, literature, and culture in the late-medieval period, to create, in effect, a distinctively Middle English literary criticism.[7]

While in these cases, changes in the status of English have been approached as concomitants to other cultural changes, John Fisher, Thorlac Turville-Petre, and others have argued that linguistic issues have been pre-eminent. Fisher's concern is specific and narrowly defined: the development of standard written English, whose origins he locates in the early fifteenth-century cultivation of Chancery English.[8] This is a significant claim in and of itself, but Turville-Petre attributes even greater consequence to Middle English in the conceptual history of the language. Focusing on several prolific and sometimes difficult writers and works, including Robert of Gloucester, Robert Mannyng, *Cursor Mundi*, and the *South English Legendary*, he argues that early in the fourteenth century a sense of English nationalism and national culture coalesced around an expanding evaluation of the vernacular and an identification of it with English nationhood. Pointing in particular to the ways English figured distinctively in religion, to the increasing production of English national chronicles, and to multilingual manuscripts that putatively arrogate elevated literary status to English, Turville-Petre sees the low social prestige of the vernacular being elevated by a nexus of simplicity, 'lewednesse,'

---

arguments that associate the sociolinguistic significance of the vernacular with literacy, see Peter Biller and Anne Hudson (eds.), *Heresy and Literacy, 1000–1530* (Cambridge: Cambridge University Press, 1994). In Ch. 3, I return to the issue of Lollardy and its implications for English linguistic history.

[7] Jocelyn Wogan-Browne et al. (eds.), *The Idea of the Vernacular: An Anthology of Middle English Literary Theory, 1280–1520* (University Park, Pa.: Pennsylvania State University Press, 1999). Also see Helen Barr, *Socioliterary Practice in Late Medieval England* (Oxford: Oxford University Press, 2001).

[8] Fisher, *The Emergence of Standard English* (Lexington, Ky.: University of Kentucky Press, 1996).

and the perceived virtue of the English language. For Turville-Petre, it is a change in linguistic attitudes that enables other literary, political, and religious transitions: 'The use of English was a precondition of the process of deepening and consolidating the sense of national identity by harnessing the emotive energy of the association between language and nationalism.'[9]

The recent *Cambridge History of Medieval English Literature* extends this line of thinking still further. In this wide-ranging and exemplary collection of papers that will influence approaches to medieval literature for years to come, notions of vernacularity and vernacular English culture function as leitmotifs, recurring ideas that sustain late-medieval culture and thereby unify the collection. The thirteenth-century scribe known as the Tremulous Hand, for instance, is understood to write 'English as the abiding articulation of a realm territorially defined, durable through time, and coherent in its religious, political and cultural interests,' while London's citizenry, in their presumed search for 'an authoritative form of the vernacular,' is judged 'a crucial force in the formation of canonical literature and in the emergence of English as an authorized language.' Chaucer's use of English rather than French, similarly, 'cannot be divorced from the political and ideological contexts (and sometimes contests) in which English acquired cultural prestige and power.'[10] In these ways, the status and social meaning of late-medieval English serve less as hypotheses to be tested than as theoretical prerequisites for the examination of various literary and historical issues in a narrative of vernacular culture's protracted struggle with late-medieval authority in its various guises.

Focusing on belletristic remains and literal meaning, all these critical accounts attribute a variety of innovative and influential

[9] Thorlac Turville-Petre, *England the Nation: Language, Literature, and National Identity, 1290–1340* (Oxford: Clarendon, 1996), 10. Similar arguments appear in several papers in Helen Cooney (ed.), *Nation, Court and Culture* (Dublin: Four Courts Press, 2001). Also see my review of *England the Nation* in the *Journal of English and Germanic Philology*, 96 (1997), 437–9.

[10] David Wallace (ed.), *Cambridge History of Medieval English Literature* (Cambridge: Cambridge University Press, 1999), 75, 298, 283, 581.

significances to English in the Middle Ages: literary trope, instrument of social unrest, form of theological dissent, and manifestation of national identity. As disparate as these accounts may be, they do however share one theoretical orientation. They all, to a greater or lesser extent, make sociolinguistic claims, for they all posit relations between language and social structure that are themselves based on particular understandings of such relations. A vernacular theology or literary criticism, for example, presupposes a stable and clear role for vernacular language at a particular cultural moment, while language rationalization of the sort imagined by Turville-Petre presupposes both this and a metalinguistic discourse framing and furthering the implication of national identity in language. Sociolinguistics is itself a discipline, of course, with its own theoretical principles and practical strategies that sometimes diverge in important ways from those of literary or religious or historical studies in general. From this vantage, which has not figured significantly in any of the discussions I sketched above, the medieval status of English would be not a presupposition or theoretical prerequisite but itself the object of study and interrogation.

Some methodological considerations

This is the particular approach of *English in the Middle Ages*—a sociolinguistic inquiry into the status of English in the late-medieval period: the meanings, reputation, and purposes of both the language in general and some of its varieties in particular. All these issues are interconnected, of course, for if the beliefs of speakers about a language, and the functions they perform with it, accord that language particular status, that status in turn encourages beliefs, justifies functions, and generally produces social meanings for uses (and users) of the language. Necessarily, I touch on several of the political, literary, and religious issues that others have explored so well, but I do so from a different, avowedly socio-linguistic perspective. My focus is not on what use Margery Kempe or John Wyclif (say) made of English but on what sociolinguistic practices underwrote the language's status irrespective of their use of it, and in this way, by beginning with language, my inquiries complement previous thinking on these topics. Since I am above all concerned with the development and use of the social meanings and functions of English, indeed, my only interest in specifically literary or theological issues is in their relation to larger concerns that inform these sociolinguistic practices.

In its modern versions, the status of English varies significantly from one region to another, with historical and social reasons distinguishing the social meanings and functions of English in the United Kingdom from its counterparts in post-colonial regions. Even among post-colonial countries such as Nigeria and India, these meanings and functions vary, as they also do in the areas Braj Kachru has called the Inner Circle—the United States, the United Kingdom, Canada, Australia, and New Zealand.[11] An abstraction of the significance of English in this Inner Circle could be put this way: the language is group-defining, authorizing, and ennobling, a historical vernacular with national and sometimes official status. For any moment in the history of English in England—the point of reference for much of this book—the concerns that would define such a status include the role of the language in England's linguistic repertoire; the relations among and social significances of varieties of English; the extent to which English could serve as a national or ethnic symbol; and the ideological and political implications of the language's uses. The breadth of these concerns has shaped my critical approach to them, for, as I suggest throughout this book, the meanings and functions of a language emerge not from the linguistic or social issues of isolated disciplines (literature, criticism, theology, and so forth) but from a broad sociolinguistic context that Einar Haugen calls the ecology of a language.[12]

---

[11] 'The Second Diaspora of English,' in T. W. Machan and Charles T. Scott (eds.), *English In Its Social Contexts: Essays in Historical Sociolinguistics* (New York: Oxford University Press, 1992), 230–52.

[12] Haugen, *The Ecology of Language*, ed. Anwar S. Dil (Stanford, Calif.: Stanford University Press, 1972).

As conventionally used, ecology refers to analyses of natural systems—to the relations that exist among individual members of a species and between various species coexisting in a particular environment. Transferring this analytic frame to linguistics, Haugen writes of the ecology of a language as the structured, learned, and analysable sociolinguistic relationships that obtain between speakers and the linguistic varieties they use—whether channels, registers, dialects, or distinct languages—in sustaining particular social and even natural environments. Recently, Salikoko Mufwene has usefully expanded this concept by focusing primarily on the grammatical structure of a language, for which ecology serves as a mechanism that accounts for language evolution, especially through language contact, in both creole and genetic developments.[13] As a way to account for the pragmatics of linguistic uses and beliefs, however, Haugen's early formulation of language ecology retains a good deal of explanatory power. Some aspects of a language ecology in this general, pragmatic sense, like some aspects of a biosystem, may remain relatively constant across time, while others may change rapidly and do so in ways that transform other features of the ecology with them. Whether its focus is diachronic or synchronic, an account of the ecology of a natural language such as Middle English, by describing who uses what linguistic varieties under which circumstances and with what social effects, characterizes the relations between a speech community's linguistic repertoire (its registers and varieties) and social practices. These ecological practices, in turn, emerge from and enact the overarching status of a language.

In a model like this, literal statements about the social significance of English and metaphorical treatments of it assume their meaning and representational value from their relation to larger sociolinguistic practices, including historiography, business, education, law, text production, and the functional distribution of languages and varieties. A language's past and future are also relevant, since they allow for a kind of interpretative triangulation:

---

[13] Mufwene, *The Ecology of Language Evolution* (Cambridge: Cambridge University Press, 2001).

if we know what happened structurally and pragmatically before a given moment in a language's history and also what happened afterwards, we gain some additional sense of the moment itself. In this way, my vantage on the status of English in the late-medieval period is indeed theoretically and practically broad, seeking to understand this status within the framework of the language's ecology, which itself must be understood within frameworks of medieval cultural practices and modern linguistic theories.

Clearly, the model of linguistic ecology—whether in Haugen's or Mufwene's formulation—diverges markedly from previous approaches to late-medieval English.[14] While structural linguistics tends to distance the form of a language such as Middle English from its social functions and interpretative criticism tends to subordinate linguistic principles to hermeneutic objectives, Haugen's analysis in particular conceives linguistic form and social process as mutually constitutive, with the meanings of specific utterances or speech acts or varieties emerging from the sociolinguistic contexts that produced them and from the regularities of sociolinguis-

---

[14] Related concepts on which I have profitably drawn are David Burnley's analyses of the 'architecture' of Chaucer's language and Michael Richter's examinations of the social status of Latin. See Burnley, 'The Sheffield Chaucer Textbase: Its Compilation and Uses,' in Ian Lancashire (ed.), *Computer-Based Chaucer Studies* (Toronto: Centre for Computing in the Humanities, 1993), 123–40; and 'On the Architecture of Chaucer's Language,' in Erik Kooper (ed.), *This Noble Craft . . . Proceedings of the Xth Research Symposium of the Dutch and Belgian University Teachers of Old and Middle English and Historical Linguistics, Utrecht, 19–20 January, 1989* (Amsterdam: Rodopi, 1991), 43–57. Also see Richter, *Studies in Medieval Language and Culture* (Dublin: Four Courts Press, 1995); and *Sprache und Gesellschaft im Mittelalter: Untersuchungen zur Mündlichen Kommunikation in England von der Mitte des Elften bis zum Beginn des Vierzehnten Jahrhunderts* (Stuttgart: Anton Hiersemann, 1979). There are in general few sociolinguistic approaches to Middle English language and literature, of which the following may be mentioned: Jeremy J. Smith, 'The Use of English: Language Contact, Dialect Variation, and Written Standardisation during the Middle English Period,' in Machan and Scott (eds.), *English In Its Social Contexts*, 47–68; Suzanne Romaine, *Socio-historical Linguistics: Its Status and Methodology* (Cambridge: Cambridge University Press, 1982); and Jacek Fisiak, 'Sociolinguistics and Middle English: Some Socially Motivated Changes in the History of English,' *Kwartalnik Neofilologiczny*, 24 (1977), 247–59. More generally see Norman Blake (ed.), *The Cambridge History of the English Language*, ii. *1066–1476* (Cambridge: Cambridge University Press, 1992); James Milroy, *Linguistic Variation and Change: On the Historical Sociolinguistics of English* (Oxford: Blackwell, 1992); Dick Leith, *A Social History of English*, 2nd edn. (London: Routledge, 1997); and Smith, *An Historical Study of English*.

tic patterning across time. These contexts need to be reconstructed out of the historical record, and much of this book is devoted to just that end, but the patterning depends (in the first instance) on the Uniformitarian Principle, the axiom on which all varieties of historiography rest.

Roger Lass formulates the most general form of the principle in this way: 'Nothing (no event, sequence of events, constellation of properties, general law) that cannot for some good reason be the case in the present was ever true in the past.'[15] In the grammatical areas that primarily concern Lass, no historical phonology ever could have lacked front vowels, nor could any historical syntax have been utterly random, for modern linguistic theory, reflecting modern linguistic understanding, proscribes such grammars. In principle, there is no reason that the Uniformitarian Principle cannot be extended from such issues of language structure to those of language use. Indeed, Suzanne Romaine inverts this principle and applies it directly to society and language, whereby the Uniformitarian Principle means that 'the linguistic forces which operate today and are observable around us are not unlike those which have operated in the past. Sociolinguistically speaking, this means that there is no reason for claiming that language did not vary in the same patterned ways in the past as it has been observed to do today.'[16] The historical absence of any regional or social variation is thus impossible, as would be the absence of structured borrowing between languages, or of the negotiation of social processes through conversation—all impossible then, whenever then was,

---

[15] *On Explaining Language Change* (Cambridge: Cambridge University Press, 1980), 55. Lass notes that this kind of reasoning 'may be "irrational," in precisely the same sense as everyday induction is; it is not strictly rational (though it may be useful) to believe that constant co-occurrence in the past will be repeated in the future. And if this is so, why should we believe that the present is in some sense a "repetition" of the past? But either we believe this or we give up' (54–5). The whole of Lass's discussion on 45–63 is valuable, as is his further consideration of these issues in *Historical Linguistics and Language Change*, 24–32.

[16] Romaine, *Socio-historical Linguistics*, 122–3. Also see William Labov, *Principles of Linguistic Change*, i. *Internal Factors* (Oxford: Blackwell, 1994), 10–27; and 'On the Use of the Present to Explain the Past,' in Philip Baldi and Ronald N. Werth (eds.), *Readings in Historical Phonology: Chapters in the Theory of Sound Change* (University Park, Pa.: Pennsylvania State University Press, 1978), 275–312.

because they are all impossible now. In any discipline, the Uniformitarian Principle does not preclude novelties; it does, however, guarantee that they will emerge according to type, that is, 'that their differentia will not involve the transgression of other necessary principles.' As Lass observes elsewhere, 'We insist not on the barring of novelty *per se*, but only a guarantee that as far as our current understanding of the world holds, all past novelties are lawful. No leap of faith is necessary to accept any novelty properly generated under these conditions.'[17] By no means, then, does the Uniformitarian Principle require an anachronistic or ethnocentric view that all speech communities are structured in the same fashion; it does not dictate which varieties will be socially advantageous, for example, or that any given vernacular must serve as a national symbol. What it does require is that the social meanings and uses of language conform to historical sociolinguistic regularities, the details of which will evolve from the details of specific language contexts.[18]

For the sociolinguistic status of a dead language such as Middle English, these are devilish details, because if imprecisely applied, the Uniformitarian Principle can lead to the misapplication of modern sociolinguistic concepts. Heuristics and expectations that

[17] Lass, *On Explaining Language Change*, 60, and *Historical Linguistics and Language Change*, 26. I would add only that the absence of a particular grammatical or sociolinguistic feature in a given language or at a particular time does not imply its impossibility. Linguistic theory continues to accommodate large-scale alterations of consonantal phonemes, even if nothing like the phenomena described by the First Consonant Shift are now evident in English; another consonant shift might well begin next week.

[18] Dell Hymes notes that 'The individual speaker of Searle's speech acts is an invalid model for the speech acts of the Ilongot of the Phillippines (as shown in the work of Michelle Rosaldo). It is an enormity to imply that the maxims of Grice, stated as imperatives, should be taken as embedded in the values systems and personality structures of every community in the world, Moslem, Chinese, Eskimo, whatever. . . . Such work on speech acts and conversational implicatures does point to *dimensions* of the use of language that may be universal, in the sense that the system of any community may involve orientation to the dimensions. But the value and weighting given them, the negative or positive attitude taken toward them, their organization, must be inductively discovered' (*Toward Linguistic Competence*, Texas Working Papers in Sociolinguistics, 16 (Austin, Tex.: University of Texas Press, 1982), 22–3). Also see Hymes, *Foundations in Sociolinguistics: An Ethnographic Approach* (Philadelphia: University of Pennsylvania Press, 1974), 148.

we might utilize in reading older linguistic history—heuristics of modern dialectology and expectations about how the vernacular contributes to nationhood—can be the result of more recent developments in linguistic theory and practice, which themselves depend on recent features of government, technology, and education. Inevitably, such heuristics and expectations will materially affect our sense of language in the Middle Ages, and for this reason alone accepting medieval statements about language at face value without considering the discursive practices that enabled them or the ways in which they relate to other language practices can render them more modern in sentiment than they may be. This is a theoretical hazard that I return to at several points in this book.

Another, more practical matter also affects sociolinguistic approaches to dead languages such as Middle English. In the modern period, sociolinguistic variation and meaning can be studied by means of tools such as interviews, matched guise and pronunciation tests, census data, and tape-recorded or videotaped conversations. Each tool can verify and expand evidence from the others, so that conclusions about a particular community's attitudes towards bilingual ballots or African American Vernacular English can be reached with a fair degree of confidence. Yet most of these tools require electronic aids and the location of a speaker in a specific physical and social environment; they may also depend on the statistical thoroughness of modern survey techniques. And this is as much to say that they are inapplicable to the study of historical languages and cultures such as Middle English. Accordingly, we can learn very little about the social semiotics of intonation, pronunciation, and proxemics, and even less about the Middle English speech community in general with the degree of statistical certainty common in modern sociolinguistic studies. We cannot know whether and how the speech of men and women differed absolutely in the late-medieval period, nor can we know how frequently speakers of English and Manx (say) confronted one another and how they communicated when they did.

These difficulties arise for at least three reasons. First, without electronic recordings we have no direct access to the actual (as opposed to reconstructed) sound of spoken Middle English,

Latin, or Old French—the three most prominent languages in the linguistic repertoire of late-medieval England—and I nowhere consider such topics in this book. Second, it is impossible to determine how well extant literary works represent the entirety of what was produced in the Middle Ages. While it is possible to make informed speculation about what was written but has not survived, therefore, the uncertain character of the evidence precludes definitive conclusions about language and society in general.[19] This difficulty, at least, is neither completely debilitating nor insurmountable. As William Labov points out, though historical data are fragmentary and inherently accidental, depending on what chanced to be recorded and what of this record chanced to survive, 'the same accidents give the record its primary advantage as objective evidence—it was not created to prove any point that we might have in mind, or to serve the purposes of some research program that we have set in motion.'[20] Further, the accuracy and thoroughness of modern sociolinguistic data are themselves sometimes illusory. In interviews, some speakers may be more voluble than other, more grammatically or pragmatically representative ones, and some data may be elicited only under specific circumstances not present in an interview.[21] The sociolinguistic interview is itself a culturally situated communicative event that can conflict with the norms of a particular speech community in such a way as to result in severely distorted or partial data reflecting the context of the interview more than unmediated linguistic usage.[22] The difficulties evolving from the fragmentary character of the Middle English corpus are thus relative, and though they may preclude categorical judgements, they do allow directed ones, particularly those that take heed of discursive conventions.

[19] See R. M. Wilson, *The Lost Literature of Medieval England* (London: Methuen, 1952).

[20] Labov, *Principles of Linguistic Change*, 74.

[21] See Ronald Macaulay, *Locating Dialect in Discourse: The Language of Honest Men and Bonnie Lasses in Ayr* (New York: Oxford University Press, 1991), 3–5; and James Milroy, *Linguistic Variation and Change*, especially 27–8 and 53–6.

[22] Charles L. Briggs, *Learning How to Ask: A Sociolinguistic Appraisal of the Role of the Interview in Social Science Research* (Cambridge: Cambridge University Press, 1986).

Such conventions figure in the third factor complicating the study of medieval sociolinguistic practice. As written remains, extant Middle English works clearly do not offer transcriptions of natural speech. Particularly in the case of poetry, Middle English writings are fundamentally rhetorical exercises that are constrained by various social factors and conditioned by medieval discursive practices as well as by strictly sociolinguistic impulses. In some instances, such as in works traditionally considered belletristic, the rhetorical stylizing may owe to the demands of metre or genre. For legal, ecclesiastical, or historical works, traditional expressions, narrative conventions, or ideological imperatives may overlie any genuine spoken usage. In this way, the speech of lower-rank individuals such as millers or women from Bath is not only always a written representation of that speech but also often the work of a fairly narrow social group—male, courtly, and devout—that might well have a vested interest in the putative character and content of this speech.

But the difficulties occasioned by this situation are again only relative. Written or spoken, all language enacts, in M. A. K. Halliday's felicitous phrase, a social semiotics.[23] Legal publications, bank statements, and advertisements may do so rather obviously in the way they fashion social identities and relations, but poetry and fiction participate in the production of social meaning as well. On a purely technical level of grammar and usage, the language of literature is not fundamentally different from the language of daily life, for spoken language is characterized by the presence of the same tropes and rhetorical strategies as literary language and therefore responds to the same kinds of study.[24] The primary differences between literary and daily language lie in the use to

---

[23] Halliday, *Language as Social Semiotic: The Social Interpretation of Language and Meaning* (London: Edward Arnold, 1978).

[24] See, e.g., studies by Monika Fludernik, *The Fictions of Language and the Languages of Fiction: The Linguistic Representation of Speech and Consciousness* (London: Routledge, 1993); Deborah Tannen, *Talking Voices: Repetition, Dialogue, and Imagery in Conversational Discourse* (Cambridge: Cambridge University Press, 1989); and Douglas Biber, *Variation across Speech and Writing* (Cambridge: Cambridge University Press, 1988). Recent criticism on this topic thus rejects the Prague School of Linguistics's claims about the peculiarity of literary language.

which such strategies are put and in the degree to which they are used at all. More importantly for the issues I explore in this book, when utterances, speech acts, or the representation of varieties serve the mimetic aspirations of a work's fictional world, they succeed or fail in accordance with how well they reproduce the linguistic semiotics of the reader's social world. To be recognized as a trial, for instance, even in the chaotic environment of *Alice's Adventures in Wonderland*, a speech event must include speech acts and speaking roles characteristic of a trial, and Alice's trial might therefore serve as a partial model of linguistic activity in historical Victorian courtrooms, just as, more generally, fictional utterances and pragmatics can offer insights into their real-life counterparts.

Beyond this, however, literary language is itself both socially situated and, like other kinds of language, performative of particular social meanings. Roger Fowler has thus argued 'that a novel or a poem is a complexly structured text; that its structural form, by social semiotic processes, constitutes a representation of a world, characterized by activities and states and values; that this text is a communicative interaction between its producer and its consumers, within relevant social and institutional contexts.'[25] By reinscribing, contesting, or bypassing particular social attitudes towards language—by ignoring the presence of bilinguals, for example, or representing characters adhering to traditional roles in traditional speech acts—literature serves as the vehicle for and endorsement of such attitudes. The non-standard language of Huckleberry Finn, thus, ultimately reinforces connections between standard language and conventional social success, while the presence of just one linguistic code in the Heaven, Hell, and Eden of *Paradise Lost* articulates a prelapsarian fantasy of uniform, transparent, and unmediated communication, a fantasy that Milton implicitly endorses throughout the poem and explicitly so at its conclusion.[26]

[25] Fowler, *Linguistic Criticism* (Oxford: Oxford University Press, 1986), 10. Also see his *Literature as Social Discourse: The Practice of Linguistic Criticism* (Bloomington, Ind.: Indiana University Press, 1981).
[26] *Paradise Lost*, XII. 24–62.

For the study of historical linguistic beliefs, functions, and social meanings, there is even an advantage to the written basis of the remains, and this is that a sociolinguistic inquiry based exclusively on written remains avoids the most debilitating factor of any contemporary analysis, the so-called Observer's Paradox that arises from the need to make a systematic study of language in its natural, unstudied state. According to this principle, if language is to be examined in anything resembling laboratory conditions with some control over the possible variables, the observed speakers will necessarily be conscious of the examination and therefore likely, depending on their attitudes towards language and society, to hypercorrect their usage in one direction or another. Inasmuch as their composition has long since been completed, medieval England's written remains clearly cannot be affected in this way—they are impervious to the critical observer, and they were not, to reprise Labov, 'created to prove any point' supporting or contesting a research programme.

The scope of this book

While the difficulties inherent in the nature of written remains prevent a broad sociolinguistic profile of the kind pursued in studies of contemporary cultures, then, they do not preclude recognition of how some language helped to produce some social practices and linguistic beliefs (and vice versa), including the medieval status of English for those who used and interacted with the language. I begin my inquiry with an examination of two royal letters that were written in English and released by Henry III in 1258, using these letters as an opportunity to talk about the many contextual factors that give utterances and codes their social meanings. How, I ask, does the status of a language such as Middle English come into being? In order to understand how such status takes shape in relation to the ecology of a language, Chapter 3 explores the relations between languages, dialects, and nations. Chapter 4 pushes the argument one step further, to consideration of how the status of a language can figure in cultural activity, by looking at two late-medieval poems and their implications for the significance of social and regional variation in Middle English; here, I do offer readings of literary works but only as platforms to talk about larger issues of social practice and the semiotics of language. In the final chapter, I consider the post-medieval history of English for the insights it can provide on the sociolinguistic meanings and practices it replaced. By returning throughout to the ecology of Middle English, I concentrate not on the eventual sociolinguistic history of English but on medieval contextual practice, in which actions or utterances that might retrospectively be seen as crucial to the formation of a modern status of English may have meant and functioned quite differently. In this way, my critical orientation differs fundamentally from that of earlier critics, who argued for the 'triumph' of English in the early modern period, and later ones, who have championed the vernacular's medieval power of dissent.[27] These are diachronic perspectives on a sociolinguistic moment, perspectives that sharply focus change or the seeds of change, while my own view is distinctly synchronic, focusing not what would be but what was.

In calling a language a population of variants moving through time and subject to selection, Lass has in mind grammatical properties, but I would extend his definition to pragmatics and add this: all language also does something socially. Sociolinguistic practices will vary synchronically and change diachronically, but at every moment every piece of language or language activity—whether a chronicle, an edict, an utterance, or a poem—will accomplish some social purpose in accordance with the ecology of the language. To understand the ecology of a historical language, the nuances of these purposes and their contexts become all important, for without them it becomes possible to see the past as the present, to presume sociolinguistic continuity where there might be none. As I will suggest throughout this book, crucial differences exist between the ecologies of Middle and modern or even early modern English, differences that frequently coun-

---

[27] Richard Foster Jones, *The Triumph of the English Language* (London: Oxford University Press, 1953).

terpoint my discussion. In comparison to its medieval predeces-
sor, the modern ecology of English in the United States or the
United Kingdom varies in linguistic repertoire, in the functions
assigned to varieties in this repertoire, in popular access to these
varieties, in the kinds of social practices that language mediates,
in a general sense of what language is and does, and, indeed, in
their respective statuses of English. The dynamics of such differences, in turn, can illuminate the modern as well as the medieval.
By examining the late-medieval status of English as it emerges
from a profile of the relations between language and society in
the English Middle Ages, I therefore hope also to contribute to
understanding of sociolinguistic processes in general, including
the inevitability of variation, the ability of language and linguistic
acts to sustain social institutions and meanings, the naturalized
and unexamined character of many such institutions and meanings, the ideological power of discursive practices, the historical
specificity of language ecologies, and the history of linguistic
beliefs. As variable grammatical and pragmatic populations move
through time, individual selection pressures produce historically
specific linguistic ecologies, among which larger linguistic principles guarantee coherence.

2

The Barons' War and Henry's Letters

Language planning and social meaning

When beliefs about a language come into being, I have suggested, they do so for specific reasons and within specific contexts. In theory, the collective means for producing such beliefs might thus be as numerous and varied as the beliefs themselves. There can be beliefs about the status of a language or the reliability of its speakers, just as beliefs could be produced by educational programmes or legislative fiat. In actuality, the broader the contributing factors for a linguistic belief, the larger the impact of that belief and the more likely that it will endure and significantly transform the ecology in which it figures. A linguistic belief held by an individual is unlikely to affect the ecology of a language, unless that individual is particularly influential, and even then the effects may be limited. As a Soviet gesture, for example, Joseph Stalin was able to impose the Cyrillic alphabet on many of the Republics. But his remained a tenuous notion, despite the institutional ruthlessness with which it could be enforced, and with the demise of the Soviet Union former Republics such as Tartarstan have increasingly rejected the Cyrillic alphabet for the Roman one, in the process actualizing a sociolinguistic vision of their own.[1]

As an individual, Cardinal Richelieu was more successful with realizing his linguistic views, precisely because they emerged

---

[1] 'Tatars to Drop Cyrillic Alphabet for Roman,' *The New York Times*, 31 August 2000, A5.

from sociolinguistic forces already at work. At the beginning of the seventeenth century he saw a general need for the French state to guarantee the security of its members by preventing social disorder. Drawing on the salon tradition of Paris and in a time when French was fast becoming widespread in diplomatic domains, Richelieu also believed that art should aspire to the order of government. It was this social vision, rather than any disinterested view of language, that inspired him to set about establishing the Académie Française, charged with making the grammar, rhetoric, poetics, and dictionary that would provide for language the regulation that government provided for society.[2]

As these examples show, the diversity of factors contributing to the successful or failed institution of a linguistic belief necessarily involves some that are not specifically concerned with language; philosophy, art, and government all played significant roles in Stalin's and Cardinal Richelieu's programmes. They also show that while an individual may have a linguistic belief, the belief takes its shape from institutions, practices, and ideas that are beyond one person's control. In this way, a specific linguistic act—such as imposing an alphabet or creating a language academy—might be best understood not as the simple introduction of a linguistic belief but as its manifestation, as an act that responds to and synthesizes, more or less successfully, broadly operative sociolinguistic practices. By this analysis, beliefs about a language and its social functions—along with the status they impute to a language—have multiple origins, perhaps originally discrete but eventually, if they are to prosper, mutually constitutive.

To understand the status of English in the Middle Ages, I want here to focus on what I consider a single linguistic act—a pair of English letters issued by King Henry III in October of 1258 (see foldout). These appeared at the onset of a seven-year conflict now known as the Barons' War, in which Henry and a diverse group of barons led by Simon de Montfort opposed each other on the issue

---

[2] Robert L. Cooper, *Language Planning and Social Change* (Cambridge: Cambridge University Press, 1989), 3–11. A recent valuable case study of how linguistic attitudes can be imposed and manipulated by political rulers is Geoffrey Lewis, *The Turkish Language Reform: a Catastrophic Success* (Oxford: Oxford University Press, 1999).

send igretinge to alle his holde clerke and ile
heom þet beoþ in chosen þurȝ vs and þurȝ þet
be loande þurȝ þ witeȝte of þan toȝ onen seide
is þes þes stedefasteliche to ailden and suwerien
to þam oðer del of heom alswo alswhuis
þis nenne þis alswo þis one of ȝe to Whoþburs
nelle witeȝe alse þon healden to Michte þan
and witeȝe .d. urnalte us þe heu Re
þis þis Wreȝi del uui from Ace
Bil of Stai e t on Gloucestre and
il a .t. bennt i soh. uf flon con om
of ȝe moȝe.

ober 1258
l City Council).

of the king's freedom to govern and to select his own councillors: Henry demanded complete discretion in these regards, while
the barons insisted that he be answerable to councillors of their
choosing. Any sociolinguistic meaning in Henry's letters would
emerge, as is the case for all linguistic acts, from the ecology that
produced them. In turn, it is the meanings of linguistic acts within
an ecology that collectively bespeak the status of a language. By
examining the various linguistic and non-linguistic determinants
of Henry's letters, then, I hope also to lay open the complex formulation of linguistic beliefs in general and to begin to sketch out
the medieval status of English in particular.

In the first of Henry's letters, dated 18 October 1258, the king
vowed to support decisions reached by his Council. He com-
manded his subjects likewise to abide by these decisions, and,
after stating that anyone who opposed the decree henceforth
would be regarded as a mortal enemy, Henry concluded the brief
missive with the injunction that duly sealed copies of it were to
be lodged in the archives of every county. Two days later, in a
slightly longer but still brief letter, Henry promised swift justice
throughout his realm and directed that sheriffs in particular were
to swear an oath of loyalty and probity. They were to act in a
non-discriminatory way, accept no bribes, employ only reliable
sergeants, and not burden the people of their districts for food
or housing; any sheriffs who violated these and other prohib-
itions were guaranteed immediate punishment, and the powers
of all sheriffs were to be curtailed by a one-year term of office.
Although this letter does not conclude with the notice of archival
publication found in the earlier letter, we do know that it, too, circulated widely, with Matthew Paris and the Dunstable chronicler
alluding to the contents of the second letter in language that parallels the original closely enough to suggest direct knowledge of it.
Additionally, the Burton annalist goes beyond simple allusion to
quote both missives in their entirety, and copies also survive in the
Patent Rolls of Henry III.

Given the letters' historical circumstances, it will become clear,
there is nothing unusual or unprecedented in any of their sentiments. What intimates the convergence of assorted sociolinguistic

factors in the letters and thereby makes them of great importance for understanding the medieval status of English is this peculiar fact. According to the Burton annalist both letters were issued in English as well as Latin and French:

In that time the following letters of the lord king were made by the mutual judgement of the lord king and the community [*communitatis*] and, written in Latin, French, and English, were sent to all the counties throughout the entire realm of England, so that read aloud by the sheriffs in those places, and understood, afterwards these letters would be firmly observed by everyone.[3]

Simply put, these English versions are aberrations in medieval English documentary practice, among the very few official royal documents in English since the days of William the Conqueror and perhaps the last until those of Henry V. And though the documentary remains are rather patchy, they do verify the annalist's claim: for the letter of 18 October, two French and two English texts survive, and for that of 20 October two French texts.[4]

[3] *Annales Monastici*, ed. Henry Richards Luard, RS 36, 5 vols. (London: Longman, 1864–9), i. 453. Also see Matthew Paris, *Chronica Majora*, ed. Henry Richards Luard, RS 57, 7 vols. (London: Longman, 1872–83), v. 720 and *Annales Monastici*, iii. 210. The Liberate Rolls, which detail approved treasury disbursements, may also refer to the October letters, for an entry from 7 November 1258 indicates that Robert de Foleham, an Exchequer clerk, was paid 50 shillings as a 'reward for his labour in composing and writing certain charters in English and French and made by ordinance of the magnates of the king's council, which are being sent through all the counties of England' (*Calendar of the Liberate Rolls Preserved in the Public Record Office*, 6 vols. (London: Her Majesty's Stationery Office, 1916–), iv. 440). M. T. Clanchy, following a suggestion originally made by R. F. Treharne (*The Baronial Plan of Reform, 1258–1263* (Manchester: Manchester University Press, 1932), 120), regards this as a certain reference to the composition of Henry's October letters, and the reference to documents being sent 'through all the counties of England' certainly does recall Henry's letters, but I think this connection is at best a possibility: the Liberate Rolls record dates to nearly three weeks after the letter of 18 October, it makes no mention of Latin versions, it leaves ambiguous whether the English and French charters contain the same (translated) text or are simply charters in English and charters in French (which would be no more linguistically unusual than the October letters), and it nowhere makes an explicit connection to the October letters. See *From Memory to Written Record: England, 1066–1307*, 2nd edn. (Oxford: Blackwell, 1993), 221–3. On the rhetorical relevance of the letters to Henry, see further below.

[4] Copies of both French letters survive in the Patent Rolls and are printed in R. F. Treharne and I. J. Sanders (eds.), *Documents of the Baronial Movement of Reform and Rebellion 1258–67* (Oxford: Clarendon, 1973), 116–22. Versions of the French letters can also be found in the *Annals of Burton* (*Annales Monastici*, i. 455–6 and i.

Like Cardinal Richelieu's creation of the Académie Française, Henry's English letters have increasingly been understood to reflect impulses of linguistic nationalism and thus to mark the emergence of a status for English as a group-defining, presumptively prestigious vernacular. A. J. Ellis, one of the earliest students of Henry's missives, asserts only that the 18 October letter took the form it did because 'to be effective this proclamation had to be made intelligible to the whole community, both gentle and simple, lay and clerical.'[5] As early as 1915, however, O. F. Emerson saw the letters not contextually but in relation to the post-medieval history of English, with the English version portrayed 'as an indication of the coming victory of English.'[6] Bruce Dickins and R. M. Wilson transformed the letters' indication of this victory—the triumph of English, to which I referred in Ch. 1—into their realization of it, describing the first letter in particular as 'the momentary emergence of English as an official language.'[7]

453–5). The second French letter is printed in Walter Waddington Shirley (ed.), *Royal and Other Historical Letters Illustrative of the Reign of Henry III*, RS 27, 2 vols. (London: Longman, 1862–6), ii. 130–2. The printed Patent Rolls of Henry III contain only modern English translations of both French letters; see *Calendar of the Patent Rolls Preserved in the Public Record Office, Henry III, A. D. 1216–1272*, 6 vols. (1901–13; rpt. Nendeln, Liechtenstein: Kraus, 1971), v. 3 and iv. 655–6. English letters for Huntingdonshire and Oxfordshire survive, the former of which is most conveniently available in Alexander J. Ellis, 'On the Only English Proclamation of Henry III.,' 18 October 1258, and Its Treatment by Former Editors and Translators,' *Transactions of the Philological Society* (1868), 1–135; William Stubbs, *Select Charters and Other Illustrations of English Constitutional History from the Earliest Times to the Reign of Edward the First*, 9th edn., ed. H. C. W. Davis (Oxford: Clarendon, 1913), 387–9; Bruce Dickins and R. M. Wilson (eds.), *Early Middle English Texts* (London: Bowes & Bowes, 1956), 7–9; and David Burnley, *The History of the English Language: A Source Book*, 2nd edn. (London: Longman, 2000), 118. Ellis and Stubbs include modern English translations. The Huntingdonshire version, a modern English rendering of it, and a translation of the French letter from 20 October appear in David C. Douglas (gen. ed.), *English Historical Documents*, iii. *1189–1327*, ed. Harry Rothwell (New York: Oxford University Press, 1975), 367–70. The Oxfordshire version (reproduced in this book), which generally differs in only minor details, can be found in Walter W. Skeat, 'The Oxford MS. of the Only English Proclamation of Henry III.,' *Transactions of the Philological Society* (1880–1), 169–78. Ellis and Skeat offer detailed commentary on the philology, codicology, and transmission histories of the two English copies. In this chapter, the English version is quoted from Dickins and Wilson, the French ones from Treharne and Sanders.

  [5] Ellis, 'On the Only English Proclamation of Henry III.,' 7.
  [6] Emerson, *The History of the English Language* (New York: Macmillan, 1915), 78.
  [7] Dickins and Wilson, *Early Middle English Texts*, 7.

More recently, David Burnley has credited the choice of English to the 'political importance' of the letters, 'since competence in English was seen as a distinguishing characteristic between the settled Anglo-Norman barony and the continental French incomers favoured by the king.'[8] And M. T. Clanchy pushes the argument about the letters and the significance they might attribute to English still further, into the written channel in particular. He maintains that no 'satisfactory contemporary explanation is given for issuing these letters in languages other than Latin, but it can be inferred that officials could not be relied upon to have them publicly read in the usual way because the letters were explicitly critical of their own conduct.' Clanchy additionally suggests that the letters may mark 'the precocious beginning of London English as the new written standard.'[9] Even more pointedly, Thorlac Turville-Petre, reading the letters within his argument for the late-medieval sociolinguistic construction of England as a nation, observes that they appropriate the common language of English 'in order to involve a wider section of the population in the political programme of reform.'[10]

---

[8] Burnley, *The History of the English Language*, 114. With the exception of brief comments on dialect or on the general emergence of English in this period, neither Henry's letters in particular nor the Barons' War in general has been discussed by historical linguists. See Robert McCrum, William Cran, and Robert MacNeil, *The Story of English* (London: BBC Books, 1992), 76–7; Jeremy Smith, *An Historical Study of English: Function, Form, and Change* (London: Routledge, 1996), 69; Charles Barber, *The English Language: A Historical Introduction* (Cambridge: Cambridge University Press, 1993), 141; and N. F. Blake, *A History of the English Language* (Hong Kong: Macmillan, 1996), 135.

[9] Clanchy, *From Memory to Written Record: England, 1066–1307*, 221–2.

[10] Turville-Petre, *England the Nation: Language, Literature, and National Identity, 1290–1340* (Oxford: Clarendon, 1996), 9. Citing the Provisions of Oxford and the Barons' War, Begoña Crespo García advances this line of thinking yet again, maintaining that one of the barons' main principles was 'the use of the vernacular, the national tongue, so that the common people could understand the institutional system in which they were immersed. Patriotic ideology connecting society and language was to involve political operations and strategic devices that would promote the emergence of English.' See García, 'Historical Background of Multilingualism and Its Impact on English,' in D. A. Trotter (ed.), *Multilingualism in Later Medieval Britain* (Cambridge: D. S. Brewer, 2000), 25.

In all these readings, Henry's letters reflect or even enact the transformation of English from a sporadically written vernacular used only in private and personal domains to a national, official, or 'standard' language that appropriates the functions and meanings of authorized discourse. These distinctions are important and would all make significant claims about the late-medieval status of English. A 'national' language is one that is recognized as both the common code and symbol of an ethnic or political group, while an 'official' one is a language that has been legally declared the language of a particular area. Categorically distinct from the official/national classification, a standard language (written or spoken) is a variety that has been consciously selected as such, has concomitantly sustained codification and an elaboration of function, and has been accepted as a standard by its users. Historically, vernaculars that have become national, official, or standard have done so not by a single political or literary gesture but (again) as manifestations of linguistic beliefs derived from a convergence of social attitudes, institutions, and identities within a language's ecology, the kind of convergence that sustained the efforts of Cardinal Richelieu, Ivar Aasen, Elias Lönnrot, and other modern language planners.

When Henry III's English letters are judged to represent 'official language' or an appeal to the 'whole community,' they are necessarily supposed to emerge from a linguistic ecology similar to that underlying nineteenth-century linguistic nationalism, the kind of methodological supposition (to which I alluded in Ch. 1) that tacitly transfers modern sociolinguistic expectations to earlier historical periods. My own method is twofold: to situate Henry's letters within their documentary, linguistic, and historical contexts, and thereby to interrogate suppositions about their putative nationalistic impulses. By concentrating on the cultural embeddedness of linguistic activity as brief as Henry's letters, I also suggest how much sociolinguistic contextualization necessarily underlies a proposition such as the medieval status of English. Ultimately, my purpose is not to use historiographic methods to make historical arguments but linguistic and rhetorical ones to offer an interpretation of historical linguistic activity.

The contexts of linguistic status I: Documentary, discursive, political

The important role documents played for Norman and Angevin kings in general and the gradual centralization of government during their reigns were among the strongest influences on the production of Henry's letters.[11] Building on structures and institutions in place during the rule of Edward the Confessor, William I and his successors elaborated programmes of legal and ecclesiastical administration that solidified their rule and began to give shape to England as a political entity. Written language, in the form of wills, charters, laws, and chronicles, was the essential medium for this administration, and though throughout the Middle English period such documents would have had essentially symbolic rather than denotative value for the largely illiterate populace, who could not read them but only perceive their semiotic import, their institutional significance was not the less for this. Within this bureaucratic lineage, the reign of Henry III figures especially prominently.[12] His sense of the power and utility of written language was already apparent when he came of age in 1227, at which time he initiated an examination of charters to verify the lands and liberties claimed by his vassals, and an interest in docu-

---

[11] On the centralizing tendencies of Norman and Angevin government, see Stubbs, *Select Charters*; M. T. Clanchy, *England and Its Rulers 1066–1272: Foreign Lordship and National Identity* (Oxford: Blackwell, 1983); Treharne, *The Baronial Plan of Reform, 1258–1263*; Michael Prestwich, *English Politics in the Thirteenth Century* (New York: St Martin's Press, 1990); W. L. Warren, *The Governance of Norman and Angevin England 1086–1272* (Stanford, Calif.: Stanford University Press, 1987); and Robin Frame, *The Political Development of the British Isles 1100–1400* (Oxford: Oxford University Press, 1990), 72–97.

[12] On the symbolic power of writing in the Middle Ages, see Clanchy, *From Memory to Written Record*; and Brian Stock, *The Implications of Literacy: Written Language and Models of Interpretation in the Eleventh and Twelfth Centuries* (Princeton: Princeton University Press, 1983). On the general bureaucratic complexity (if not always efficiency) of Henry's reign, see E. F. Jacob, *Studies in the Period of Baronial Reform and Rebellion, 1258–67*, Oxford Studies in Social and Legal History, 8, ed. Sir Paul Vinogradoff (1925; rpt. New York: Octagon Books, 1974); F. M. Powicke, *King Henry III and the Lord Edward: The Community of the Realm in the Thirteenth Century*, 2 vols. (Oxford: Clarendon, 1947), i. 84–122; Robert C. Stacey, *Politics, Policy, and Finance under Henry III 1216–1245* (Oxford: Clarendon, 1987); and Richard Mortimer, *Angevin England 1154–1258* (Oxford: Blackwell, 1994), 37–76.

ments remained distinctive of his entire reign.[13] Even allowing for the fact that his 56-year rule gave him far greater opportunity to produce documents than his father, John, who ruled 17 years, or his son Edward, who ruled 35, the sheer mass of written material connected to Henry is staggering. In modern printed editions, the reign of Henry III accounts for: one volume of *post mortem* and other miscellaneous documents; six volumes of patent rolls; one volume of miscellaneous inquisitions; fourteen volumes of close rolls; two volumes of charter rolls; one volume of building accounts; one volume of pleas and assizes; one volume of cases conducted without writ; and two volumes of letters.[14] And I do not here count the Pipe Rolls of the Exchequer and the Plea Rolls of the king's courts—largely unpublished and perhaps as imposing as the Chancery material—nor poems such as the *Song of Lewes* or historical works such as Matthew Paris's *Chronica Majora*, which, however much antipathy they express towards Henry, were for that very reason conditioned by his reign.

Producing many of these documents and the institutions they sustained was a special class of administrators whose very existence both furthered the expansion of written bureaucracy and witnessed its success. As Clanchy describes a situation that occurred, with permutations, on the Continent as well as in England,

The nobility were up against a new type of royal counsellor, who was typically a graduate from a law school and a specialist in finance or record keeping . . . They deprived traditional counsellors of their influ-

---

[13] Sir F. M. Powicke, *The Thirteenth Century 1216–1307*, 2nd edn. (Oxford: Clarendon, 1962), 38.

[14] *Calendar of Inquisitions Post Mortem and Other Analogous Documents Preserved in the Public Record Office*, 12 vols. (1904–38; rpt. Nendeln, Liechtenstein: Kraus, 1973); *Calendar of the Patent Rolls*, 6 vols.; *Calendar of Inquisitions Miscellaneous (Chancery) Preserved in the Public Record Office* (1916; rpt. Nendeln, Liechtenstein: Kraus, 1973); *Close Rolls of the Reign of Henry III Preserved in the Public Record Office*, 14 vols. (1902–38; rpt. Nendeln, Liechtenstein: Kraus, 1970); *Calendar of the Charter Rolls Preserved in the Public Record Office*, 6 vols. (1895; rpt. Nendeln, Liechtenstein: Kraus, 1972); H. M. Colvin (ed.), *Building Accounts of King Henry III* (Oxford: Clarendon, 1971); Doris Mary Stenton (ed.), *Rolls of the Justices in Eyre, Being the Rolls of Pleas and Assizes for Yorkshire 3 Henry III* (London: Bernard Quaritch, 1937); H. G. Richardson and G. O. Sayles (eds.), *Select Cases of Procedure without Writ under Henry III* (London: Bernard Quaritch, 1941); Shirley (ed.), *Royal and Other Historical Letters*, 2 vols.

ence because they were the masters of the bureaucracy through which advanced monarchies such as Frederick II's and Henry III's operated. Decisions no longer had to be made orally at large meetings of counsellors. Instead, little conclaves of experts executed their orders by written instructions to sheriffs and bailiffs in the localities.[15]

In this way, a new bureaucracy ultimately appointed by the king began to vie for influence with traditional, sometimes inherited positions, and government and its administration gradually developed an existence separate from the barons and other nobility whose power and economic reserves had traditionally determined English policy. These old and new traditions existed side-by-side at Oxford, where during Henry's reign a group of teachers unaffiliated with the university operated what might be considered one of England's earliest technical colleges, specializing in the Latin, French, charter writing, and accounting that the new bureaucrats required.[16]

Given the increasing Angevin emphasis on writing, and without meaning to minimize the blood shed between 1258 and 1265, recognition that the Barons' War was to a significant extent a war of words exposes some important underpinnings of Henry's letters and the status of English they embody. This was a war in which both sides were well armed, for while they may have lacked the administrative mechanisms available to the king for the production of written charters and the like, the barons evinced as refined a sense of the potential of documents as did Henry. R. F. Treharne once suggested, indeed, that in several of the letters and proclamations vital to the barons' cause 'we can almost certainly see the expert civil servant at work, advising the reformers how best they might attain their ends, and even suggesting new problems

---

[15] Clanchy, *England and Its Rulers 1066–1272*, 215. Elsewhere Clanchy notes that Robert de Foleham, whom Clanchy regards as the author of the October letters, epitomizes this new, bureaucratic function; he was 'a clerk who had been in the king's service before the civil war and remained so afterwards. Robert is the prime example of the multilingual competence of English administrators at the time, since he must have known Latin to perform his ordinary duties and he probably understood some Hebrew too as he was a justice of the Jews' (*From Memory to Written Record*, 221–2).

[16] Margaret Wade Labarge, *A Baronial Household of the Thirteenth Century* (Totowa, NJ: Barnes & Noble, 1980), 60.

for solution and the means by which they might be solved.'[17] Whether due to baronial influence or simply a fortuitous conflux of sentiments, moreover, the chroniclers were almost uniformly pro-baronial and therefore provided de Montfort and his allies with a textual platform from which they could respond to Henry's documentary salvos.

Without a war of words, in any case, there could have been no Barons' War at all. The 1258 Provisions of Oxford, which imposed a council of fifteen advisers on Henry, was one of the barons' first documentary offensives. Circulated with other pro-baronial documents and repeatedly invoked by king and barons alike, the Provisions served at once as the political constant whose implementation was the measure of all subsequent activity and (therefore) as a symbol of baronial–royal conflict whose meaning became as contested as Henry's administrative policy.[18] In the following October Henry issued the letters that occasion my discussion, while one year later

---

[17] Treharne, *Simon de Montfort and Baronial Reform: Thirteenth-Century Essays,* ed. E. B. Fryde (London: The Hambledon Press, 1986), 179.

[18] J. R. Madicott points out that, strictly speaking, the Provisions of Oxford was not formally published as a document but rather 'took the form of a series of memoranda drawn up by a section of the committee of twenty-four' (*Simon de Montfort* (Cambridge: Cambridge University Press, 1994), 157). Only two copies of these survive—one in the *Annals* of Burton, one in London, British Library MS Cotton Tiberius B.IV—but a seventeenth-century abstract that John Selden made of a roll in Sir Edward Coke's possession implies that a third existed at that time. All three texts were copied with other documents relating to the Barons' War, and much of the collecting was evidently done in June and July of 1258, when the barons and not Henry sat atop Fortune's Wheel. The collections would thus seem to bespeak an attempt to control Henry by controlling the production of documents that validated governmental activities, and in this vein it is important to note that as a group the barons, like many involved in the Peasants' Revolt late in the next century, never sought to eliminate the king or his administration. Rather, from at least 1237 what the barons desired was a share in the government with Henry, and their request of 1244 (repeated in 1248) that the positions of justiciar and chancellor be restored, like their cultivation of pro-baronial documents, declares an aspiration to manage bureaucracy as a means for managing the king. See Richardson and Sayles, 'The Provisions of Oxford: A Forgotten Document and Some Comments,' *Bulletin of the John Rylands Library,* 17 (1933), 291–321. Reference to what was presumably a fourth copy occurs in *Flores Historiarum,* ed. Henry Richards Luard, RS 95, 3 vols. (London: Eyre & Spottiswoode, 1890), ii. 473–4; see Treharne, *The Baronial Plan of Reform, 1258–1263,* iv. As was often the case during the Barons' War, Simon de Montfort is a possible exception here, for he seemed on occasion to have at least entertained the notion of deposing the king and replacing him with his own line. See Maddicott, *Simon de Montfort,* 322.

the Provisions of Westminster revised judicial procedure, codified some of the reforms already underway, and enquired into additional administrative difficulties. In the Treaty of Paris that December, Henry surrendered Normandy, Maine, Anjou, and Poitou to Louis IX of France and thereby brought closure to English–French hostilities, but only after complicated negotiations regarding money that he owed to Simon de Montfort. The following July, by which time Fortune's Wheel had begun to elevate Henry, there appeared a document recording various personal and political accusations that Henry had lodged against de Montfort, while on 13 April 1261 and 25 February 1262 Papal bulls sided with Henry and absolved him of any obligation to comply with the Provisions of Oxford. By the Mise of Amiens on 23 January 1264, Louis IX, Henry's brother-in-law and the man the barons had improbably accepted as a mediator of the conflict, also sided with Henry and pronounced the Provisions null and void.[19] This decision against the baronial party led eventually to a major baronial victory at Lewes that resulted in two more significant documents—the *Song of Lewes*, which commemorated the victory, and the Mise of Lewes, which served as a peace treaty and by which Henry yet again vowed to uphold the Provisions of Oxford and to restore a number of royal castles to the barons. As with every other document associated with the Barons' War, the Mise of Lewes had few lasting effects, inspiring instead still other documents and still other conflicts. On 20 October 1264, thus, the papal legate formally excommunicated and interdicted the baronial opposition, and within a year, after the Battle of Evesham, Simon de Montfort, the symbolic leader of the barons, had been captured and beheaded, and the War itself was over. With the Dictum of Kenilworth, issued in December of 1266, all legal manœuvres and regulations made since the Provisions of Oxford, including those regarding baronial presence on the king's Council, were effectively repealed; constitutionally, the rebellion was thus concluded, even if scattered insurrection continued for some time.

---

[19] Maddicott points out, however, that prior to the Mise of Amiens Louis had at least been favourably disposed towards the barons. See *Simon de Montfort*, 243–4.

Although even a glance at the historical record reveals that this account omits many essential documents, such a summary still sufficiently foregrounds just how important documents were to the conduct of the War. The Provisions of Oxford catalysed succeeding events and served as a reference point for them, while Henry's subsequent proclamations, rallying his loyal troops or acquiescing to the barons' demands, constituted the dynamic that defined the course of events. The Mise of Amiens led to war, just as surely as the Mise of Lewes, in its testimony for the barons' victory, guaranteed that war was not yet finished. All these documents were quite literally speech acts that were answered sometimes by other documents, sometimes by physical force, so that the weapons of the Barons' War, unlike those of the Norman Conquest, were indeed as much words as pickaxes and swords.

Given the importance of this verbal ordnance, and given the importance that documents had in Henry's administration, it might seem incongruous that several of the key documents survive fragmentarily or not at all. While there are two extant copies of the Provisions of Oxford, for example, neither survives in the official Chancery or Exchequer rolls. Moreover, both the copies use Latin only for the opening statements about general reform of the system of sheriffs, and then switch to French for the details of administrative duties specified by the Provisions. The implication would seem to be that memoranda for the meeting of the Council and king were originally, as was customary, taken in French but that only the portion covering administration of the realm in general was translated into Latin because that was the only part meant for broad distribution.[20] Informal French rather than authorized Latin is again the language of the July 1260 document recording charges of sedition levelled against Simon de Montfort and also his responses to them, and it is the language of a document from the spring of 1261 that lists Henry's grievances against the Council and the Council's rebuttals.[21] These are both lengthy and signif-

[20] Treharne, *The Baronial Plan of Reform*, 82; Treharne and Sanders, *Documents of the Baronial Movement*, 96; E. F. Jacob, 'What Were the "Provisions of Oxford"?' *History*, 9 (1924), 188–200.

[21] Treharne and Sanders, *Documents of the Baronial Movement*, 194–210 and 218–38.

icant documents in the fortunes of the baronial and royal parties during these years, as are the 1259 Provisions of Westminster. Yet these Provisions are extant in just five copies, none of which is complete. Further, part of the Provisions of Westminster, the part that contains legal resolutions for the whole of England, survives in authorized Latin enrolled on the Close Rolls, while the part that describes administrative and political resolutions is extant (again) only in French. This linguistic split once more seems to reflect something of the origin and status of these Provisions. Of an initial, informal French draft of the Council's deliberations, only that portion that related to general legal issues merited formal proclamation; the parts of the draft that did not require public announcement were evidently neither translated into Latin nor recorded in the Close or Patent Rolls. As informal and incomplete as some of these records may be, they are still more informative than the Mise of Lewes, of which there are no extant copies.

Henry's letters, emerged, then, from a context in which documents were generally vital but specifically—in relation to the Barons' War—perhaps curiously incomplete. The documents themselves and by extension Henry's letters also drew on discursive traditions that allocated particular functions to particular languages in these documents, the issue to which I now turn. At the time of the Conquest, English had long been established in the domains of charters and government records, but this situation was to change shortly, whether due to William of Normandy's desire to undermine any bases for the last efforts of Anglo-Saxon resistance or simply to the fact that Lanfranc and other Norman prelates had far greater familiarity with Latin than with English.[22] From 1070 to the end of the twelfth century, in any case, Latin so prevailed in official documents in Norman and Angevin England that its use might well be considered one of their conditions of existence.

By the early thirteenth century, however, as the Norman descendants assimilated with the Anglo-Saxon ones and as the power of the barons increased in relation to that of the church and crown, a linguistic gap had opened between this Latin used for official pur-

---

[22] Clanchy, *England and Its Rulers*, 46.

poses and the French and English spoken and read by the nobility. Latin may have marked official discourse, but at a time when the semantic content of documents was beginning to rival their symbolic import, intelligibility demanded, in some cases, translation into French. Thus, Magna Carta, the document by which King John assented to many baronial demands for reform in the judicial and administrative systems, was officially issued in a Latin version. But when it was proclaimed to the barons gathered at Runnymede, this proclamation was almost certainly in Anglo-Norman, as would have been all subsequent proclamations in shire courts, and an Anglo-Norman translation of Magna Carta is in fact extant.[23] In the many documents that survive from Henry III's reign Latin certainly remains dominant, but the presence of sporadic French records before and during the Barons' War points further to the linguistic gap I have noted.[24] The distribution of Latin and French in the Provisions of Oxford and Westminster offers one relief map for the contours of this gap—one that demarcates general and legal concerns from local and administrative ones—and two sets of grievances, one in Latin and another in French, probably datable to March or April of 1261, offer another, similar map. The former would seem to be Henry's official dated complaints to the arbitrators established in March of 1261, while the latter preserves the arbitrators' informal minutes of their meeting.[25]

---

[23] J. C. Holt, *Magna Carta*, 2nd edn. (Cambridge: Cambridge University Press, 1992), 257, 474–7. Cf. Clanchy, *From Memory to Written Record*, 220–1. London, British Library MS Harley 458 offers some confirmatory evidence for changes in the status of French. This is a bifolium that contains Anglo-Norman charters of Stephen and Henry II and also Henry I's Charter of Liberties, which figured prominently in the deliberations surrounding Magna Carta. As Holt points out, such a manuscript seems to be a reference document for baronial consultation and therefore testifies to the language the barons associated with formal proceedings. See further below.

[24] See, e.g., a letter affirming the power of the Council of Twenty-four, from August of 1258, and a document (dated 24 June 1266) pardoning and restoring land to Hugh de Nevill, who had followed Simon de Montfort but then swore allegiance to the king (*Calendar of the Patent Rolls*, iv. 644–5, v. 608–10).

[25] Treharne and Sanders, *Documents of the Baronial Movement*, 212–13; more generally see 210–38. Given this linguistic map of the relations between Latin and French, I think Clanchy exaggerates the functions of French at this period when he explains its appearance in the Provisions of Oxford by saying: 'What had happened was that French had at last achieved literate status for legal purposes' (*From Memory to Written Record*, 208).

English is rather more difficult to locate on this linguistic map. From the beginning of William the Conqueror's reign until the end of Henry II's (1189), only fifty-five royal documents survive that either are bilingual or were issued in both Latin and English; over forty of these date to the Conqueror's reign, and the great majority concerns the granting of land or the confirmation of jurisdictional rights. After William's 1067 writ affirming the validity of laws dating to the reign of Edward the Confessor, evidently no other general legal and administrative proclamations in English are extant until Henry's letters, and no such proclamations survive again until early in the fifteenth century. Beyond these scattered royal uses, English also had limited currency in other prestigious domains, as at Canterbury, where a few charters were recorded in both Latin and English during the reign of Henry II.[26] At Peterborough, English remained prominent in the *Anglo-Saxon Chronicle*, which was kept until 1154, and the copying of Old English manuscripts throughout the twelfth and thirteenth centuries implies at least limited awareness of and competence in the language at that time.[27] But in the light of the sociolinguistic roles of Latin and

[26] David E. Pelteret, *Catalogue of English Post-Conquest Vernacular Documents* (Woodbridge: Boydell, 1990). As Pelteret notes, there almost certainly are other extant English documents after the reign of Henry II, though the terrific volume of thirteenth- and fourteenth-century writing complicates any systematic search. Identification of a few other English charters in this period would in no way undermine either the peculiarities of Henry's letters or the distinctive purposes they served early in the Barons' War. On the Canterbury Charters, see Clanchy, *England and Its Rulers*, 58. Isolated English phrases or sentences also appear in other official (but not royal) documents of the period. See Lionel Stones and Seymour Phillips, 'English in the Public Records: Three Late Thirteenth-Century Examples,' *Nottingham Medieval Studies*, 32 (1988), 196–206. For a brief account of the languages used for law in the Middle Ages, see Sir Frederick Pollock and Frederic William Maitland, *The History of English Law before the Time of Edward I*, 2nd edn., 2 vols. (Cambridge: Cambridge University Press, 1903), i. 80–7.

[27] Christine Franzen, *The Tremulous Hand of Worcester: A Study of Old English in the Thirteenth Century* (Oxford: Clarendon, 1991); and Mary Swan and Elaine M. Trehare (eds.), *Rewriting Old English in the Twelfth Century* (Cambridge: Cambridge University Press, 2000). Even as late as the beginning of the fourteenth century, the Dominican Nicholas Trevet at Oxford evidently could read some Old English, for his commentary on Boethius's *De Consolatione Philosophiae* contains several references to King Alfred's translation. See B. S. Donaghey, 'Nicholas Trevet's Use of King Alfred's Translation of Boethius, and the Dating of His Commentary,' in A. J. Minnis (ed.), *The Medieval Boethius: Studies in the Vernacular Translations of 'De Consolatione Philosophiae'* (Cambridge: Boydell & Brewer, 1987), 1–31.

French, all these uses combined do not delineate a place—much less an expanding place—for English in the powerful and prestigious domains of the late-medieval period.

Outside official domains, other uncertainties enveloped the status of English. From the first 150 years after the Conquest, comparatively little English of any kind survives, and even through the middle of the thirteenth century English remains suggest sporadic and isolated efforts at cultivation—such as those associated with the AB dialect in the south-west or the romances of the north-east Midlands—rather than a coherent and well-defined functional role across all England for what could be called 'English language and literature.' Seth Lerer has in fact argued that the fragmentary character of English writing throughout this period offers a 'collocation of images commensurate with the broken quality of an Anglo-Saxon afterlife' and that within this context early Middle English lyrics both expressed alienation and also located 'the speaking subject in a landscape of displacement.'[28] By its very nature, that is, English of the post-Conquest period both lacked connection with dominant institutions and linguistically mediated the dislocation of itself and its speakers. As heartfelt and potent an emotion as such dislocation may be, however, its contribution to the status of either the language or its speakers is ambiguous, since it is typically social tradition rather than dislocation that renders a language a mediation of national or cultural sentiment. The Finnish language helped to construct nineteenth-century Finnish ethnic identity, for example, precisely because its speakers strove to connect the language to what Lerer calls the cultural landscape and to invest symbolic significance in this connection.

In European consciousness of that time the English had certainly acquired a general reputation as curious and lowly creatures, drinking hard and sporting tails.[29] Moreover, in the twelfth- and thirteenth-century works that do survive, such as *The Owl and*

---

[28] Lerer, 'The Genre of the Grave and the Origins of the Middle English Lyric,' *Modern Language Quarterly*, 58 (1997), 151–2.

[29] Clanchy, *England and Its Rulers*, 248.

the Nightingale or Laȝamon's *Brut*, some nativist sentiments
are expressed, and it's certainly possible to read the alliterative
metre of the latter or the largely Anglo-Saxon vocabulary of both
as forms of ethno-linguistic identification. But those who pinned
a tail on the English did not distinguish Germanic or Gallic
descendants from one another and conceived England's population in general less as a rigid political entity than as a group of
individuals sharing traditions and history. The very dislocation
that Lerer describes, indeed, works against any but the loosest
kinds of association between the English language and ethnic,
cultural, or national identity. Accordingly, the possibility of using
the English language itself to mark thirteenth-century Englishness
is neither topicalized nor demonstrated in *The Owl and the Nightingale* or the *Brut*.[30] Events of the later thirteenth century affirm
these sociolinguistic limitations, for some of the most vocal critics of Henry III and his alleged favouritism of foreigners (including Matthew Paris and the anonymous poet of the *Song of Lewes*)
voiced their criticism not in English but in Latin or French. These
languages, in turn, could little further any specifically English
national consciousness, both because most inhabitants of England were not conversant with them and because by the thirteenth
century French as well as Latin had pan-European implications.
When Henry issued his letters in October 1258, consequently, not
only was English excluded from the domains of the church and
government as well as the communication gap that was opening
between authorized Latin and the conduct of government business in councils, parliament, and the like in French, but it also
lacked the status to mediate English ethnicity, cultural identity,
or political resistance, whereby composition in it could constitute
the kind of ideological statement that Lönnrot's compilation of
Kalevala did.

[30] Laȝamon, of course, concludes the *Brut* before the advent of the Anglo-Saxons,
though the nature of the poem as in part a commentary on Anglo-Saxon England is
everywhere apparent. At the same time, as Daniel Donoghue has pointed out, scholarly
focus on the putative nationalism of the *Brut* is anachronistic exaggeration of the thirteenth-century political situation. See 'Laȝamon's Ambivalence,' *Speculum*, 65 (1990),
537–63.

The contexts of linguistic status II: Language, ethnicity, and the foreigner question

For every English monarch since William the Conqueror, the Continent had represented economic, military, and political opportunities of such consequence as to shape the character of England and English rule. Both William Rufus and his brother and successor Henry I struggled with their brother Robert over the solidification and expansion of Normandy, and when Henry's grandson ascended the throne as Henry II, Anjou also entered the purview of the English crown. Ultimately, the English kings wanted to curtail the power of the French monarchy by expanding in the north, west, and south of modern-day France, but John's loss of the dukedom of Normandy in 1204 concentrated these efforts in the south and west. For Henry III as for his predecessors, acquisition and protection of land in these areas were not acts of mere aggression or avarice but rather attempts to maintain territory they truly believed to be their own; to back down in such circumstances would have invited international ridicule if not French invasion.[31]

Henry III cultivated connections with two Continental groups in particular, the Savoyards and the Poitevins. Most prominent among the former group were relatives and acquaintances of Henry's wife, Eleanor of Provence; among the latter group, who were already a presence in England during the time of King John and his Poitevin wife, Isabella of Angoulême, the most famous (even infamous) representatives were Henry's four half-brothers from Isabella's second husband, Hugh de Lusignan: William, Aymer, Guy, and Geoffrey. In the light of England's historical Continental interests and even disregarding kinship, alliances with the Poitevins and Savoyards offered Henry great strategic advantages. The house of Lusignan controlled land that extended across seven modern French departments—from Poitou eastwards to the Creuse and Vienne river valleys. The connections and geographic position of his wife Eleanor's family in Provence-Savoy

---

[31] Clanchy, *England and Its Rulers*, 231.

made it even more influential. Situated where it was, the family occupied important territory near the junction of modern France, Italy, and Switzerland and could also serve as mediators in relations between England, France, Emperor Frederick II, and the papacy. The Savoyards' relations with the latter were particularly important to Henry, though he also saw them as an opportunity to further his ambition of containing Louis of France from the south and west. Both the Savoyards and the Poitevins, indeed, sent knights to aid Henry in his 1252–4 campaign in Gascony.[32]

This is just the kind of Continental assistance that had been vital to England's interests dating back to the Conquest—even before, if one considers the Norman asylum and aid that Edward the Confessor received. But while the barons thus might have agreed at least in principle to Henry's interest in Anjou, Gascony, Maine, and Poitou, and while many of them had Continental holdings and interests of their own, the king's foreign ambitions proved divisive. It was, for example, a thoroughly Continental matter that immediately precipitated the Provisions of Oxford: following a history of taxes imposed to finance campaigns in Scotland and on the Continent, Henry sought baronial help to pay off Pope Alexander IV, who had promised Sicily to the king's son Edmund.[33] Further, throughout the Barons' War the status of foreigners, particularly the Poitevins, proved increasingly contentious. Before I consider this latter issue in detail, however, I want to put the divisiveness associated with foreigners in Henry's reign into a discursive context of its own. Specifically, just as a tradition of Continental opportunity dated back to the time of the Conquest, so did a tradition that suspected foreign influences and intentions in England.

In the discursive practices of Anglo-Norman historiography, this suspicion emerges in the representation of language contact. Within the context of the Uniformitarian Principle, language con-

---

[32] Powicke, *The Thirteenth Century*, 89; Clanchy, *England and Its Rulers*, 232, and H. W. Ridgeway, 'King Henry III and the "Aliens," 1236–1272,' in R. Coss and S. D. Lloyd (eds.), *Thirteenth Century England* (Woodbridge: Boydell, 1988), ii. 82–3.

[33] Treharne, *The Baronial Plan of Reform*, 50–1, and Powicke, *King Henry III and the Lord Edward*, i. 156–258.

tact among individuals or institutions might be regarded as the inevitable result of the unavoidable movements and interactions associated with commerce, exploration, and war, and contact between French and English was in fact one of the most pervasive and far-reaching consequences of the Conquest. Yet the chroniclers, who were themselves often descendants of foreigners, characteristically associate language contact and the foreign involvement it implies not with the ordinary course of human events but with social divisiveness and preternatural phenomena. This association continues right through Henry's reign, as in the thirteenth-century continuation of John of Worcester's *Chronicle*. There, language contact correlates with religious error when the acquisition of Hebrew leads to apostasy: 'In London, one of the order of preachers (called brother Robert of Reading), an extremely accomplished preacher and someone most learned in Hebrew, apostatized and converted to Judaism. Taking a Jewish wife, he was circumcised and renamed Haggai. When he was speaking boldly and publicly against Christian Law, the king summoned him and committed him to the care of the Archbishop of Canterbury.' A subsequent 'great earthquake, at London and throughout almost all of England' rhetorically projects the dangers of language difference beyond the social into the natural world.[34] In this way, contact between English (or French) and Hebrew undermines the safety of society and the countryside alike.

By this same discursive tradition, language contact evokes the marvellous as well as the dangerous in various supernatural events such as marvels, prophecies, and miracles wherein humans encounter devils or other unearthly creatures and where language serves as one of the mediations of larger spiritual or social differences. Ralph Coggeshall thus relates the story of a bilingual evil spirit named Malekin, who, during the reign of Richard I, haunted the house of Osbern de Bradewelle and in the voice of a

---

[34] John of Worcester, *Florentii Wigorniensis Monachi Chronicon ex Chronicis*, ed. Benjamin Thorpe, 2 vols. (London: Sumptibus Societatis, 1899), ii. 214. For an explanation of why the figure formerly known as Florence of Worcester is now called John of Worcester, see R. Darlington, P. McGurk, and Jennifer Bray (eds. and trans.), *The Chronicle of John of Worcester*, 3 vols. (Oxford: Clarendon, 1995 and 1998), ii.

1-year-old child spoke Latin and English 'according to the idiom of that region.'[35] More benignly, in hagiographic situations sudden ability to speak may correlate with the visionary character of an episode in such a fashion that the marvellous associations of linguistic diversity are twice-told: once in the transformation of an original mute condition, and again in a speaker's newfound multilingualism. A compilation of miracles about St John of Beverly, for instance, recounts how early in the twelfth century when John was visited by Archbishop Gerard of York, a previously deaf and dumb servant suddenly began to speak in both English and French. And another miracle in the collection involves St John and a boy rendered dumb as a consequence of his carefree behaviour; as soon as the boy began to speak again, his father directed him to learn English and French.[36] Language contact similarly marks sanctity for the Anglo-Saxon St Edmund, for when his body was exhumed 'a little sheet of parchment' was found, 'with words thereon written in the English tongue, containing, as is believed, the salutations of Ailwin the monk.' When the body was reinterred near the high altar, Samson, abbot of Bury St Edmunds, ordered that this parchment be joined by another (presumably in Latin) recording that Samson had touched the body of St Edmund in the sight of eighteen monastic witnesses.[37]

In these ways, chroniclers of the eleventh and twelfth centuries intimate the dangers of foreigners by fabricating a world in which all residents of England speak the same language and in which interactions with speakers of other languages could signify an aberrant and disruptive if not other-worldly experience. The chroniclers also correlate threats to social and national security with those who do not speak the language of England—whatever that language may be. The *Anglo-Saxon Chronicle*, accordingly, represents the Francophone Normans as a violent and irreligious

---

[35] Ralph of Coggeshall, *Radulphi de Coggeshall Chronicon anglicanum*, ed. Joseph Stevenson, RS 66 (London: Longman, 1875), 120–1.

[36] R. M. Wilson, 'English and French in England 1100–1300,' *History*, 28 (1943), 58.

[37] Jocelin of Brakelond, *The Chronicle*, ed. and trans. H. E. Butler (London: Thomas Nelsons & Sons, 1949), 115.

peril for England, while in the 1120s William of Malmesbury lamented the fact that Edward the Confessor's vision of an England dominated and debilitated by foreigners had come to pass: 'England has become the habitation of foreigners and the tyranny of aliens. Today there is no English duke, or bishop, or abbot, and strangers of all sorts gnaw away at the wealth and entrails of England. There is no hope that the misery will end.'[38] Later, in 1191, when Richard Cœur de Lion was crusading and his chancellor William Longchamp served as his surrogate, arguments for Longchamp's deposition emphasized his foreign birth, his ignorance of the English language, and the insults he had extended to England. Still later, several chroniclers insisted on John's partiality to foreigners, particularly the Poitevin relations of his wife, Isabella, while Magna Carta specifies actions against foreigners in a number of places, with one clause requiring the dismissal of Tourangeaux bailiffs and another the removal of foreign mercenaries.[39] Similar complaints were made up to the dawn of the Barons' War. Having been chastised for speaking in English, Robert Grosseteste lamented in 1252 that native people were being fleeced by aliens who could not even speak their language. To the chronicler William De Rishanger, such fleecing was serious enough to render foreigners a grave threat to national security:

In those days flourished Aymer (bishop of Winchester), William de Valence (brother of the lord king), Peter of Savoy (uncle of her majesty the queen), and a great many aliens (councillors of the said king) who were more special and preferred than all the inhabitants and natives of the kingdom. With them taking religious and lay alike by surprise in various ways, and immoderately despising the inhabitants of the land,

[38] The *Anglo-Saxon Chronicle* for the year 1083 describes an incident in which the abbot of Glastonbury, unable to control his charges, calls in certain 'frencisce men' who defile the altar with blood and leave three dead and eighteen wounded monks. See Cecily Clark (ed.), *The Peterborough Chronicle, 1070–1154*, 2nd edn. (Oxford: Clarendon, 1970), 7–9. Also see Malmesbury, *De gestis regum Anglorum libri quinque; Historiae novellae libri tres*, ed. William Stubbs, RS 90, 2 vols. (London: Eyre & Spottiswoode, 1887–9), i. 278.

[39] Clanchy, *England and Its Rulers*, 140, 191; *Magna Carta*, clauses 50 and 51. Also see Machan, 'Language and Society in Twelfth-Century England,' in Irma Taavitsainen et al. (eds.), *Placing Middle English in Context: Selected Papers from the Second Middle English Conference* (Berlin: Mouton de Gruyter, 2000), 43–66.

their tyranny occasioned so much harm that no one could be found who could anticipate getting any kind of legal remedy against them when necessity demanded it.[40]

By the time of the Barons' War, then, the Continent had acquired a double-edged history and discursive tradition: foreign ambition and assistance remained vital to England's interests, even as this same ambition and assistance had become political flashpoints, areas that could focus a variety of conflicts. When documents of 1258 represent foreigners as a divisive problem in Henry's reign and make several specific demands to resolve the difficulties associated with them, they necessarily participate in this discursive tradition of foreign suspicion. This criticism takes various forms, but its most basic concern is to claim the pernicious influence of foreigners as a reason for them to be driven from the country for the betterment of all. According to the Tewkesbury annalist, at a London council in April of 1258, Roger Bigod, the earl of Norfolk, led a group of barons and other powerful men before the king, who asked whether they meant to take him captive. '"No lord,"' the earl replied, '"no, my king. But the unbearable Poitevins now held captive and all the aliens should flee from your face and ours, just as from the face of a lion, and glory will be to God in the highest, and peace will be in your land to men of good will."'[41] As early as this meeting, moreover, the nobles made aid for Henry's predicament with the pope contingent on the expulsion of the Lusignans and the subsequent reorganization of the kingdom by native-born men. In a petition the following month, the barons specified both that 'royal castles situated on a harbour, into which ships might sail, should be entrusted to true-born Englishmen, on account of many evident perils which could arise were they entrusted to others,' and 'in the matter of marriages pertaining to the lord king, that the [women] shall not be married

---

[40] Clanchy, *England and Its Rulers*, 222; Ridgeway, 'Foreign Favourites,' 605; D. A. Carpenter, *The Reign of Henry III* (London: The Hambleton Press, 1996), 192–3; Luis Iglesias-Rábade, 'Norman England: A Historical Sociolinguistic Approach,' *Revista canaria de estudios ingleses*, 15 (1987), 104; De Rishanger, *The Chronicle of William de Rishanger, of The Barons' Wars: The Miracles of Simon de Montfort* (London: The Camden Society, 1840), 3.   [41] *Annales Monastici*, i. 164.

in such a way as to disparage them—that is, to men who are not true-born Englishmen.'

A letter from July of that year records that the response to a Lusignan request for reconciliation was another demand for their expulsion:

Answer was given them that since at the beginning they had sworn to provide, together with the others, for the reformation and good of the lord king and the realm, and nevertheless had fled from Oxford such as traitors to the lord king and the community, and as men forsworn, opposing the barons' articles and provisions, no confidence whatsoever could be placed in them; and that therefore it was necessary that they should all leave the kingdom, with all their followers, until the state of the realm should have been reformed, and after that the lord king would make orders for them according to the advice which would be given him.

The Lusignans did in fact leave on 14 July 1258, only to reappear in England in 1261–2 upon Pope Alexander IV's abrogation of the Provisions of Oxford and the reassertion of royal authority.[42] Henry had further exacerbated the situation in April 1260, when he returned to England from France with an army of foreign mercenaries, an inflammatory action that his son Edward duplicated three years later, when he introduced foreign mercenaries on the pretence of fighting Welsh insurgents.[43] From a sociolinguistic perspective the activities of both father and son could easily be accommodated within the discursive tradition of foreign suspicion, which they thereby helped to sustain.

Remaining volatile throughout the period 1258–65, the foreigner question, with its history and the very general way in which it opposed aliens to the native-born, constituted yet another important context for the status of English underlying Henry's letters. When barons and chroniclers foregrounded anti-alien attitudes in the events of 1258, they did so from within a broad and long-developing tradition. Poitevin abuses and the remedies for them were real enough, in other words, but equally real, in tex-

---

[42] Treharne and Sanders, *Documents of the Baronial Movement*, 81, 93, 241–3.
[43] Carpenter, *The Reign of Henry III*, 269–70; Maddicott, *Simon de Montfort*, 223.

tual and conceptual terms, was a sociolinguistic perspective that saw relations with foreigners as a nexus of complex and competing political impulses, a perspective that becomes clear when one considers the fashion in which anti-foreign sentiment became increasingly more detailed and more predominant in accounts written as the Barons' War progressed.

By way of rationales for the Barons' War, these accounts both extend nativist enmity beyond the Poitevins to the Savoyards and foreigners in general and wrongly posit foreign influence as the specific cause of the Provisions of Oxford. Of the Savoyards and Poitevins alike the *Chronicle of Bury St Edmunds* observes, for example, 'wherever they held sway, they behaved unbearably, like tyrants.'[44] The chronicle of Osney Abbey merely records Henry's preference for foreigners—'He loved aliens more than all the English, and he enriched them with countless gifts and valuables'—but to the Waverly chronicler, the vile plans of the many non-localized foreigners included regicide and genocide: 'Already for many years so many aliens, speaking diverse languages, had multiplied in England, enriched by so many gifts, lands, estates, and other goods, that they held the English in the greatest contempt, as if they were inferior. It was revealed by some who knew their secrets that if their power should continue, they would destroy all the more powerful people of England; and once they deprived king Henry of the kingdom, in place of him they would set up someone else according to their own design, and in this way they would at last permanently subjugate all England to their power.'[45] The incorrect representation of the presence of foreigners in England as the primary impetus of the Barons' War appears in several sources, including the anonymous chronicler of St Benet Hulme, John Trokelowe, de Rishanger, the Waverly annalist, and Robert of Gloucester. Other chroniclers, such as the annalists of Tewkesbury and Bury St Edmunds, accelerated anti-

---

[44] *The Chronicle of Bury St. Edmunds, 1212–1301*, ed. and trans. Antonia Gransden (London: Nelson, 1964), 23. As Carpenter makes clear in *The Reign of Henry III*, criticism of the Savoyards, who aided the reactionary interests of Henry's wife, Eleanor, was not without merit.

[45] *Annales Monastici*, iv. 254, ii. 349.

alien sentiment with a different misunderstanding, by projecting to the time of the Provisions of Oxford a later statute mandating expulsion of all foreigners.[46]

Matthew Paris epitomizes this tradition as an evolving one that attributed increasingly greater treachery to foreigners. For him, the Poitevins and Savoyards were engaged in an orgy of acquisition that pitted them against each other as well as against the English: 'With the king's faction thus set against the queen's, the Poitevins against the Provincals, and with all of them frenzied because of their many valuables, they rage against the sleeping English, as if once they eliminated the native inhabitants, they would struggle to determine which of them could earn control of the . . . kingdom.' 'England,' he says elsewhere, 'has indeed been trampled underfoot by aliens,' so much so that in Matthew's historiography aliens serve as a metonymy of the malevolence and deception that threatens to undermine England. At one point in his narrative, Matthew tells of the appearance of a mysterious fleet that arrives from an unidentified but decidedly foreign country. The ships are searched, and weapons and armour are discovered, whereupon the linguistic practices of the sailors confirm their by now obviously hostile intentions: 'And when the English asked who they were, they did not wish to reveal to those in the castle who, why, whence, or wherefore they had come. Nor did anyone from the castle understand their language.' With this anti-foreign sentiment pervading his *Chronica Majora*, Matthew by himself reflects the two false rationales of the Barons' War that the chronicles in general cultivated. Not only does Matthew believe that at the 1258 Oxford Parliament the barons expressly desired the expulsion of foreigners, but also he projects the Savoyard and Poitevin difficulties to foreigners in general. In 1255, he contends, 'The city of London teems not only with Poitevins, Romans, and Provincals, but also with Spanish, who contrive miseries for the

---

[46] Ridgeway, 'King Henry III and the "Aliens,"' 88; De Rishanger, *Chronicle*, 8–9, *Annales Monastici*, ii. 349–50; Gloucester, *The Metrical Chronicle*, ed. William Aldis Wright, RS 86, 2 vols. (London: Spottiswoode, 1887), lines 10987–11005; *Annales Monastici*, i. 174–5; *The Chronicle of Bury St. Edmunds*, 23.

English, especially the citizens of London, by means of adultery, fornication, quarrelling, injury, and murder; and the king not only does not restrain them but protects them.'[47]

Perhaps the most intense and articulate statement of this evolving anti-foreign sentiment comes in the pro-baronial *Song of Lewes*, composed shortly after the barons' victory in 1264. Drawing on biblical paradigms that conceived Simon de Montfort as Christ and the putatively native English as the Israelites striving to flee Egypt, the *Song* points out that Moses, David, and Samuel, unlike Henry, did not install foreigners over native citizens.[48] Henry, consequently, is urged to surround himself with reliable native advisers:

> And the king should have natives
> surrounding him as councillors, as leaders
> of the kingdom, not strangers or favourites,
> who overthrow other people and good customs alike.   (955–8)

The *Song* frequently opposes the native to the foreign and, indeed, conceives the entire conflict of 1258–65 in these terms, extolling the English, who once lay as low as dogs but now stand triumphant over the aliens, and advising these same aliens to return home:

> Foreigners may come, if they are about to depart quickly,
> even instantly, but they may not remain.   (316–17)

What rested in the balance between barons and king, English and aliens, was England itself:

> Because if victory had come to the conquered,
> the living memory of the English would have become
>   worthless.   (415–16)

Without denying that the Poitevins merited a good deal of genuine hostility, I want to suggest that there is something oppor-

[47] Matthew Paris, *Chronica Majora*, v. 352, 357, 426, 531.

[48] Thomas Wright (ed.), *Political Songs of England: From the Reign of John to that of Edward II*, rev. edn., ed. Peter Coss (Cambridge: Cambridge University Press, 1996), lines 345–6, 73–4, 615–18, 747–52. The following three translations from the *Song of Lewes* are my own, not Wright's.

tunistic about this cultivation of generalized anti-foreign sentiment and that this opportunism appears already in accounts of
King John's relations with foreigners—that it is a feature of the
discourse. As in Henry's reign, John's rule witnessed a conflux
between powerful and well-placed foreigners and a contraction of
the land available for grants. Also as in Henry's reign, it was then
possible to exaggerate the wrongs committed by foreigners. J. C.
Holt acknowledges that 'the foreigners were harsh and efficient
administrators, who also exploited office in their own interests.'
'But,' he continues, 'this was true of many sheriffs and bailiffs.
Their iniquities did not depend directly on their nationality.' When
Magna Carta specified the exile of foreign mercenaries and specific individuals such as Gerard d'Athies or Engelard de Cigogné,
consequently, it did so not because foreigners as such were the
barons' primary source of complaint but to deprive John of the aid
of foreigners, who were resented less for their foreignness than
for the king's patronage and their influence.[49] The rhetorical utility and opportunism of the foreigner question also emerges from
the 1216 reissue of Magna Carta, produced shortly after Henry
had been crowned a boy king. Given Henry's age (9), Poitevins
were once again vital to the administration of a state still threatened by a rebellious faction seeking to make Louis IX the King
of England, and the 1216 issue accordingly omits the original
demands for the expulsion of alien administrators and soldiers.[50]

When Matthew Paris likened Henry's relations with his barons
to John's relations with his and then circularly used his critique
of the latter's reign to underwrite his critique of the former's,
his historiography thus reproduced a discourse of convenience,
one that traditionally and reflexively represented foreigners as a
threat to England's cultural and political structures.[51] As in effect
a trope, foreigners invoked notions of immorality, autocracy,
taxation, seizure of property, judicial impropriety, and nearly any
other social wrong. And as a trope, the foreigner question could

[49] Holt, *Magna Carta*, 344–5; Prestwich, *English Politics in the Thirteenth Century*,
81–2.
[50] Holt, *Magna Carta*, 381; also see Powicke, *The Thirteenth Century*, 4–5.
[51] Holt, *Magna Carta*, 402–3.

be strategically extended beyond its narrow application in the royal–baronial conflict. In 1264, thus, Henry's son Edward appropriated the foreigner question by vowing to Gilbert de Clare, earl of Gloucester, that he would urge his father to banish aliens from the Council and henceforth to consult none but native-born Englishmen.[52] The barons could even use the foreigner question to discriminate among themselves, as in a pro-baronial song that describes factionalization within the baronial party and calls on de Montfort and others to unite their forces in pursuit of a common goal. Some of the baronial party, the song notes, have fled back to France, while those that remain quarrel among themselves, with the foreign barons—to the detriment of England—growing stronger than the native-born ones:

> Thus the nation is wasted, the land destroyed;
> a foreign nation grows strong and rises up,
> while the native man grows worthless.[53]

In light of the traditions for talking about aliens, the opportunistic growth of anti-foreign sentiment after 1258 could be understood as a heuristic fostered by the barons (especially Simon de Montfort) for their own advantage. Despite what several chronicles imply, for instance, the demands that all royal advisers be native-born and that all foreigners be exiled do not date to 1258 and the environment that produced the Provisions of Oxford. They appeared, rather, in successive petitions of June, 1263 and followed Edward's February appearance with foreign mercenaries and several weeks of indiscriminate anti-alien hostilities, led by a number of Edward's former confidants who had transferred their allegiance to de Montfort. Indeed, by the summer of 1263, according to the *Flores Historiarum*, the populace hated everyone unable to speak English: 'For whoever could not speak English was commonly vilified and held in contempt.'[54] Written in emotive language asserting that foreigners were never to return ('ulterius non reversuri'), the second petition of 1263 tapped into this

---

[52] Maddicott, *Simon de Montfort*, 334.
[53] Wright, *Political Songs of England*, 122. The translation is my own, not Wright's.
[54] *Flores Historiarum*, ii. 481.

growing apprehension and jeopardy associated with foreigners as a trope, projecting their putative sentiments onto the past, and for this reason the petition would potentially have had resonance not just with the nobility but with all ranks of English society, whether peasants, clergy, merchants, or barons. 'Essentially,' R. A. Carpenter concludes, 'the new clause [about the exile of foreigners] was produced by the actual events of that month. It marked the decision of the Montfortians to sanction and exploit the popular tide of xenophobia in the hope of winning wide support for their cause.'[55] The documentary prominence of these anti-alien provisions in subsequent events testifies for the success of the opportunistic baronial strategy: in a letter patent of July, 1263 Henry explicitly accepted both clauses, which Louis IX in turn paraphrased and obviated in the Mise of Amiens the following January.[56]

That the barons' commitment to the expulsion of foreigners was rhetorical and strategic as well as ideological also appears in their response to Louis and in the Mise of Lewes following their victory. In March of 1264, before the battle, they acceded to all Louis's decisions save the ones to do with the aliens. According to the *Annals of London*, the barons sent a group of bishops as messengers to Henry, 'humbly and devotedly asking the king that if he would yield on one and only one clause—namely that with the aliens expelled from England he would govern by means of the native inhabitants—they would assent to all the statutes, provisions, and arrangements of the French king.'[57] In Carpenter's analysis, 'The statute of 1263 thus became Simon de Montfort's final rallying-point. It was cunningly chosen, for it linked the irreducible minimum of the Provisions of Oxford—some restriction on the King's choice of councillors and ministers—to the popular cry of "down with the aliens." '[58] Yet once they had won

---

[55] Carpenter, *The Reign of Henry III*, 272. Carpenter's entire analysis of these petitions (261–80), which includes Latin texts of both, is valuable and informs my discussion.

[56] Treharne and Sanders, *Documents of the Baronial Movement*, 289.

[57] *Chronicles of the Reigns of Edward I and Edward II*, ed. William Stubbs, RS 76, 2 vols. (London: Longman, 1882–3), i. 61.

[58] Carpenter, *The Reign of Henry III*, 275.

the battle and met in August of 1264 to finalize a resolution, the barons effected a reversal over foreigners similar to that reflected by the 1216 issue of Magna Carta. Perhaps realizing the necessity of some foreigners and the delicate status of some of their own, including Simon de Montfort, they changed their demand, still insisting on the exclusion of foreigners from government, but abandoning their demand that all aliens leave the country.[59]

Equally indicative of the strategic value of anti-foreigner sentiment is the manipulative fashion in which political affiliations could be assigned or claimed against ambiguous ethnic and national boundaries. The familial relations of the principals of the Barons' War are emblematic: Henry's wife was the sister of King Louis IX of France, while Henry's sister was married to Simon de Montfort, whose eldest son was named for the English king. More particularly, for all his interest in Continental affairs and for all his reliance on the foreign advisers at the centre of the political maelstrom of the Barons' War, Henry cultivated more than an affection for the Anglo-Saxon past. He named his sons Edward and Edmund after English saints, he fostered a cult for Edward the Confessor—whom he chose as his patron saint—and he rebuilt Westminster Abbey. Born in Winchester Castle, which he substantially restored during his reign, the king was often called Henry of Winchester and also was the first English monarch since the Conquest to have resided principally in England. All this would seem to have entitled him as much to a pro-English reputation as to a pro-alien one.

Simon de Montfort even more pointedly embodied the ambiguity of nationality, ethnicity, and their social meanings in late-medieval England. On the one hand, de Montfort, self-styled champion of English nativism, held an English earldom, had children born and raised in England, and, though responsible for bringing a number of aliens into England, did not rely as heavily on the counsel of aliens as did King Henry. Further, the earl had been a prominent figure in Henry's campaigns in Gascony, and when Henry's wife Eleanor threatened to invade and recapture control of the country

---

[59] Treharne and Sanders, *Documents of the Baronial Movement*, 299.

late in the summer of 1264, he quickly manipulated nativist senti-ments.[60] But on the other hand, de Montfort was born the son of a French noble in France, almost certainly spoke no English, and throughout the Barons' War repeatedly aligned himself with the Welsh prince Llywelyn ap Gruffudd against Henry. Technically, the petitions of June, 1263 required that de Montfort, along with all the other aliens, be excluded from government and England itself, and there is some indication that he did not always elude the anti-foreign sentiments that he helped to foster at the time.[61] De Montfort's ambiguous ethnic status is well reflected in the exten-sive efforts he took to Anglicize himself through marriage and the English *famuliares* with whom he surrounded himself. The vested interest he had in the barons' demands displays this ambiguity as well. After having been Henry's confidant for several years, the earl initially broke with the king over financial issues involving his wife's dowry, and though at times he was clearly committed to the baronial cause, the degree of his commitment often varied with the progress of his financial negotiations. However much popu-lar sentiment at the end of the thirteenth century transformed de Montfort to the cult-like position of the selfless national hero, self-gain and self-preservation were always implicated in his desire for constitutional reform. And the same could be said of a good many other powerful barons, with the result that if the foreigner question serves as a trope for thirteenth-century political and social conflict, de Montfort's life might well be considered a trope for the contin-gency of ethnicity and nativist leanings in the period.

But the crucial implication of this analysis is not whether Henry or de Montfort might be characterized as the more pri-

---

[60] Arnold Fitz-Thedmar, *De Antiquis Legibus Liber. Cronica Maiorum et Vicecomi-tum Londoniarum et Quedam, que Contingebant Temporibus illis ab Anno MCLXXVIII ad Annum MCCLXXIV*, ed. Thomas Stapleton (1846; rpt. New York: Johnson Reprint Corp., 1968), 67–9; *Annales Monastici*, iii. 233.

[61] Robert of Gloucester's *Metrical Chronicle* narrates that certain 'frensse men' whom Simon had made wardens of castles oppressed the land so severely that by order of Parliament 'iremewed al clene. þe frenssemen were' (lines 11448–56). See further Carpenter, *The Reign of Henry III*, 274 and, for de Monfort's manipulation of anti-for-eign sentiment, 231. Some writers, such as the chronicler of Melrose Abbey, acknow-ledged the irony that de Montfort, a foreigner, should champion the expulsion of other foreigners (Carpenter, *The Reign of Henry III*, 220).

marily sympathetic to the English or to the foreigners. It is, rather, that such sentiments were themselves strategic. Just as twelfth-century chroniclers used the labels 'Norman' and 'English' for specific rhetorical effects and not to reflect clear and conventional national identities, so the king's or baron's claims opportunistically depended on specific circumstances.[62] And like the sociolinguistically subordinate status of English in medieval England's linguistic repertoire, such strategic use of national and ethnic affiliations supports neither the literal claims of medieval comments on ethnicity nor the projection to the Middle Ages of a modern conception of English as unifying and embodying a fixed and well-defined political entity.

Henry's opportunism and the audience of the letters

By 18 October 1258, when he issued his first English letter, Henry III was in desperate straits. Throughout the previous summer, the Council of Fifteen had held jurisdiction over England and its administration, and in a letter patent dated 4 August Henry announced this Council's plan to conduct a formal inquiry of injustices perpetrated in his kingdom. Four knights were to travel to each county to inquire 'by the oaths of trusted and law-worthy men of the county, by whom the facts of the matter can best be elicited, into all excesses, trespasses, and acts of injustice committed in the said county from past times, by no matter what persons, done to anyone whatsoever, and this should cover our justices, sheriffs, and our other bailiffs, and all other persons whatsoever.' These knights were enjoined to bring their findings to Westminster on 6 October. When Parliament met at Westminster on 13 October, five days before Henry's first English letter, the king was about to confront evidence of the moral and administrative failures of his

---

[62] On de Montfort's life, see Maddicott, *Simon de Montfort*. For some account of the miracles associated with him after his death, see Wright, *Political Songs of England*, p. xxix, and de Rishanger, *Chronicle*, 67–110. On the treatment of ethnicity by twelfth-century chroniclers, see John Gillingham, *The English in the Twelfth Century: Imperialism, National Identity and Political Values* (Woodbridge: Boydell, 2000), 123–60.

reign.[63] If Henry's conduct here was at all consistent with how he responded to the barons throughout his reign, he presumably hoped to act in a way that gave the appearance of acquiescence to baronial demands, at the same time it allowed him some measure of freedom and the opportunity to advance his own interests.

The language of the letters would have constituted just such a calculated action, with the significance of English that underwrites them emerging from several mutually constitutive sociolinguistic concerns that I have drawn together: increasing dependence on written language and a centralized bureaucracy, functional allocation of linguistic varieties, foreign expansion, and anti-foreign sentiment. Collectively, such concerns extend the determinants of the letters far beyond literal or disciplinary meanings, defining certain sociolinguistic suppositions and implications and excluding other ones. As I have presumed throughout this chapter, for instance, the speaking subject of the letters is best understood as Henry. Both Ellis and Skeat considered Simon de Montfort to be responsible for the letters' appearance,[64] and at this time, the letter of 4 August seems to suggest, Henry was in fact subject to the Council to some extent. Yet the Burton annalist describes the October missives as 'letters of the lord king,' written at least in part on his initiative, and they are, indeed, royal letters, each beginning (in the French versions), 'Henri, par la grace deu rey de Engleterre.' Given baronial reticence about claiming for the movement anything other than status as a reform, it seems improbable that de Montfort would have appropriated the power effectively to speak in the king's voice in this fashion at this date; it was in fact only after the Battle of Lewes in 1264 that de Montfort began to use the royal seal for letters.[65]

---

[63] Treharne and Sanders, *Documents of the Baronial Movement*, 115, 13.

[64] Ellis, 'On the Only English Proclamation of Henry III,' 8, and Skeat, 'The Oxford MS,' 175. Clanchy is ambiguous on the matter of the letters' authorship, describing them as Henry's but attributing them to Robert de Foleham and regarding their use of English as a baronial expedient. See *From Memory to Written Record*, 222–3.

[65] Maddicott, *Simon de Montfort*, 280–2. In the spring of 1261, however, Henry did complain that he had 'no control over his own seal, but they [the Council] do as they like without the king's knowledge,' though the Council, for its part, maintained that it had never done anything improper with the seal and that Henry did in fact still control it, subject to the Council's oversight. See Treharne and Sanders, *Documents of the Baronial Movement*, 225/227.

Further, in expressing their specific demands the preceding May the barons had used a Latin petition that spoke of Henry in the third person, while a royal letter of March of 1259 that recorded (among other items) the promises of the king's Council to submit to formal review any wrongs it had committed did so in a way that clearly distinguished the Council's words from those of Henry, who speaks in the first person at the beginning of the letter.[66] In a different vein, the barons had the almost universal support of the chroniclers to make their case in writing, and so they did not need the sociolinguistic forum of the October letters. But the strongest argument for Henry's responsibility comes from the anti-foreign sentiment of the time. Ellis felt that de Montfort's putative 'object was to enlist the sympathies of the people on his side against the other foreigners who were of the royal faction.' An English letter written by the barons and attributed to the king surely would have done quite the opposite: to construct the king as speaking pro-baronial notions in the popular language of England would have undermined any attempt by de Montfort to capitalize on traditional discourse in order to render himself as thoroughly English and Henry as sympathetic to aliens.

Whatever the specifics of the letters' appearance—whether the Council issued them on its own or, as I would maintain, with Henry's consultation if not direction—within the social, linguistic, and political contexts of the thirteenth century the October proclamations make good sense as royal letters. This is so not simply because they are delivered by 'Henri . . . rey de Engleterre' but also because to a medieval audience the king would have been the one to benefit the most from their rhetoric. Historically, opposition between the kings and baronial class of England owed significantly to the Angevin programme of governmental centralization, at the heart of which were the documents—the letters, charters, petitions, and writs—that Henry's reign so prolifically produced. Since Henry as much as the barons wanted to forestall civil war, the English, French, and Latin letters of Octo-

---

[66] Treharne and Sanders, *Documents of the Baronial Movement*, 76–91, 130–7. Treharne and Sanders regard both of the October 1258 letters as Henry's (13–14).

ber, 1258—rather than, say, immediate military confrontation—offered a way to further his ambitions that was at once logical and consistent with his administrative practice of using documents to actualize his power. As the barons themselves had evidently recognized, in Angevin England documentation validated government, and by conducting so much of his conflict with the barons in letters, proclamations, and papal bulls, Henry effectively co-opted the conflict and the issues. The barons were thus in a double bind: if they engaged in documentary warfare with the king, they fought on a field that he controlled and was sure to maintain; and if they initiated open conflict, they declared themselves above the law they claimed to want to preserve. It is in this regard, I think, that the casual preparation and poor survival of many key documents besides the October letters make the most sense. To the king, these documents were merely stratagems containing provisional sentiments and not policy statements.

Stratagem, indeed, is an apt word to describe Henry's use of the letters as well as many of his other administrative manœuvres. As a ruler, Henry was both calculating and ineffective, resilient and reactionary, the sort of person a modern popular psychologist might call passive-aggressive. The seven years beginning with 1258 witnessed Henry vacillating between humiliated and despairing acquiescence to baronial demands and, immediately upon acquiescence, concerted effort to circumvent the restrictions he had accepted. He seems to have deeply resented any constraints being placed on his royal will, even as he seems never to have defined for himself just what it was that he wanted, in England or abroad. One of the qualities that kept Henry a viable ruler was this sheer calculation, which is sociolinguistically evident in a letter written from his court in July of 1258. By the evidence of this letter, Henry then understood the rhetorical power of the foreigner question and was able to make good use of it himself, for the letter represents the king initiating the issue as one the barons had resisted. Henry, the letter states, 'has often begged them [barons] that none but Englishmen shall stay around him, and so it will be.' The barons, however, have had difficulty complying with Henry's alleged desire: 'The barons have to make great and difficult arrangements, which cannot be quickly or easily consummated and brought to effect. Soon they will make provision at London, together with the lord king, on many matters touching aliens, both Romans and merchants, money-changers, and others.'[67] The barons' resistance is hereby conceived less ideologically than circumstantially—they and the king alike appear desirous to resolve the foreigner question—but the important rhetorical point is that it is resistance none the less. Henry, this rhetoric implies, is the more upright, for it is he who reminds the barons of the need to contain alien influences.

This letter's early witness to Henry's manipulation of the foreigner question foreshadows the calculation that I have suggested underlies the later proclamations. There is, for example, nothing spontaneous about the English of the 18 October letter, nothing that suggests a sincere attempt to speak to the populace at large in the most widely used vernacular, for the original document was quite clearly composed in French, the language typically used for note-taking, political resolutions, and drafts of public documents. The fact that the English copies are directed to specific counties but the French are not suggests this line of transmission, as do several grammatical features in the letters. Syntactically, 'to halden amanges ȝew ine hord' makes for awkward Middle English but follows logically from 'a demorer la en tresor'; the presence of the second-person pronoun here and elsewhere further distinguishes the Middle English version from the French one, giving it a slightly more colloquial style that is easily understood as an adaptation of the impersonality of law French in a language that had had no legal register since the eleventh century. Twice 'feaus et leaus,' with its look of a legal collocation such as 'clers et lais,' is simply and vaguely rendered by the substantive adjective 'treowe,' while the collocation 'nul u nus' is similarly obscured by the substantive adjectives 'oni oþer onie.' Perhaps most compelling is the English equivalent to French 'Et kil sentre eident a ce fere par meismees tel serment cuntre tutte genz dreit fesant et prenant'—literally, 'And that they, making and holding a right against all people, will aid each other to do that by the very same

---

[67] Ibid. 95/97.

oath.' The English translator misconstrues the participial clause as modifying 'genz' rather than 'il' and thus renders this as 'and þæt æhc oþer helpe þæt for to done bi þan ilche oþe aȝenes all men riȝt for to done and to foangen.'[68] Just as the split between Latin and French in documents such as the Provisions of Westminster reflects the more ephemeral and localized status of the latter, so the stylistic variation between copies of these letters attests to the derivative and even more casual status of the English version.

If the composition of the letters does not advance a claim for the status of English as a national symbol, neither does their audience, which is more easily understood as the baronage than England at large. This was the audience that historically had made and furthered the foreigner question, and also the audience that represented Henry's only real opposition in England at this time. As I have already stressed, there are no indications that the barons ever contemplated a popular overthrow of the king or the monarchy. Consequently, I would argue that when the 18 October letter speaks of the 'rædesmen alle . . . þæt beoþ ichosen þurȝ us and þurȝ þæt loandes folk on vre kuneriche,' it does not posit an audi-

---

[68] Treharne and Sanders advocate 'bribe' as the meaning of *dreit*, presumably on the implications of the subsequent sentence: 'And that none shall take land nor goods in any way which would infringe or impair this provision in any way.' They thus translate the relevant clause as 'against all men who either give or receive a bribe.' There are several problems with this reading. The referent of 'fesant et prenant' is again displaced, while the meaning of *dreit* is stretched. The Töbler-Lommatzsch *Altfranzösisches Wörterbuch* (Berlin: Weidmann, 1925–) does not record this meaning, nor does J.-P. Bourdon et al. (eds.), *Dictionnaire normand–français* (Paris: Conseil international de la langue française, 1993); the word used for 'bribe' in the Provisions of Oxford is in fact *loer*. In the Provisions, further, a similar construction in 'e nus e les nos cuntre tute genz dreit fesant' clearly modifies the clause's subject, as Treharne and Sanders's translation suggests (*Documents of the Baronial Movement*, 102, 100). Ellis offers a tortured justification of the English version and then faults the Burton annalist for confusing matters, when in fact his substitution of *dun* for *dreit* clarifies the sense considerably, even if it also alters it. See Ellis, 'On the Only English Proclamation of Henry III,' 86–7. Clanchy's assertion that whether the original version of the letters was 'Latin or French or English is anybody's guess' is thus disprovable (*From Memory to Written Record*, 221). Common practice dictated that administrative letters like these would be composed in French, while linguistic evidence indicates translation from French to English. Recently, Paul Brand has acknowledged as much but also curiously suggests that the 18 October letter was issued only in French and English (not Latin) and the 20 October letter only in French. See Brand, 'The Languages of the Law in Later Medieval England,' in Trotter (ed.), *Multilingualism in Later Medieval Britain*, 62–76.

ence of commoners who, in Ellis's words, for the first time 'were made to feel that they were worth addressing.' The context of the letters in general and the wording of the French version in particular suggests instead that the reference here is to the political coalition of the barons: 'nostre cunseil . . . ki est eslu par nus ou par la commune de nostre reaume.' Dating back to the previous century, a medieval English *commune*—conceptually and etymologically derived from Latin *communis* and French *comune*—was an alliance such as a municipal corporation in which individuals pledged mutual support. The barons were thus a 'commune' because they constituted a voluntary, self-governing alliance seeking mutual gain and willing to offer mutual aid if need be, an arrangement to which the Bunton annalist points by naming them a 'communitas'. This was in fact their declared status on 12 April 1258, when, even before the barons confronted the king, seven magnates symbolized their enterprise by affixing their seals to a charter of confederation, the word that Matthew Paris uses to describe the baronial opposition.[69] The broader conception that Ellis had in mind—of the 'commons' as the third estate or, even more broadly, as the realm in its entirety—is not recorded in English until the fourteenth century and not itself common until the fifteenth or sixteenth.[70] While Magna Carta certainly did extend liberties across society in an unprecedented fashion, the 'commune' that gave rise to it was also exclusively baronial, as was the dominant orientation of the country it imagined.[71] Like Magna Carta, Henry's letters—indeed, much of the documentation of the Barons' War—made sporadic use of a general notion of England as a realm inhabited by English

[69] This charter is now known only through an eighteenth-century drawing. For a picture and discussion, see Maddicott, *Simon de Montfort*, 152–3. Also see Matthew Paris, *Chronica Majora*, v. 689: 'Meanwhile the most powerful men in England, namely, the dukes of Gloucester, Leicester, and Hereford, as well as the earl Marshall and all the most illustrious men, in order to protect and watch out for themselves, were confederated [sunt confœderati].'

[70] See Clanchy, *England and Its Rulers*, 268; *Oxford English Dictionary*, s.v. 'commons'; *Middle English Dictionary*, s.v. 'commune', sense 3; Tobler-Lommatzsch, *Altfranzösisches Wörterbuch*, s.v. *comune*; *Dictionary of the Middle Ages*, 10 vols., ed. Joseph R. Strayer (New York: Charles Scribner's Sons, 1983), iii. 493; David Nicholas, *The Growth of the Medieval City: From Late Antiquity to the Early Fourteenth Century* (London: Longman, 1997).

[71] Holt, *Magna Carta*, 56–7, 296, and Mortimer, *Angevin England*, 103–4.

people. Further, the peasantry certainly participated in and benefited from the programme of reform, sometimes genuinely so and not simply as a means to baronial gain, particularly after 1263, by which time the reform movement did in fact include various lower ranks of society in the towns and countryside alike.[72] This development, however, represents a clear transformation of what Henry faced in October of 1258.

As with any translation, 'loandes folke' inevitably effects a slight connotative shift from 'la commune,' for Middle English 'folk' in particular can indeed evoke the populace in several ways. But as with Old French *comune*, it can also refer generally to the members of a council or advisory body, as in Chaucer's *Man of Law's Tale*, when the Sultan's mother

> . . . right anon . . . for hir conseil sente,
> And they been come to knowe what she mente.
> And whan assembled was this folk in-feere,
> She sette hire doun, and seyde as ye shal heere.[73]

In effect, like 'tocius regni Anglie' in a baronial petition of the preceding May or 'le commun de Engleterre' in the Provisions of Oxford,[74] 'loandes folk' is thus ambiguous—perhaps purposely so—potentially eliding a distinction between the barons and England at large. The compelling issue here is contextual: the letters negotiated not the rights or character of the realm of England but the relative responsibilities and privileges of the monarch, the bar-

---

[72] On these matters and how they point to an incipient sense of a realm with legal rights for all individuals, irrespective of social rank, see Carpenter, *The Reign of Henry III*, 309–48. More generally, see Jacob, *Studies in the Period of Baronial Reform*, 147–333.

[73] *Canterbury Tales*, ii. 326–9 (Larry D. Benson (ed.), *The Riverside Chaucer*, 3rd edn. (Boston: Houghton Mifflin, 1987)); also see the *Tale of Melibee, Canterbury Tales*, vii. 1008. For the various operative meanings, see the *Middle English Dictionary*, s.v. 'folk,' senses 1a and 2. The *Middle English Dictionary* itself cites 'loandes folk' from the letters as a specific collocation meaning 'the inhabitants of the country' (s.v. 'lond', sense 1b); 'inhabitants' begs the question, however, and in any case only three other passages are cited as comparable.

[74] Treharne and Sanders, *Documents of the Baronial Movement*, 82, 100. I would thus disagree with Turville-Petre's contention that in the phrase 'le commun de Engleterre' the barons expressed 'their concept of a united group of leaders representing the interests of the country as a whole' (*England the Nation*, 5). Matthew Paris also sometimes refers to the whole of the English realm at this time; see *Chronica Majora*, v. 704, 716.

ons, and the sheriffs who administered their wishes. Historically and linguistically, 'loandes folk,' following from 'la commune,' is most comprehensible as a reference to a confederation of discontented individuals from the upper social ranks whose use of the general English populace was demonstrably as opportunistic as Henry's. And even this baronial group was limited, since the support for de Montfort was localized in the southern and eastern Midlands. It is the saintlike altruism attributed to the earl, in fact, that underlies the claim for the pan-English character of the baronial movement, but de Montfort achieved this status only after death. Not until the Parliament of June 1264 could he be said to speak for the country, and within just over a year he and his army would be destroyed by a vastly superior force.

If in 1258 Henry had no nationalistic sentiments for preserving the realm of England, thus, neither did he have any reason to believe that the entire realm would rise up against him. What could happen was that the baronage, with whom he had struggled over this issue for twenty years, could circumscribe the king's powers; the letter of 4 August indicates that it had already done so to some extent. For Henry, with his knowledge of John's acquiescence at Runnymede and after a hundred years of centralizing efforts by his Angevin predecessors, this would have been bad enough. Both baronage and king alike may have publicly declared their shared interests with the populace at large, and both may have invoked this populace as a rhetorical strategy. De Montfort's capitalization on the foreigner question testifies, further, that among the lower social ranks there was some genuine anti-alien sentiment. But with what we today would call constitutional matters at issue, the only combatants to have significant parts in the struggles unfolding between 1258 and 1265—the ones to whom their outcome mattered most—were Henry and the nobility.

Language planning and the status of late-medieval English

Like most instances of language planning, Henry's letters originated in a powerful domain—royal government; they reproduced the ideology of an elite; and they were concerned more with social than linguistic behaviour.[75] On the documentary battlefields of the Barons' War, anti-foreign sentiment constituted one of the strongest and best-tested weapons, ordnance that had proved its efficacy against John and remained a reliable feature of the barons' arsenal. Part of this efficacy lay in the fact that as a weapon the foreigner question had a tradition of manipulation for rhetorical purposes. Whatever the ethnic affiliations of the participants or the governmental issues that they debated, anti-foreign sentiment served as an emotive issue whose very murkiness increased its potency: perhaps like labels of 'liberal,' 'conservative,' 'fundamentalist,' or 'traditional' in the modern world, references to aliens were powerful precisely because they had a history of vitriolic collocation that subsumed and obscured the specifics of any particular application.

Rather than accuse the baronage of pro-alien feelings or defend himself from those same accusations, then, Henry responded to the events of 1258 with situationally unusual language that evoked on his behalf this powerful but vague foreigner question and the antipathies and histories associated with it. Put simply, the English of the letters used the foreigner question to express a loosely constructed sense of Englishness for Henry's benefit. Put with greater sociolinguistic nuance, by speaking in English to an audience of English barons, the king took up the issue that would be the heart of Simon de Montfort's arguments—nativism and its relations to administrative probity—and turned it to his own advantage. In fact, the language of the letters rhetorically manipulated the foreigner question in several ways: it aligned Henry with England and not the France of the Savoyards and Poitevins; it implied his putatively anti-alien inclinations; it summoned the

---

[75] On language planning generally, see Cooper, *Language Planning and Social Change*; Joshua Fishman (ed.), *Advances in Language Planning* (The Hague: Mouton, 1974); Norman Fairclough, *Language and Power* (London: Longman, 1989); James W. Tollefson, *Planning Language, Planning Inequality: Language Policy in the Community* (London: Longman, 1991); Robert Hodge and Gunther Kress, *Language as Ideology*, 2nd edn. (London: Routledge, 1993); and Tove Skutnabb-Kangas and Robert Phillipson (eds.), *Linguistic Human Rights: Overcoming Linguistic Discrimination* (Berlin: Mouton de Gruyter, 1994).

murky but potent spectre of the foreigner question; and it thereby articulated the justness of his cause to the barons. The language thus served as a rhetorical mask to cover what Henry truly sought to defend: his own power. Participating as it does in the discursive traditions of Angevin documentary practice, the functional distribution of languages, and anti-foreign sentiment in medieval England, this is a strategy much different from an attempt to declare and appeal to nationalism by evoking a national language and addressing the country at large. And building on the opportunism inherent in the foreigner question and the period's provisional construction of ethnic identity, this strategy embodies a significance for English that is much more amorphous and much less consequential than one that would render English an authoritative language, ennobling vernacular, or medium of resistance.

From a perspective that contextualizes the October letters as I have, Henry's linguistic act can be judged successful. It is true enough that since Henry never again used English or language planning, the rhetorical potency of the foreigner question remained the barons' alone; until the end of the War the king continued in a posture of defending his right to consult aliens, not of arrogating anti-alien sentiment to himself. But within eight years and with the aid of the pope and Louis IX, the king did extract himself from the limitations imposed on him by the Provisions of Oxford and he did finally eliminate Simon de Montfort as a threat. If Henry's calculated co-opting of the foreigner question as a rhetorical weapon did nothing to forestall imposition of the Provisions of Oxford or prevent the Battle of Lewes, he eventually did find other weapons and other ways to defuse the question, divide the baronial opposition, and reassert his right to govern England by unrestricted will.

Perspectives that see the October letters as emergent 'official' language, appeals to the 'whole community,' attempts to involve the populace at large in political reform, or the 'beginning of London English as the new written standard' are more difficult to maintain and render the letters far less successful or even comprehensible. It is not until well into the seventeenth century (or even the eighteenth) that English can be said to have something like official status—indigenous in powerful domains of business and government, codified, and widespread as the vehicle and subject of education. And even this status would not make seventeenth- or eighteenth-century English technically official. Nor, as I have already argued, do the letters seem directed at an especially wide spectrum of English society. Given their sociolinguistic circumstances, indeed, it is difficult to see how they could be. The status of English within the linguistic repertoire of late-medieval England figures in this regard. Without any recent history of administrative use and without any role in educational, business, or political domains, written English had no implications as the channel for official activities or as a manifestation of government policy; and Henry had no Cardinal Richelieu to cultivate and contextualize these kinds of uses for the vernacular. At the same time, however, neither did English have any implications as a medium for social unrest. The dislocation of what might be called Anglo-Saxon sensibility, the lack of a discourse of protest in English, and the absence of topicalization of vernacular language as a public issue gave the language no history to produce the cultural identity associated with Nynorsk or the nationalistic feelings conveyed by Finnish in the nineteenth century. As the Middle Ages advanced, so did the survival rate for English writing of all genres, suggesting commensurate increases in interest in English and in the institutional means for producing it. Whether and how such increases were ideological depends, however, on the extent to which they mediated educational, financial, political, and other general cultural concerns within the ecology of Middle English. At the time of the Barons' War—at the very least—English figures negligibly in all these connections.

Perhaps the strongest arguments against Henry even conceptualizing—much less actualizing—a nationalistic notion of English in the letters come from the practices by which such notions have typically been implemented. As ubiquitous as the connection between language, linguistic beliefs, and national identity has become in the modern world, this connection remains not intrinsic but contingent and naturalized, a modern framework for approaching modern linguistic phenomena. Most generally, the implementation of beliefs about language as social and governmental policy has been, historically, a Western, post-medieval strategy that Europeans, as with standard languages, have introduced around the world.[76] And this has been the case more particularly because the link between such beliefs and national identity characteristically depends on a constellation of sociolinguistic factors unavailable to other times and cultures, such as the English Middle Ages.

Late-medieval England lacked, for instance, the intellectual and technological currents that carried along the linguistic nationalism in the Norwegian and Finnish examples I have mentioned several times. A key feature of the language planning in these cases was the identification of a language with an ethnic or social group through language rationalization, by means of which, as I noted in the previous chapter, such identification serves as a functional feature of government or social policy. In western Europe, French and Spanish are the earliest languages to be rationalized in this fashion, and this happens only in the sixteenth and seventeenth centuries.[77] As late as the Congress of Vienna in 1815, international treaties typically conceived religion, not language or ethnicity, as the definitive characteristic of a social group; this Congress produced the first international agreement to concentrate on and protect national and, by implication, linguistic minorities.[78] Global acceptance of language's role in the definition of a culture or people would seem to be later still. The United Nations' 1948 Universal Declaration of Human Rights mentions language only in passing, and it is not until the 1996 Universal Declaration of Linguistic Rights that language and its relations to national and

---

[76] On the connections between the concept of a standard language and Western culture, see John Earl Joseph, *Eloquence and Power: The Rise of Language Standards and Standard Languages* (New York: Blackwell, 1987). For historical and contextual reasons such as these, Clanchy's interpretation of 'al on þo ilche worden' at the conclusion of the 18 October letter as an 'obvious' implication that 'a uniform orthography was adopted in every county's copy' is highly doubtful if not untenable. See *From Memory to Written Record*, 222.

[77] David D. Laitin, *Language Repertoires and State Construction in Africa* (Cambridge: Cambridge University Press, 1992), 3–23.

[78] Tove Skutnabb-Kangas and Robert Phillipson, 'Linguistic Human Rights, Past and Present,' in eid. (eds.), *Linguistic Human Rights*, 74–9.

ethnic identity were formally (if not universally) recognized as fundamental human civil rights.

In the aftermath of the Congress and under the impetus of the nineteenth century's twin emphases on romanticism and nationalism, Ivar Aasen and Elias Lönnrot thus framed their plans within a political context that generally (if not rigorously) sanctioned the sociolinguistic identifications they sought to make. As linguists, further, Aasen and Lönnrot thought and wrote with the assistance of the neo-grammarian tradition. In less than a century since Sir William Jones's pioneering work on Sanskrit and the hypothetical reconstruction of Indo-European, the neo-grammarians had made terrific advances in comparative and descriptive studies and had thrust linguistics to the forefront of academic disciplines, legitimizing the vernacular as a focus of intellectual endeavours and rendering its ideological potential tangible to the public at large. And if the neo-grammarians had made language study a science that mediated nationalistic impulses across Europe, rising literacy rates, lower printing costs, and increased availability of schooling provided the technology and institutions necessary to implement new thinking on language. Without these means of dissemination—none of which was available in the English Middle Ages—all Aasen's and Lönnrot's linguistic ideas would have come to naught.

Henry's letters were as contextually determined as Aasen's and Lönnrot's efforts, but the contexts that gave them meaning differed radically from those that enable connections between language and national identity in the modern world. No language planning for English preceded Henry's letters, and none would follow them for some time. Management of Chancery English implies a kind of corpus planning, but the first English grammars and rhetorics appear only in the sixteenth and seventeenth centuries. As for status planning, while the church engaged in it as early as the 1407 Constitutions of Arundel and while Henry V's exclusive use of English in royal letters after 1417 implied it, the sixteenth century and such provisions as the 1536 Act of Union of England and Wales again inaugurate the practice as government policy. Without the notion of the general immanence of language in national identity or of established roles for English in the definition of medieval England, English could neither construct nor symbolize culture and nationhood in the ways Nynorsk has in Norway, Finnish in Finland, or, for that matter, English itself now does in the United Kingdom and the United States.

The very ideas of 'nationhood' and 'nation' that underwrite much modern language planning, indeed, are doubtfully applicable to England in the Middle Ages. When contemporary laws and schools have proscribed or privileged particular languages in the national self-interest, they have done so perhaps as opportunistically as the foreigner question demonized aliens but from a distinctively different perspective with distinctively different objectives. In the former case, in the United States for example, courts and schools have sustained a legal status for language as a means for at once the inculcation of patriotic values and the curtailment of the dangerous social instability sometimes attributed to parochial schooling, immigration, and religious and ethnic diversity; the restriction of non-English languages has thereby putatively served as a forge for national unity, good citizenship, and safety alike.[79] At the time of the foreigner question, however, English had neither legal status nor a demonstrated role in the transmission of cultural and political sentiments that were presumed to be the foundation of national identity. Nor were English and the foreigner question implicated in the issues of social diversity or citizenship that English has mediated in the United

[79] Such efforts have often focused on efforts to designate English as the official language of the United States, on which see: Dennis Baron, *The English-Only Question: An Official Language for Americans?* (New Haven: Yale University Press, 1990); James Crawford, *Hold Your Tongue: Bilingualism and the Politics of 'English Only'* (Reading, Mass.: Addison-Wesley, 1992) and *Language Loyalties: A Source Book on the Official English Controversy* (Chicago: University of Chicago Press, 1992); William G. Ross, *Forging New Freedoms: Nativism, Education, and the Constitution, 1917–1927* (Lincoln, Nebr.: University of Nebraska Press, 1994); Raymond Tatalovich, *Nativism Reborn? The Official English Language Movement and the American States* (Lexington, Ky.: University Press of Kentucky, 1995); and Shirley Brice Heath and Frederick Mandabach, 'Language Status Decisions and the Law in the United States,' in Cobarrubias and Fishman (eds.), *Progress in Language Planning: International Perspectives* (Berlin: Mouton, 1983), 87–105. On the role of English in the formation of early American identity, see Christopher Looby, *Voicing America: Language, Literary Form, and the Origins of the United States* (Chicago: University of Chicago Press, 1996).

States. What focused the foreigner question during the Barons' War was less the broad preservation of national safety than the barons' desire to check the king's power and thereby protect their own influence and wealth.

My discussion of Henry's letters affirms a view that individual acts, whether of rulers, governments, or educators, are often not the most significant factors for the construction of linguistic beliefs, sociolinguistic meanings, and the status they project for a language. Of greater impact are the cumulative effects of speech communities across the social spectrum, effects that can, however, find their nexus in a single linguistic act such as the issuance of a letter. Or, as R. L. Cooper puts the matter, 'Symbols are created not by legislation but by history. Irish and Kiswahili are not national symbols because the Irish and Tanzanian constitutions proclaim them as national languages. They are national symbols because of their association and identification with their national liberation movements and with their citizens' shared memory.'[80] A conceptualization of English as a mediation of nationalism and ethnicity, as naturalized as it has become today, could not lie behind Henry's letters because, unlike the efforts of Aasen, Lönnrot, or adherents of the movements to designate English the official language of the United States today, they could not draw on the kinds of discursive traditions, institutions, and technologies that enable such thinking. As I suggest throughout this book, in fact, during the whole of the Middle Ages and not just the thirteenth century, there was no sociolinguistic history to sustain significance for English as a broadly national symbol or to foster a shared memory of its meaning. For these same reasons, Henry's letters should not be regarded as portents of the linguistic future, either of a modern status of English or of the language's eventual use in powerful domains such as government and education. The rhetorical and linguistic opportunism that produced Henry's letters were as distinctively medieval as subsequent technological, institutional, and cultural transformations of the ecology of English were not.

[80] Cooper, *Language Planning and Social Change*, 103.

3

Language, Dialect, Nation

Variation and significance

In expressing the late-medieval status of English, Henry III's letters were shaped by processes as diverse as the role of documents
in governmental practice, the functional distribution of languages
in the period, and the dynamics of what I have called the foreigner
question. Rather than the creation of a single political gesture or
of an individual discipline's tropes, this status developed from a
complex sociolinguistic nexus of institutions and cultural activities, some of which (at least superficially) would seem to have
had little to do with language as such and none of which involved
change from above in the areas (such as belletristic writing) most
overtly concerned with language. Within this kind of nexus,
Henry's English letters cannot be said to reflect or even initiate a
conception of English as ennobling vernacular, medium of resistance, or group-defining mediation of nationalism; the opportunism of his letters, indeed, suggests that such a conception would
be a long time coming for English. In this chapter I take another
approach to the medieval status of English by shifting my inquiry
from the construction of linguistic beliefs to the ways in which
they convey meaning. If Middle English was not a group-defining mediation of nationalism, I ask, what role did it play within
the linguistic repertoire of late-medieval England? How were its
social meanings formed in relation to other languages?

The Uniformitarian Principle and its explanation of historical
consistencies provide one way to approach such questions. By a

sociolinguistic application of this Principle, a natural language that never had any individual or institutional contact with other natural languages would be unusual (if not strictly impossible), since languages come into contact whenever speakers move about. Even more unusual—in fact truly improbable or impossible—would be a language that displayed no social or regional variation. Indeed, because of ordinary linguistic processes such as acquisition and because language so readily serves as what Halliday calls a social semiotic—as a means to encode social disparities in age, class, education, and so forth—the language of even an isolated monoglot community will necessarily embody synchronic variation. The British Isles of the late-medieval period, which were by no means monoglot anyway, certainly embodied a good deal of such variation. By itself, the Uniformitarian Principle offers only a general framework for approaching these linguistic phenomena. While it does predict language contact and variation among the languages in contact, it cannot predict the precise social significance of such contact and variation—whether multilingualism (say) will be strongly identified with religion or economic success, whether language planning will serve as a nationalistic strategy, whether a specific regional variety will correlate with specific social status, or whether linguistic variation will in fact correlate at all with social variation. The Uniformitarian Principle cannot make such predictions, because as the outgrowths of particular sociolinguistic situations these strategies and features are fundamentally contingent on historical circumstances. The degree of contact speakers of different varieties have with one another, the extent to which speakers notice one another's variations in speech, the discursive practices by which varieties are represented, the potential interplay between variety and social class, education, or employability—these are all contextual products of other social institutions and attitudes. All languages may vary both structurally and pragmatically, but they do not all vary in the same ways.

To extend my discussion from the development of linguistic beliefs to their meaning—and specifically to the status of English in the late-medieval period—I need to consider both the role of English within the linguistic repertoire of the period (its relations to Latin and French in particular) and also the relative status among varieties of English.[1] Discursive conventions, which shape all meta-linguistic utterances, inevitably figure in both issues, for when we talk about language—as when medieval chroniclers talked about foreigners—our utterances are not decontextualized, value-free observations but very much the products of specific metalinguistic traditions. To be sure, such metalinguistic awareness may still have some sociolinguistic verisimilitude. To talk about Standard American English, for example, may be to participate in a tradition that wrongly conceives this particular variety as invariable, accentless, and inherently superior to other varieties of English in the United States. None the less, Standard American English also refers to a loosely defined variety of educated, largely northern, speech that dominates national government, the media, and education. Rather than accept metalinguistic utterances at face value, then, I am interested in exploring the rhetorical and institutional conventions that make them possible and in which they convey meaning.

Truisms, diglossia, and discursive practices

The linguistic truisms of the English Middle Ages, which I briefly described in the previous chapter, are easily stated. Though lack-

---

[1] In this chapter I am not concerned with the several Celtic languages that were spoken in late-medieval England as the birth languages of thriving monoglot populations: Cornish in the south-west, Welsh in Wales, Gaelic in Scotland, and Irish in Ireland. Norse speakers remained in the Shetland and Orkney Islands, and though a Flemish-speaking colony in Wales probably shifted to Welsh or English by the end of the thirteenth century, Flemish was among several languages spoken by immigrant merchants in London, including Italian, German, and Dutch. See R. I. Page, 'How Long Did the Scandinavian Language Survive in England? The Epigraphical Evidence,' in Peter Clemoes and Kathleen Hughes (eds.), *England Before the Conquest: Studies in Primary Sources Presented to Dorothy Whitelock* (Cambridge: Cambridge University Press, 1971), 165–81; M. L. Samuels, 'The Great Scandinavian Belt,' in Margaret Laing (ed.), *Middle English Dialectology: Essays on Some Principles and Problems* (Aberdeen: Aberdeen University Press, 1989), 106–22; Austin Lane Poole, *From Domesday Book to Magna Carta 1087–1216*, 2nd edn. (Oxford: Clarendon, 1955), 88, 290; M. T. Clanchy, *From Memory to Written Record: England, 1066–1307*, 2nd edn. (Oxford: Blackwell, 1993), 201–2. I take the title of this chapter from the same title of an article by Einar Haugen that is reprinted in Anwar S. Dil (ed.), *The Ecology of Language* (Stanford, Calif.: Stanford University Press, 1972), 237–54.

ing a native speaker for nearly a millennium and greatly restricted
in its domains, Latin was widely read, written, and, in monasteries
and schools, even spoken; it was the dominant written language
in ecclesiastical and many civil activities, including theology, science, philosophy, and law. French was a similarly widely used language with similar restrictions among its users. The descendants of
the original Norman monoglots had mostly shifted to English by
the late twelfth century, but the resurgence of French immigration
during Henry III's reign and the fourteenth-century cultivation of
French literature and manners rendered the language a continual
marker of the aristocracy.[2] Despite its persistent minority status, it
was spoken by the most powerful civil, social, and ecclesiastical
individuals in post-Conquest England, who thereby guaranteed a
long, if limited, history for French in the government, church, and
court. And English was the region's majority language, the only
language of most of its perhaps four million inhabitants. Lacking
traditions in all the areas dominated by Latin and French, however, English was the ephemeral language of daily transactions, a
language with a developing literary record and an abundance of
native, monoglot speakers but without status or purpose allocated
to it in any of the sociolinguistically powerful domains. Given
the limitations of vernacular literacy, indeed, for the population at
large English remained a largely oral language.

Such distribution of languages means that the linguistic ecology
of early medieval England was structurally diglossic, a situation
in which two (or more) linguistic varieties coexist in functionally
specialized and complementary ways: the high variety (Latin or
French in medieval England) is used in prestigious and authoritative domains, and the low variety (Middle English) appears
in domestic and casual ones.[3] This functional distribution was
already well-established in the twelfth century, when both Gerald

[2] Judith A. Green, *The Aristocracy of Norman England* (Cambridge: Cambridge
University Press, 1997), 13–15.

[3] For brief introductions to the phenomenon of diglossia, see R. A. Hudson, *Socio-
linguistics*, 2nd edn. (Cambridge: Cambridge University Press, 1996), 53–5; Ralph
Fasold, *The Sociolinguistics of Society* (Oxford: Blackwell, 1984), 34–60; and Suzanne
Romaine, *Bilingualism*, 2nd edn. (Oxford: Blackwell, 1995), 33–8.

of Wales and William of Malmesbury associated serious, learned writing primarily with Latin.[4] At that time, Latin was also specified as the language used by papal legates and the pope himself when expounding the gospel,[5] though a prelate such as Odo, abbot of Battle, could, if need be, modulate his speech into the two other codes in order of prestige: 'In explaining divine scripture and in his treatises—whatever the matter he took up, whether he was writing or preaching in Latin or French or often, for the instruction of the ignorant mass, in the mother tongue—he was so lucid, so eloquent, and so agreeable to all, that what seemed obscure and not clarified by the doctors of old he made clear and very plain.'[6] In the extreme case of Samson, abbot of Bury St Edmunds, such modulation became desirable rather than simply possible. When a certain Herbert protested his appointment as prior on the grounds that he did not 'know how to preach a sermon in Chapter,' Samson,

for his consolation and (as it would seem) to the prejudice of the literate, replied at length, saying that he could easily commit to memory the sermons of others and inwardly digest them as others did; and he condemned rhetorical ornament and verbal embellishments and elaborate general reflections in a sermon, saying that in many churches sermons are preached before the Convent in French or better still in English, for the edification of morals and not for the display of literary learning.[7]

Samson's liberality is predicated, of course, on general recognition that rhetorical ornament and Latin are in fact characteristic of just the kind of preaching Herbert unsuccessfully sought to avoid. This same association of Latin with the domains of rhetoric, theology, and education remained constant throughout the Middle English period, prominently appearing two hundred years later in

[4] Gerald of Wales, *Expugnatio Hibernica: The Conquest of Ireland*, ed. and trans. A. B. Scott and F. X. Martin (Dublin: Royal Irish Academy, 1978), 264–5; William of Malmesbury, *De Gestis Regum Anglorum Libri Quinque; Historiae Novellae Libri Tres*, ed. William Stubbs, RS 90, 2 vols. (London: Eyre & Spottiswoode, 1887–9), i. 1–3.

[5] William of Malmesbury, *The Historia Novella*, ed. and trans. K. R. Potter (London: Thomas Nelson & Sons, 1955), 29; Orderic Vitalis, *The Ecclesiastical History of Orderic Vitalis*, ed. and trans. Marjorie Chibnall, 6 vols. (Oxford: Clarendon, 1969–80), vi. 255.

[6] *The Chronicle of Battle Abbey*, ed. and trans. Eleanor Searle (Oxford: Clarendon, 1980), 307/9.

[7] Jocelin of Brakelond, *The Chronicle*, ed. and trans. H. E. Butler (London: Thomas Nelson & Sons, 1949), 128.

Langland's *Piers Plowman*, wherein ignorance of Latin in effect defines 'lewed' men, just as knowledge of it defines the learned:

> *Ignis deuorabit tabernacula eorum qui libenter*
> *accipiunt munera & c.*
> Among þise lettrede lordes þis latyn amounteþ
> That fir shal falle & forbrenne at þe laste
> The hous and þe hom of hem þat desireþ
> Yiftes or yeresyeues bycause of hire Offices.   (III. 96–100)[8]

Beyond simply being the language of ignorance, however, English is depicted in *Piers Plowman* as grammatically unable to represent truth in the way Latin does. In Passus XV, for example, Patience uses Latin to define poverty, at which the simple Haukyn objects:

> 'I kan noȝt construe . . . ye moste kenne me þis on englissh.'
> 'Al þis in englissh,' quod Pacience, 'it is wel hard to expounen.'
> (XIV. 277–8)[9]

Functionally situated between Latin and English, French—or rather knowledge of French—remained the most distinctive sociolinguistic marker of social rank throughout the period I am considering, though its status did change in significant ways, far more so than did Latin's. Throughout the eleventh and well into the twelfth century French maintained its role in medieval England's linguistic repertoire by virtue of the fact that it was the primary, birth language of the original Normans and their descendants. The chronicler Gerald of Wales attests to this sociolinguistic marker when he narrates an encounter between Henry II and a strange ascetic on Easter morning at Cardiff. As Henry leaves the church, the man uses English to admonish him that so long as the king prohibits markets and work on Sundays, he will be prosperous. Henry in turn uses French to ask a knight, Philip de Mercros, to enquire of the man whether he had dreamt what he foretold. Here, the peasant knows only English, the king only French, and the

---

[8] All quotations are from William Langland, *Piers Plowman: The B Version*, ed. George Kane and E. Talbot Donaldson, rev. edn. (Berkeley and Los Angeles: University of California Press, 1988). I do not here include diacritics indicating emendation or the expansion of an abbreviation. Also see XV. 119 and XV. 319.

[9] Cf. IV. 143–5, X. 460–1, XV. 28, XV. 56, XIX. 327–8.

knight both languages.[10] Following the twelfth-century shift of Francophones to English—whether as monoglots or bilinguals—and the next century's resurgent interest in French during the reign of Henry III, the late thirteenth century witnessed the elevation of the status and prestige of French in various forums: the cultivation of French literature, the introduction of the language to law courts and practices, and the production of French grammars and language aids such as Walter of Bibbesworth's *Tretiz*.[11] By the fourteenth century, French's role in the linguistic repertoire of England had shifted yet again, then including this developing Anglo-French, with its own distinctive grammar and pragmatics, alongside the Continental French that continued to be brought to England via literature, diplomacy, and business.[12]

The force of diglossia lies not simply in the coexistence of several languages, however their roles may change over time, but in the dynamics between these languages and the social tasks they perform in business, government, education, and so forth. Beyond any literal reference, an utterance in or command of a given language, by virtue of the language itself, can maintain or challenge any number of social relations. In the late-medieval period, for instance, the multilingualism of individuals helped sustain the hierarchical structure of English society, since those commanding several languages were characteristically educated, upper-rank individuals who administered social and religious institutions.

---

[10] Gerald of Wales, *Expugnatio Hibernica*, 111–13.

[11] Evidence of the twelfth-century amalgamation of the Anglo-Normans and the native English has recently become overwhelming and has been widely discussed. See e.g. William Rothwell, 'A quelle époque a-t-on cessé de parler français en Angleterre?' in *Mélanges de Philologie Romane offerts à Charles Camproux*, ed. Robert Lafont et al., 2 vols. (Montpellier: Université Paul-Valéry, 1978), ii. 1075–89, and 'The Role of French in Thirteenth-Century England,' *Bulletin of the John Rylands Library*, 58 (1976), 445–66; and Ian Short, '*Tam Angli quam Franci*: Self-Definition in Anglo-Norman England,' in Christopher Harper-Bill (ed.), *Anglo-Norman Studies*, 18 (Woodbridge: Boydell, 1996), 153–75. French was not employed regularly in English law courts and practices until well into the thirteenth century, though there are some indications of sporadic use already in the twelfth century. On this latter point see Paul Brand, 'The Languages of the Law in Later Medieval England,' in D. A. Trotter (ed.), *Multilingualism in Later Medieval Britain* (Cambridge: D. S. Brewer, 2000), 63–76.

[12] William Rothwell, 'Chaucer and Stratford atte Bowe,' *Bulletin of the John Rylands Library*, 74 (1992), 3–28.

From the twelfth century alone one can point to such polyglots as Gilbert Foliot, bishop of London; Henry II, who 'had a knowledge of all the tongues used from the French sea to the Jordan, but spoke only Latin and French'; the chronicler Orderic Vitalis, who was educated if not upper-rank; Richard of Leicester, abbot of Saint Évroul; Odo, abbot of Battle; Samson, abbot of Bury St Edmunds; St Edmund Rich; and Ailred of Rievaulx.[13] In one sense, this association of multilingualism with a select group of the population is to be expected, since an uneducated, lower-rank Anglophone would perforce have no schooling for studying Latin and little opportunity or need to pick up French. None the less, as a characteristic of only certain speakers, the multilingualism of these individuals confirms and enacts language-mediated social divisions of education and rank: to know Latin and French as well as English was, typically, to be educated, upper-rank, and socially powerful.

By medieval discursive practices, an individual's inability to acquire another language could also dynamically sustain these kinds of social divisions. In Orderic Vitalis's *History*, for example, William the Conqueror's failed attempts to learn English emblemize both the social implications of language and the rigidity of the structures it maintains:

The king's passion for justice dominated the kingdom, encouraging others to follow his example. He struggled to learn some of the English language, so that he could understand the pleas of the conquered people without an interpreter, and benevolently pronounce fair judgements for each one as justice required. But advancing age prevented him from acquiring such learning, and the distractions of his many duties forced him to give his attention to other things.[14]

Despite his good intentions, William cannot transcend the social barriers mediated by language and conduct himself, linguistically and otherwise, as a common man: his inability to acquire English

---

[13] Walter Map, *De Nugis Curialium: Courtiers' Trifles*, ed. and trans. M. R. James, rev. C. N. L. Brooke and R. A. B. Mynors (Oxford: Clarendon, 1983), 37, 477; Orderic Vitalis, *The Ecclesiastical History*, vi. 555, 489; *The Chronicle of Battle Abbey*, 307/9; Jocelin of Brakelond, *The Chronicle*, 40; R. M. Wilson, 'English and French in England 1100–1300,' *History*, 28 (1943), 59. Orderic Vitalis mentions only that Richard of Leicester knew English, though I assume that as the abbot of a French abbey he must have known French and Latin as well.

[14] Orderic Vitalis, *The Ecclesiastical History*, ii. 257.

manifests an unbridgeable distinction between the Norman rulers
and their Anglophone subjects. And just as medieval England's
diglossia sustained social distinctions such as that between William and his subjects, so these distinctions, as in any diglossic
situation, were implicated in various features of the social landscape. Since the Norman presence was strongest in the south, for
instance, a Francophone visitor to other parts of the country was
likely to encounter communication problems. Such was the case
in a story told by Richard of Devizes in which he recounts the
life of a French youth 'of low condition and of extreme poverty.'
A friend encourages the youth to visit England, 'a land flowing
with milk and honey,' but at the same time warns him against Durham, Norwich, and Lincoln, where he would 'hear almost no-one
speaking French.'[15] In this case, geographic advice is economic as
well as linguistic, since in the twelfth century social and financial
power lay with the Francophones of the south; by restricting his
visit to places where his language is known, the youth simultaneously increases his opportunities for advancement.

Such mediation of social structure by language appears with
particularly dramatic effect in the case of William, bishop of Ely,
in whose remarkable life language figures briefly but significantly.
Depicted as arrogant, unjust, wilful, and (not surprisingly) partial
to foreigners, William is the very model of vanity:

Although, therefore, all of England zealously served him on bend-
ed knee, he was nevertheless always aspiring to the Franks' lack of
restraint, and he removed to Oxford his knights and servants and his
entire household. And there, despising the nation of the English in every
way, he walked pompously, surrounded by a band of Franks and Flem-
ings, bearing—as the decoration of a priest—a sneer in his nostrils,
derision in his mouth, mockery in his eyes, and arrogance in his brow.

Finally chased to the Tower and deposed by Richard I, William flees
to Canterbury to ready himself for pilgrimage to Rome. At Dover,
he disguises himself as a woman, at which Roger of Hoveden cries

---

[15] Richard of Devizes, *The Chronicle of Richard of Devizes of the Time of King
Richard the First*, ed. and trans. John T. Appleby (London: Thomas Nelson & Sons,
1963), 64/66. On the south-east localization of French, see Rothwell, 'Language and
Government in Medieval England,' *Zeitschrift für Franzöische Sprache und Literatur*,
93 (1983), 258–70.

out, 'Oh, the agony! A man was made into a woman, a chancellor into a chancelloress, a priest into a whore, a bishop into a buffoon.' A fisherman, mistaking the bishop for a prostitute, quickly grasps the truth about William and calls others to see him: 'Meanwhile, a certain woman, leaving the town and seeing the linen cloth that he (or she) was carrying as if it were displayed for sale, walked up and began to ask how much the price was, and for how much he would sell an ell. He said nothing in response, because he was wholly ignorant of the English language.'[16] Here, William's vanity and immorality correlate with his Continental sentiments and his attempts to transgress gender, social, and linguistic distinctions: his character, national allegiances, social rank, sexuality, and language are all revealed at once. The stability and probity of these distinctions, in turn, are figured in the ease with which his transgressions are discovered and in the fact that the story concludes with William being dragged through the streets and imprisoned.

Necessarily brief, these examples are meant to suggest two important features of the social meanings, functions, and status of a language. First, as sociolinguistic markers, languages such as medieval Latin, French, and English were at once linguistic codes and forms of social behaviour: to speak a given language in given circumstances was inevitably to assume a particular role within a nexus of social relations. And second, since our access to these sociolinguistic markers is only through discursive representations of them, our perception is necessarily influenced by ideological considerations as well as by linguistic reality. Put another way, statements about a particular variety or utterances in it have sociolinguistic implications that transcend literal meaning and that need to be factored into any account of historical linguistic reality.

In the case of French, such broad considerations produced continual sociolinguistic reinterpretation of the language's introduction and survival in England. For Norman and Angevin historians, as I suggested in the last chapter, political circumstances dictated

---

[16] Roger of Hoveden, *Chronica Magistri Rogeri de Houedene*, ed. William Stubbs, RS 51, 4 vols. (London: Longman, 1868–71), iii. 141–7. The story also appears in Roger of Wendover, *Rogeri de Wendover Chronica, sive Flores Historiarum* (London: Sumptibus Societatis, 1841), iii. 50–3.

that contact between English and French, despite the latter's association with the aristocracy, should be effectively erased from
England's linguistic ecology. Norman historians may well have
regarded the events of 1066 as justifiable and divinely sanctioned,
that is, but the linguistic disparity between the nobles and their
native subjects testified for the social disruption occasioned by
the Conquest, giving the lie to any claim the Normans could make
that their presence represented a continuity with the Anglo-Saxon
past. In business, religious, and military matters, and whenever
twelfth-century kings or nobles travelled beyond the south-east of
England, language contact embodied the fact that a Francophone
minority had invaded and colonized the land of an Anglophone
majority. When Norman and Angevin chroniclers employed discursive practices that depicted language contact as the aberrant
consequence of encounters with monsters, marvels, and angels,
they incorporated French and English within a discursive practice
that transformed the Conquest's sociolinguistic reality and political implications. If language contact was represented as unnatural, in other words, it could not exist in the presumptively natural
social situation occasioned by the Norman presence in England;
and if it did not exist, neither did one of the clearest markers of any
disjunct between the native English and immigrant Normans.[17]

This discursive practice might seem superfluous, since by the
middle of the twelfth century the vast majority of the Normans and
their descendants had already become bilingual if not monoglot
Anglophones, leading to further contraction of the already small
number of Francophones. Yet this same apparent superfluity
points to the ideological underpinning of the chronicles' representations of language and of beliefs about language status in
general. Even if the linguistic future could have been predicted
and the chroniclers could have foreseen that Francophones would
shift overwhelmingly to English, their sociolinguistic mythology would have been well motivated, since linguistic attitudes
and cultural practices are mutually constitutive, sometimes irre-

[17] See further Machan, 'Language and Society in Twelfth-Century England,' in Irma
Taavitsainen et al. (eds.), *Placing Middle English in Context: Selected Papers from the
Second Middle English Conference* (Berlin: Mouton de Gruyter, 2000), 43–66.

spective of empirical linguistic reality. A century and a half later, indeed, after the foreigner question of Henry III's reign and as England's relations with France continued to deteriorate, French was no longer erased from the sociolinguistic landscape but was instead foregrounded and interpreted as a sign of that country's insidious intentions. In a 1295 royal letter to the archbishop of Canterbury, Edward I of England thus claimed that Philip IV of France 'proposes, if his power should prove equal to the horrid purpose of his wicked plan, to destroy completely the English tongue from the land.'[18]

As the Hundred Years War developed in the fourteenth century, the threat of the French army may have seemed even more genuine, and, perhaps as a response, linguistic representation became more nuanced. On the one hand were additional contemporary concerns that French victory would result in the elimination of English, concerns that were reiterated in addresses to open Parliament in 1340, 1344, 1346, and 1376.[19] On the other were historical concerns, with additional claims about the status of English immediately after the Conquest dating to this period. Some of these merely exaggerate the historical situation, whether by demonizing the Normans or by rendering language as a then-current issue. Robert Holcot, for instance, claimed that William the Conqueror had attempted to amalgamate the English and Normans under one speech—French.[20] Others were outright frauds

---

[18] William Stubbs (ed.), *Select Charters and Other Illustrations of English Constitutional History from the Earliest Times to the Reign of Edward the First*, 9th edn., ed. H. W. C. Davis (Oxford: Clarendon, 1913), 480. Also see Woodbine, 'The Language of English Law,' *Speculum*, 18 (1943), 424; and Rolf Berndt, 'French and English in Thirteenth-Century England. An Investigation into the Linguistic Situation after the Loss of the Duchy of Normandy and other Continental Dominions,' in *Aspekte der Anglistischen Forschung in der DDR: Martin Lehnert zum 65. Geburtstag* (Berlin: Akademie-Verlag, 1976), 147, and 'The Period of the Final Decline of French in Medieval England (Fourteenth and Early Fifteenth Centuries),' *Zeitschrift für Anglistik und Amerikanstik*, 20 (1972), 347.

[19] John Fisher, *The Emergence of Standard English* (Lexington, Ky.: University of Kentucky Press, 1996), 45, 160–1. The Rolls of Parliament preserve these concerns, ironically, in French, though Fisher contends that the oral versions must have been given in English.

[20] For this and other examples, see Michael Richter, *Sprache und Gesellschaft im Mittelalter: Untersuchungen zur Mündlichen Kommunikation in England von der Mitte*

that served as historical witnesses of such activities. While there was an eleventh-century Ingulf, abbot of Croyland and secretary of William the Conqueror, for example, *Ingulph's Chronicle of the Abbey of Croyland* is a fourteenth-century forgery. In projecting linguistic propaganda born of contemporary circumstances onto the events of post-Conquest period, the *Chronicle* mythologizes both the French character and language contact:

So inveterately did the Normans at this period detest the English, that whatever the amount of their merits might be, they were excluded from all dignities; and foreigners, who were far less fitted, be they of any other nation whatever under heaven, would have been gladly chosen instead of them. The very language even they abhorred with such intensity, that the laws of the land and the statutes of the English kings were treated of in the Latin tongue; and even in the very schools, the rudiments of grammar were imparted to the children in French and not in English. The English mode of writing was also abandoned, and the French manner adopted in charters and in all books.[21]

Similar mythologizing is present in Robert of Gloucester's early fourteenth-century assessment of England's linguistic history. After England came into Norman hands, Robert asserts,

> & þe normans ne couþe speke þo . bote hor owe speche .
> & speke French as hii dude atom . & hor children
>   dude also teche .
> So þat heieman of þis lond . þat of hor blod come .
> Holdeþ alle þulke speche . þat hii of hom nome .
> Vor bote a man conne frenss . me telþ of him lute .
> Ac lowe men holdeþ to engliss to hor owe speche ȝute .
> Ich wene þer ne beþ in al þe world . contreyes none .
> Þat ne holdeþ to hor owe speche . bote engelond one .
> Ac wel me wot uor to conne . boþe wel it is .
> Vor þe more þat a mon can . þe more wurþe he is.[22]

des Elften bis zum Beginn des Vierzehnten Jahrhunderts (Stuttgart: Anton Hiersemann, 1979), 36–8.

[21] Quoted in Woodbine, 'The Language of English Law,' 403.

[22] Robert of Gloucester, *The Metrical Chronicle*, ed. William Aldis Wright, RS 86 (London: Spottiswoode, 1887), lines 7538–47.

Here Robert represents the Normans as a foreign aristocracy, insulated from intermarriage and the English language, which common people, who remain more faithful to themselves than the upper rank does, have not rejected as 'hor owe speche ȝute.' English, in Robert's view, is unmistakably the proper language of the land, so that while he acknowledges the utility of multilingualism, he also asserts the unnaturalness—and uniqueness—of the English linguistic condition. In the adverb 'ȝute' and (ironically) at a moment when French literature and manners remained cultivated among English aristocrats, Robert ominously invokes a potentially unnatural conclusion to England's unnatural linguistic situation—the loss of English throughout the land.

The myth of the Norman threat to English likewise figures in John Trevisa's translation of the *Polychronicon*, where he, too, notes that English children have construed 'hir lessouns and here þynges in Frensche, and so þey haueþ seþ þe Normans come first to Engelond.' The strategic use of discursive practices is especially clear in this passage, however, for having evoked the putative shift of Anglophones to French, it fabricates a subsequent linguistic history for medieval English in Trevisa's often-cited testimony for the status of English and French in English schoolrooms. By the end of the fourteenth century, Trevisa observes, the schoolmasters John of Cornwall and Richard Pencriche taught their pupils not in French but English, 'so þat now, þe ȝere of oure Lorde a þowsand þre hundred foure score and fyue, and of þe secounde kyng Richard after þe conquest nyne, in alle þe gramere scoles of Engelond, children leueth Frensche, and construeþ and lerneþ an Englische.'[23] In the light of the historical record, Trevisa's triumph of English would seem to be as exaggerated as the threat to it that the forged *Chronicle* of Ingulf of Croyland attributes to William the Conqueror. But importantly, both views—held simultaneously by Trevisa—do eloquently attest to the ideological

[23] *Polychronicon Ranulphi Higden Monachi Cestrensis together with the English Translations of John Trevisa and an Unknown Writer of the Fifteenth Century*, ed. Churchill Babington and J. R. Lumbly, RS 41, 9 vols. (London: Longman, 1865–86), ii. 159, 161.

underpinnings of linguistic beliefs and to the ways in which such beliefs alter alongside the social reality they sustain.

Nuances in the representations of Latin reflect not the political reconceptualization of a country and its people—necessarily, since Latin was not a national language—but a dilatory re-evaluation of England's diglossia and its social and cultural implications. This re-evaluation, which has figured prominently if implicitly in many recent critical discussions of late-medieval literature, literary theory, and religion, enlivens several late fourteenth-century works, particularly *Piers Plowman*, which displays both the initial and evolving perspectives on Latin. Even as the poem affirms the traditional diglossic situation of England, that is, *Piers Plowman* reveals this situation's inherent contradictions and instabilities. Although the poem depicts Latin as the language of authority, it also grants that an utterance in it can be grammatically false; and when the utterance is false, so, by implication, may be the text and document in which it appears, as well the authority that the three in their entirety construct. As Trajan comments,

> A chartre is chalangeable bifore a chief Iustice;
> If fals latyn be in þat lettre þe lawe it impugneþ,
> Or peynted parentrelynarie, parcelles ouerskipped.   (XI. 303–5)

According to *Piers Plowman*, the falseness of grammar, text, and document are all too common. Despite thirty years as a priest and a parson, Sloth says of himself:

> 'Yet kan I neyþer solue ne synge ne seintes lyues rede;
> But I kan fynden in a feld or in a furlang an hare
> Bettre þan in *Beatus vir* or in *Beati omnes*
> Construe clausemele and kenne it to my parisshens.
> I kan holde louedayes and here a Reues rekenyng,
> Ac in Canoun nor in decretals I kan noȝt rede a lyne.'   (V. 416–21)

Moreover, while Sloth inadequately knows the Lord's Prayer, he 'kan rymes of Robyn hood and Randolf Erl of Chestre' (V. 395). Reflective of fourteenth-century England in general, then, the language associated with institutional authority in *Piers Plowman* is Latin. But the poem provocatively suggests that such authority can sometimes rest on inadequate linguistic competence, just as it can be claimed by those without any competence in Latin at all.[24]

At its most general level, the linguistic repertoire of late-medieval England thus involved a structured, developing distribution of Latin, French, and English. Shaped as it was by discursive conventions, this repertoire allotted a fairly restricted role to English that emerged from broader institutions and ideas. Though these conventions evolved to reflect evolving social concerns, the restrictions on English retained certain consistencies throughout the period. In many ways, the status of English within medieval England's linguistic repertoire rests on a set of exclusions: English was excluded from powerful domains, from powerful ranks, from the negotiation of ethnic status, from the evaluation of moral character, from the ideological construction of history, and from an evolving role in society. Perhaps the most encompassing and influential exclusion of all was that from the institutions and discursive practices—universities, education, exegesis, and law, for example—that negotiated for Latin and French their sociolinguistic significance. With only a limited role in such socially powerful domains, English participated much less fully than either of these languages in the kinds of metalinguistic commentary that might help to address or adjust its status in England's ecology of languages.

Registers, varieties, and meanings

The relations among varieties of English within this ecology and the discursive traditions used to represent them offer additional insights into the status of late-medieval English. As a natural language, Middle English was necessarily both regionally and socially diverse, so much so, at least in the written channel, that histories of English routinely describe the Middle English period as pre-eminently dialectal. And at least some Middle English speakers seem to have been well aware of the variation around them. One such speaker was Roger Bacon, who as early as the thirteenth century observes, 'We see also that within the same lan-

[24] See further Machan, 'Language Contact in *Piers Plowman,' Speculum*, 69 (1994), 359–85.

guage there are various idioms [diversa idiomata], that is manners and peculiarities of speech, as there are in English among northerners, southerners, easterners, and westerners.'[25] As the copying of vernacular manuscripts proliferated in the following centuries, it created greater opportunities for scribes to encounter texts produced in the linguistic varieties of distant locales, resulting in the phenomenon of dialect translation. This, too, testifies for a sense of regional variation. When scribes accustomed to using a southern variety encountered works written in a northern one, for instance, they might simply reproduce the linguistic forms in front of them or they might translate these forms, with varying levels of consistency, into ones they would ordinarily use, such as *schal* for *xal* or *foryiveþ* for *forgives*.[26] In these latter cases, the scribes' translation efforts bespeak both an awareness of vernacular variation and, particularly in the professional production of manuscripts, a sense that in some regions a particular variety was more appropriate, intelligible, and desirable than others. More direct recognition of Middle English variation and its sociolinguistic significance emerges from Dan Michel's remark that he composed the *Ayenbite of Inwyt* 'mid engliss of kent' or from colophons like that in Thomas Bareyle's copy of Richard Rolle's *Form of Living*, which observes that the text has been 'translat out of Northarn tunge into Sutherne that it shulde be the bettir vnderstondyn of men that be of the selve countre.'[27]

---

[25] Bacon, *Opera Quædam Hactenus Inedita*, ed. J. S. Brewer (London: Longman, 1859), 467.

[26] See Laing (ed.), *Middle English Dialectology: Essays*. Also see James Milroy, 'Middle English Dialectology,' in N. F. Blake (ed.), *The Cambridge History of the English Language*, ii. *1066–1476* (Cambridge: Cambridge University Press, 1992), 156–206; and Felicity Riddy (ed.), *Regionalism in Late Medieval Manuscripts and Texts: Essays Celebrating the Publication of 'A Linguistic Atlas of Late Medieval England'* (Woodbridge: D. S. Brewer, 1991). There are many good introductions to the methods and objectives of dialectology in general, including G. L. Brook, *English Dialects*, 3rd. edn. (London: Andre Deutsch, 1978); Lawrence M. Davis, *English Dialectology: An Introduction* (University, Ala.: University of Alabama Press, 1983); W. N. Francis, *Dialectology: An Introduction* (London: Longman, 1983); and Peter Trudgill, *On Dialect: Social and Geographical Perspectives* (New York: New York University Press, 1983).

[27] Dan Michel, *Ayenbite of Inwyt*, ed. Richard Morris, EETS os 23 (London: Trübner, 1866), 262; and M. B. Parkes and Richard Beadle (eds.), *The Poetical Works of Geoffrey Chaucer: A Facsimile of Cambridge University Library MS Gg.4.27*, 3 vols. (Norman, Okla.: Pilgrim Books, 1979–80), iii. 55. Also see *Cursor Mundi*, ed. Richard Morris, EETS os 57, 59, 62, 66, 68, 99, 101 (London: Trübner, 1874–93), lines 20061–4.

Indications of such dialect awareness increased as the Middle English period progressed. From the eleventh, twelfth, and thirteenth centuries, I can locate no remarks in English about synchronic variation, but a self-consciousness about dialect does figure significantly in Chaucer's *Reeve's Tale* (which the next chapter examines in depth) and at the end of his *Troilus*; Mak's use of a 'Sothren tothe' in the *Second Shepherds' Play* also foregrounds the issue briefly and prominently. By the end of the fourteenth century and the beginning of the fifteenth, the topic of vernacular variation appears frequently enough—even if in a still very limited way—that it might be regarded as a kind of rhetorical setpiece. In his *Mappula Angliae* Osbern Bokenham extends several Latin traditions going back through Higden to William of Malmesbury and Roger Bacon. Bokenham maintains, specifically, that William the Conqueror had mandated French as the language of English grammar schools and also offers a linguistic map of the regional variation of fifteenth-century England that includes the value judgements of his predecessors. In his *Legendys of Hooly Wummen*, he places himself on the map in this way:

> . . . spekyn and wrytyn I will pleynly
> Aftyr the language of Suthfolk speche.[28]

The author of the fifteenth-century *Promptorium Parvulorum* similarly (albeit in Latin) aligns his language with one particular regional variety: 'I have followed only the fashion of speech [loquendi modum] of the county of Norfolk, which is the only one I learned from youth and the only one I know fully and completely.'[29] And a prologue to the *Myroure of Oure Ladye* maintains that language diversity within England has become so great as to affect communication: 'Oure language is also so dyuerse in yt selfe, that the commen maner of spekyng in Englysshe of some contre can skante be vnderstood in some other contre of the same

---

[28] For the *Mappula*, see David Burnley, *The History of the English Language: A Source Book*, 2nd edn. (London: Longman, 2000), 186–9. Also see Bokenham, *Legendys of Hooly Wummen*, ed. Mary S. Serjeantson, EETS os 206 (London: Oxford University Press, 1938), lines 4063–4.

[29] A. L. Mayhew (ed.), *The Promptorium Parvulorum*, EETS es 102 (London: Oxford University Press, 1908), col. 3.

londe.'[30] One of the best-known examples of this setpiece occurs
in William Caxton's preface to the *Eneydos*, where he notes both
synchronic variation (social as well as regional) and diachronic
change: 'our langage now vsed varyeth ferre from that. whiche
was vsed and spoken whan I was borne.' [31]

None the less, in comparison to contemporary French comments on regionalisms and their sociolinguistic potential, English references to regional and social variation are rather limited.
French traditions, for example, include extensive recognition of
not only the divergence of Anglo-French from Continental French
but also the dialect divisions of the latter.[32] The more prominent
rhetorical setpiece in late-medieval England's discursive traditions involves recognition of English—simply English—as the
language of the land and especially its common people in the very
general fashion that I have described above and that underwrites
Henry III's English letters: lacking both political self-consciousness and linguistic rationalization. By these traditions, Latin,
French, and English are all conceived and presented as individually coherent but regionally and socially undifferentiated languages.
It is just such general language contact that is foregrounded in
Trevisa's reference to John of Cornwall, which elaborates on Trevisa's source Ralph Higden, which is itself largely Higden's add-
ition to his own source, William of Malmesbury.[33] The Northern
English Homily Cycle advances a similarly general conception

---

[30] John Henry Blunt (ed.), *The Myroure of Oure Ladye*, EETS ES 19 (London: Trübner, 1873), 7–8.

[31] W. J. B. Crotch (ed.), *The Prologues and Epilogues of William Caxton*, EETS OS
176 (1928; rpt. New York: Burt Franklin, 1971), 108.

[32] See Andres M. Kristol, 'L'intellectuel "anglo-norman" face à la pluralité des
langues: le témoignage implicite du MS Oxford, Magdalen Lat. 188,' in Trotter (ed.),
Multilingualism in Later Medieval Britain, 37–52.

[33] *Polychronicon Ranulphi Higden Monachi Cestrensis*, ii. 160/162 and 161/163.
While Latin, French, and English are understood to correlate with certain speakers and
domains, the languages themselves are not characteristically represented as antagonis-
tic—the use of French around Anglophones, for example, does not in itself sufficiently
correlate with social identity in such a way as to produce conflict. Such is not the case
with Flemish in a late-medieval account of the 1381 Peasants' Revolt: 'And many fflem-
mynges loste here heedes at that tyme, and namely they that koude nat say Breede and
Chese, But Case and Brode' (*Chronicles of London*, ed. Charles Lethbridge Kingsford
(1905; rpt. Dursley: Alan Sutton, 1977), 15).

of English by observing that 'Bathe klerk and leued man' who have been born in England can understand the language,[34] as does *Of Arthour and Of Merlin* in its itemization of late-medieval England's languages:

> Of Freynsch no Latin nil y tel more
> Ac on Inglisch ichil tel þerfore:
> Riȝt is þat Inglishce vnderstood
> Þat was born in Inglond.
> Freynsche vse þis gentil man
> Ac euerich Inglische Inglische can.[35]

Such comprehensive identification of language with homeland also occurs in Lollard discourse, which sometimes collapses linguistic and rank distinctions along national lines. *De officio pastorali* observes of the Bible that 'þe comyns of englisschmen knownen it best in þer modir tunge.'[36]

For Thomas Usk, territorial conceptions explicitly merge with rank-based ones that associate language with social position as well as country: 'Let than clerkes endyten in Latin, for they have the propretee of science, and the knowynge in that facultee; and let Frenchmen in their Frenche also endyten their queynt termes, for it is kyndley to their mouthes; and let us shewe our fantasyes in such wordes as we lerneden of our dames tonge.'[37] Here Latin is the studied language of academics and French the cultivated language of rhetoric, but English is what children learn on their mothers' knees; in effect, the *academic* environment of clerks is thereby juxtaposed to the *physical* places inhabited by Francophones and Anglophones. Many other writers connect language with social grouping in this way. As in Norman and Angevin chronicles, later medieval traditions characteristically associ-

---

[34] Quoted in Berndt, 'French and English in Thirteenth-Century England,' 141.

[35] *Of Arthour and Merlin*, ed. O. D. Macrae-Gibson, EETS os 268 and 269 (London: Oxford University Press, 1973, 1979), lines 19–24.

[36] *The English Works of Wyclif*, ed. Frederic David Matthew, EETS os 74 (London: Trübner, 1880), 430.

[37] Thomas Usk, *Testament of Love*, in W. W. Skeat (ed.), *Complete Works of Geoffrey Chaucer*, vii. *Chaucerian and Other Pieces* (Oxford: Oxford University Press, 1897), 2.

ate knowledge of non-English languages, particularly Latin and French, with the wealthy, educated, or noble classes. In *King Edward and the Shepherd*, for example, the shepherd Adam enters the court of King Edward III, and

> When he French and Latyn herde,
> He hade mervell how it ferde.[38]

The poet of *Richard Coer de Lyon* delineates associations among rank, education, and language in a Troy book:

> In Frenssche bookys þis rym is wrouȝt,
> Lewede men ne knowe it nouȝt.
> Lewede men cune Ffrensch non,
> Among an hondryd vnneþis on.[39]

Floris and Blancheflour, William of Nassyngton's *Speculum Vite*, Robert of Gloucester's *Chronicle*, and Robert Mannyng's *Handlyng Synne* all advance similar associations, which in the *Book* of Margery Kempe and the Northern Metrical Version of the *Rule of St Benet* assume additional gendered implications:

> Monkes & als all leryd men
> In latyn may it lyghtly ken,
> And wytt þarby how þay sall wyrk
> To sarue god and haly kyrk.
> Bot tyll women to mak it couth,
> Þat leris no latyn in þar ȝouth,
> In ingles is it ordand here,
> So þat þay may it lyghtly lere.[40]

---

[38] Walter Hoyt French and Charles Brockway Hale (eds.), *Middle English Metrical Romances* (New York: Prentice-Hall, 1930), lines 1013–14.

[39] Karl B. Brunner (ed.), *Die Mittelenglische Versroman über Richard Löwenherz*, Wiener Beiträge zur Englischen Philologie 42 (Vienna: Wilhelm Braumüller, 1913), lines 21–4.

[40] *Three Middle-English Versions of the Rule of St. Benet*, ed. Ernst A. Kock, EETS os 120 (London: Kegan Paul, 1902), 48, lines 9–16. Also see *Floris and Blancheflour*, lines 155–8, in *Middle English Metrical Romances*, ed. French and Hale; William of Nassyngton, *Speculum Vite*, in *Englische Studien*, 7 (1884), ii. 61–96; Robert of Gloucester, *The Metrical Chronicle*, lines 7538–47; Robert Mannyng, *Handlyng Synne*, ed. Idelle Sullens (Binghamton: Medieval and Renaissance Texts and Studies, 1983), lines 7–8; *The Book of Margery Kempe*, ed. Sanford Brown Meech and Hope Emily Allen, EETS os 212 (London: Oxford University Press, 1940), ch. 47.

Perhaps the most eloquent and encompassing version of these generalizing sociolinguistic sentiments that collapse English, social rank, and national identity comes from the beginning of *Cursor Mundi*:

> And on Inglysch has it schewed
> Not for þe lerid bot for þe lewed:
> For þo þat in þis land wone
> Þat þe Latyn no Frankys cone.[41]

When modern readers encounter these setpieces of language contact and dialect variation, they may well have the sense of the familiar, the sense that in these areas at least the status of Middle English mirrored that of Modern English. By this sense, the facts that several contemporary Anglophone countries both demonstrate linguistic rationalization and have one typically urban variety of English that is more socially advantageous than other varieties support the assumption that such rationalization and dialect stratification must be sociolinguistic universals. But in late-medieval England, the sociolinguistic significance of English, as I have teased it out so far, suggests otherwise. Indeed, the general conception of nationhood that this status sustained has few of the sociolinguistic implications of modern nationalism. In Benedict Anderson's landmark formulation, which has become a touchstone for recent discussions, nationalism is an act of communal imagination fundamentally dependent on literacy, capitalism, industry, and other cultural developments of the eighteenth and nineteenth centuries.[42] Adrian Hastings and others have countered Anderson's positions by identifying English nationalist impulses as early as the Battle of Hastings, if not before that.[43] Where Anderson and Hastings agree is on the central role vernaculars

---

[41] *Cursor Mundi*, lines 5-8. Also see lines 21–6, 237–40.

[42] Benedict Anderson, *Imagined Communities: Reflections on the Origin and Spread of Nationalism*, rev. edn. (London: Verso, 1991). Also see Ernest Gellner, *Nations and Nationalism* (Ithaca: Cornell University Press, 1983); Aldo Scaglione, 'The Rise of National Languages: East and West,' in id. (ed.), *The Emergence of National Languages* (Ravenna: Longo Editore, 1984), 9–49; and Joshua A. Fishman, *Language and Nationalism: Two Integrative Essays* (Rowley, Mass.: Newbury House Publishers, 1972).

[43] Hastings, *The Construction of Nationhood: Ethnicity, Religion and Nationalism* (Cambridge: Cambridge University Press, 1997). Also see Alfred P. Smyth, 'The Emergence of English Identity, 700–1000,' in Smyth (ed.), *Medieval Europeans: Studies in*

play in the formation of national identity, with Hastings seeing 'linguistic nationalism' in Robert of Gloucester's *Chronicle* and *Cursor Mundi* and Anderson arguing for the nineteenth-century incorporation of vernaculars as distinctive national symbols.[44]

The larger issues here lie far outside my present sociolinguistic concerns, but I do want to note that the 'linguistic nationalism' to which Hastings refers and that some have seen underlying several of the passages I have examined is categorically distinct from the kind that figures in Anderson's arguments. The latter, indeed, depends on distinctly modern developments in print, education, government, linguistics, and so forth, while Robert of Gloucester and others merely posit a connection between English and England. Inasmuch as the role of vernaculars in modern nationalist discourse is fundamentally institutional and depends on a variety of contextual factors, the mere acts of writing in a vernacular, testifying to its existence, or translating the Bible into it do not constitute linguistic rationalization, nor are they, as Hastings's position would require, sufficient for the transformation of a language's ecology. When medieval universities referred to *naciones* or *Cursor Mundi* to 'Ingland the nacion,' the reference is not to a clearly defined and sociolinguistically sustained political and geographic entity as such but to a confederation of people sharing common language, history, and traditions. As the Anglo-Norman chronicles, the sociolinguistic contexts of King Henry's October letters, and Henry's appropriation of Anglo-Saxon traditions all indicate, England the medieval country stood in loose and general sociolinguistic opposition to (say) France the country, beginning only in the early modern period to exhibit the political self-consciousness and linguistic rationalization that enables sociolinguistic appeals to the population at large or meaningful uses of language in political programmes of reform.[45] For reasons such as these, a medieval

Ethnic Identity and National Perspectives in Medieval Europe (London: Macmillan, 1998), 24–52; and John Gillingham, *The English in the Twelfth Century: Imperialism, National Identity and Political Values* (Woodbridge: Boydell, 2000).

[44] Anderson, *Imagined Communities*, 67–82, and Hastings, *The Construction of Nationhood*, 46.

[45] See *OED*, s.v. 'nation' sb. 1. See further Pearl Kibre, *The Nations in the Mediaeval Universities* (Cambridge, Mass.: Mediaeval Academy of America, 1948).

origin of English nationalism has itself become a tenuous idea for some critics, as for Derek Pearsall, who points in particular to the desultory fashion in which such notions develop:

while particular circumstances produced a momentary surge in asser-tions of Englishness around 1290–1340 and again in 1410–20, there was no steadily growing sense of national feeling. French culture retained much of its customary hegemony during the fifteenth century, in court as in the work of Malory and Caxton, and the establishment of the author-ity of English written culture went along slowly and haltingly.[46]

Whatever the origin of England's nationalism, English linguistic nationalism emerges neither from such disconnected growth of national feeling nor from the literal sense or discursive contexts of medieval comments on the linguistic repertoire of England.

Likewise, though in the modern United Kingdom and United States synchronic variation (in the form of social or regional dia-lects) correlates with social variation and power in ways broadly recognized by the relevant speech communities, this kind of cor-relation is absent from the ecology of Middle or, for that matter, Old English. In Anglo-Saxon England, Northumbrian, Mercian, and West Saxon all consecutively held prestige status but never for very long and never in the institutionalized fashion that Stand-ard American English has in the United States today.[47] Nothing in the record of Old or Middle English, moreover, implies the kind of correlation between regional variety and social stratification present in the geographic and linguistic implications of Latin *rus-ticus*, which from the republic period signifies both a rural dweller and someone who is coarse, awkward, clownish, or linguistically

---

[46] Pearsall, 'The Idea of Englishness in the Fifteenth Century,' in Helen Cooney (ed.), *Nation, Court and Culture: New Essays on Fifteenth-Century English Poetry* (Dublin: Four Courts Press, 2001), 15. Also see Pearsall, 'Chaucer and Englishness,' *Publications of the British Academy*, 101 (1999), 79–99. For an explicit rejection of the increasingly common transference of modern notions of nationalism and nationhood to the Middle Ages, see Patrick J. Geary, *The Myth of Nations: The Medieval Origins of Europe* (Princeton: Princeton University Press, 2002).

[47] Thomas E. Toon, 'The Social and Political Contexts of Language Change in Anglo-Saxon England,' in T. W. Machan and Charles T. Scott (eds.), *English in Its Social Contexts: Essays in Historical Sociolinguistics* (New York: Oxford University Press, 1992), 28–46.

backward.[48] Indeed, both the diglossia of medieval England and the relative rigidity of the estates worked against the sociolinguistic utility—even viability—of mapping any social rank onto any variety of English. Of interest here is a 1364 plea about bigamy heard at York, in which there is testimony from a man who was born in Scotland but who lived twenty years in England. Because the man code-switched from southern English, to northern, to Scottish, the magistrate disregarded his testimony as unreliable, and in relation to the status of modern English the episode could seem to point to an anti-regional—or at least anti-northern—bias. Within the discursive traditions I have been examining, however, it is more likely that it was the witness's mixing of varieties, rather than his use of any one particular variety, that undermined his credibility.[49]

Two better-known invocations of regional variation are potentially just as misleading. Chaucer's allusion to alliterative poetry with the 'rum, ram, ruf' of the *Parson's Prologue* (*Canterbury Tales*, x. 43) does not, as is sometimes implied, need to point to a regional linguistic chauvinism, since within the context of the Parson's rejection of fable for 'a myrie tale in prose' the allusion functions as a metonymy for poetical diversion. Indeed, the plentiful existence of alliterative poetry in fifteenth-century southern manuscripts argues strongly against just such putative chauvinism.[50] Trevisa's description of northern English, which occurs in a passage I have already discussed, does gesture towards a correlation between linguistic and social hierarchies: 'Al þe longage of þe Norþumbres, and specialliche at ȝork, is so scharp, slitting, and frottynge and vnschape, þat we Souþerne men may þat longage vnneþe vnderstonde.'[51] Yet this description forms a context

---

[48] P. G.W. Glare (ed.), *Oxford Latin Dictionary* (Oxford: Clarendon Press, 1982), s.v.

[49] Cecily Clark, 'Another Late-Fourteenth-Century Case of Dialect-Awareness,' *English Studies*, 62 (1981), 504–5.

[50] See A. I. Doyle, 'The Manuscripts,' in David Lawton (ed.), *Middle English Alliterative Poetry and Its Literary Backgrounds* (Cambridge: D. S. Brewer, 1982), 88–100.

[51] *Polychronicon*, ii. 163. The linguistic antagonism that Trevisa describes apparently coincided with some regional antagonism as well, for Knighton describes conflicts that pitted southerners against northerners. See Henry Knighton, *Knighton's Chronicle, 1337–1396*, ed. and trans. G. H. Martin (Oxford: Clarendon, 1995), 431, 529.

far more slender than is often acknowledged. Trevisa's comments expand on Higden's metalinguistic observations in the original Latin version of the *Polychronicon*, which are themselves largely taken from William of Malmesbury's remarks in his twelfth-century *Gesta Pontificum*:

> Indeed, the entire language of the Northumbrians, especially in York, grates so stridently that none of us southerners is able to understand it. This situation came about because the north is in the proximity of the barbarians, with the result that it was distant from the former English kings and the current Norman ones, who are known to be situated more in the south than the north.[52]

Trevisa and Higden thus demonstrate faithfulness to their sources as much as they testify for the status of dialects in fourteenth-century English culture. As *Cursor Mundi* and Bokenham's *Mappula Angliae* indicate, such recycling of phrasings and ideas is in fact one of the hallmarks of the rhetorical setpieces I have here considered.

Standard languages and language ecology

In situations where regional or social varieties have individualized meanings within the ecology of a language, a number of factors are typically present, including clear class (rather than rank) distinctions, a standardized variety, and ideological structures that maintain sociolinguistic attitudes. Actualized in tools such as dictionaries and grammar books, which prescribe correct forms and proscribe non-standard ones, a standard sustains itself through a circular route from inculcation of the standard in education to the necessity of education for advancement in powerful domains such as government and business, which in turn require the use of a standard language and motivate its use in education.[53] A standard language thus correlates language and social variation in such a way

---

[52] William of Malmesbury, *De Gestis Pontificum Anglorum*, ed. N. E. S. A. Hamilton, RS 52 (London: Longman, 1870), 209.

[53] Hudson, *Sociolinguistics*, 32–4. Also see James Milroy and Lesley Milroy, *Authority in Language: Investigating Language Prescription and Standardisation*

that language use, both spoken and written, can correspond with socioeconomic achievement and serve as a measurement of personal and intellectual worth. The determining influence of standard English today—in its several forms—is in fact so strong that it can distort the historical situation, for standard languages are no more inevitable than is the sociolinguistic stratification of regional varieties. In the office of the Chancery and other governmental venues of the early fifteenth century, Chancery English—like some earlier varieties, such as the so-called AB dialect—served as a kind of standard, somewhat elaborated in function and somewhat regular in orthography and grammar. But lacking broad acceptance and still restricted in its domains, Chancery was sustained neither by formal, published codification nor by cultivation in education, and a truly standardized written variety of English did not exist until the eighteenth century.[54]

What makes a standard language important in the cultivation of sociolinguistic meanings for regional and social varieties is not

(London: Routledge, 1985). The distinctly institutional character of modern language hierarchies is also suggested by pre-colonial Papua New Guinea, in which there were hundreds of competing languages. Though speakers of each typically regarded their variety as superior to other varieties, the total number of speakers for any one language was small, and the societies were neither individually nor collectively stratified, nationalistic, or imperialistic. There was thus no opportunity for language variation to correlate with social variation or power, as it has in England and the United States. See Gillian Sankoff, *The Social Life of Language* (Philadelphia: University of Pennsylvania Press, 1980), 10.

[54] In addition to Fisher, in *The Emergence of Standard English*, Thomas Cable has argued for Chancery English as effectively the beginning of Standard English. See 'The Rise of Written Standard and English,' in Scaglione (ed.), *The Emergence of National Languages*, 75–94. Arguments for a more disparate, nuanced origin for Standard English can be found in Laura Wright (ed.), *The Development of Standard English, 1300–1800* (Cambridge: Cambridge University Press, 2000). Jeremy Smith has recently provided a valuable corrective to the misapplication of the entire concept of a standard language. See 'Standard Language in Early Middle English?' in Taavitsainen et al. (eds.), *Placing Middle English in Context*, 125–39. Cf. the remarks of R. D. Grillo: 'That the British, at any rate the English, are obsessed with "class" (whatever we mean by that) is, among ourselves, a commonplace. A feature of that obsession, and one that can be traced continuously from at least the fifteenth century, is the belief that we signal class by grammar, vocabulary and perhaps above all accent' (*Dominant Languages: Language and Hierarchy in Britain and France* (Cambridge: Cambridge University Press, 1989), 151). Also see Joseph M. Williams, '"O! When Degree Is Shak'd!": Sixteenth-Century Anticipations of Some Modern Attitudes toward Usage,' in Machan and Scott (eds.), *English in Its Social Contexts*, 69–101.

simply the identification of the standard with powerful domains. More generally, standards, by inviting comparison of linguistic forms, enable conceptualization of non-standard varieties and, therefore, metalinguistic discussion that furthers stratified roles for social and regional variation in the ecology of a language. In this way, standards, like all acts of language planning, ultimately serve objectives beyond communication or the refinement of a linguistic code. These objectives may be presumptively ethical—the betterment of society—but they may also support a ruling elite's economic, political, or administrative initiatives. To realize these objectives, J. K. Chambers has noted, metalinguistic discussion must use linguistic concerns to mask social ones:

the root of . . . dialectal differences is ideological, not linguistic. In the sphere of language, it is not the content of non-standard dialects that arouses criticism but their form. The arbiters of 'good' language are less concerned about breakdowns in meaning or comprehensibility than they are about deviations from an imposed form. Taking umbrage at someone's use of *ain't* for *isn't*, to take a simple example, has no linguistic basis when the interchangeability of their meanings is known to everyone, but it has an ideological basis in so far as the usage marks a class distinction in the community.[55]

When written and spoken varieties of English were standardized in the eighteenth, nineteenth, and twentieth centuries, the forms and theoretical underpinnings of these standards sustained institutional and linguistic correlations between language, intelligence, reliability, and social class. Both public and grammar schools, along with phonetics handbooks, worked to erase regional accents by stigmatizing such features as dropped inital [h] or final [ɪn] as the infallible markers of low education and status. At the same time, printed language in general helped to reproduce the ideology of a standard language—including subordination of non-standard varieties—while novelists in particular developed strategies for eliding differences between spoken and written English and utilizing these same sociolinguistic meanings

---

[55] J. K. Chambers, *Sociolinguistic Theory: Linguistic Variation and Its Social Significance* (Oxford: Blackwell, 1995), 232.

in their efforts. Widely available because technological improvements made printed texts cheaper and more accessible, standard language and orthography allowed writers such as Fielding, Dickens, Eliot, Gaskell, and Meredith to use aberrant orthography, punctuation, capitalization, and the like as methods of characterization, as devices that announced to readers a character's social class along with all the personal qualities this class was understood to imply. What mattered was neither the absolute accuracy of a feature as a marker of class nor even the integrity of the feature; a real upper-class speaker might be just as likely to drop an [h] as a lower-class one, and early in the modern period, in fact, such dropping was recognized as a characteristic of the upper class, as was the affectation of word-final [ɪn] at the beginning of the twentieth century. What mattered was the widespread impression, actualized in discursive practice, that aberrant written forms correlated with aberrant spoken forms and their sociolinguistic implications. When Dickens credits Joe Gargery with words such as *elth* for *health* and *air* for *are*, he implies sociolinguistic deviance that is absent from the depictions of socially successful characters such as Jaggers, whose speech is represented with standard orthography. In this way, marked speech (such as Joe's) has an accent, but unmarked speech (such as Jaggers's) is accentless—a linguistic impossibility. This rhetorical manipulation of the ideology immanent in a standard language is especially striking when a non-standard form entails no phonological significance. Joe's *giv'*, for instance, would seem as adequate a representation of [gɪv] as *give*, just as Mr Peggoty's *dootiful* seems no less accurate than *dutiful* for [dutɪful]. But both *giv'* and *dootiful* carry additional meanings simply by virtue of their deviation from dictionary usage. Dickens could use such spellings only because he knew that his readers knew their social implications.[56]

---

[56] See Tony Crowley, *The Politics of Discourse: The Standard Language Question in British Cultural Debates* (London: Macmillan, 1989); Robert Phillipson, *Linguistic Imperialism* (Oxford: Oxford University Press, 1992); Alastair Pennycook, *The Cultural Politics of English as an International Language* (London: Longman, 1994); and Lynda Mugglestone, *'Talking Proper': The Rise of Accent as Social Symbol* (Oxford: Clarendon, 1995).

More recently, schoolboard policy, court decisions, and even popular films have been vehicles for the disinformation, trivialization, and marginalization that can define a non-standard variety in a way that disadvantages its speakers and advantages those who speak varieties closer to the standard. When schoolboards and courts presume that adults can easily change accents or that some accents are intrinsically more difficult to understand than others—and use such presumptions to justify their policies and decisions—they affirm the thinking that underpins language subordination. This is also true of films in which a disproportionate number of the villains speak with foreign or regional accents, as is the case in Disney cartoons. Under the influences of such ideological forces, non-standard speakers themselves can become complicit in this subordination process, coming to judge their own variety as linguistically and socially deficient.[57]

A late-medieval conception of English as means of nationalism, ennobling vernacular, or medium of resistance must rely on belletristic remains and the literal meanings of passages such as the ones I have discussed in this chapter. In contrast, I have here focused on linguistic history, sociolinguistic principles, and discursive practices. By so doing I have emphasized the absence of the ideology of a standard and of the most common practices for formulating it to suggest that medieval England lacked the means for the systemization of regional or social varieties that supports modern notions of English. In this vein, while it is convenient to speak about Kentish or East Midlands as if they were stable and well-defined varieties, the recorded evidence of Middle English suggests otherwise. The manuscripts in fact display considerable variation not only between dialects (as traditionally conceived) but also within dialects and documents; ultimately, regional and even idiolectal forms of Middle English are sociolinguistic variables, not the immutable structures of contemporary print culture.[58] Further, without widespread, institutionalized access to powerful domains such as education, government, and business and with-

---

[57] See Rosina Lippi-Green, *English with an Accent: Language, Ideology, and Discrimination in the United States* (London: Routledge, 1997).

[58] This is a point that has been well made many times. See e.g. Michael Benskin,

out the codification of printed grammar books and dictionaries—
the very factors that established a tenacious connection between
language and class in the early modern era—English remained
without a standard variety, spoken or written, throughout the
entire medieval period. Lacking these institutional supports and
a standard variety, in turn, speakers of Middle English had neither the means to represent social stratification in language nor a
sociolinguistic context in which such a representation could have
been easily conceived. A form such as *xal* for *shal* simply could
not bear the ideological weight that *elth* or *giv'* do; nor could it,
by extension, support a conception of English as a rationalized
language with popularly and institutionally stratified varieties.

The common, modern use of dialect writing for humorous
effect is of interest here. Such humour emerges from the structural contrasts between regional language and standard language
and also between each variety's concomitant social associations.[59]
Because his cockney accent marks him as lower-class, we are
invited to laugh at Sam Weller, and we laugh with Huck Finn
because his non-standard language unexpectedly and ironically
articulates insight into the educated class's violence, racism, and
ignorance. Without a literary history for such usages or the institutional contexts to support them, however, Middle English cul-

'Some New Perspectives on the Origins of Standard Written English,' in J. A. Van Leuvensteijn and J. B. Berns (ed.), *Dialect and Standard Language, Dialekt und Standardsprache in the English, Dutch, German and Norwegian Language Areas* (Amsterdam:
North-Holland, 1992), 71–105.

[59] Blake observes that since non-standard language always has an unsophisticated air,
and since literature 'has until the recent present been written by the educated, it is not unnatural that non-standard language has been widely looked down on as being the appropriate language for the lowly born, the foolish and the ignorant' (*Non-Standard Language
in English Literature* (London: Andre Deutsch, 1981), 13). But the key point, again, is not
whether literature is written by the educated but whether there is a sociolinguistic context
in which a distinction between standard and non-standard languages applies. Einar Haugen has shown, for example, that among Norwegian immigrants to the United States,
a good deal of humour was elicited from dialect writing that emphasized immigrants'
inadequate command of English or Norwegian or their mixing of more than one code.
Humour in this case is to be expected, since the patterns Haugen describes occurred in
the late nineteenth and early twentieth centuries and therefore in a context not dissimilar
to that in which Dickens and his contemporaries produced their own dialect writing. See
The Ecology of Language, 112–26. Also see Muriel Saville-Troike, *The Ethnography of
Communication: An Introduction*, 2nd edn. (Oxford: Blackwell, 1989), 181–218.

ture lacked the discursive traditions that enabled the rise of such dialect writing in the eighteenth and nineteenth centuries. Even when in *Henry V* Shakespeare parodied Welsh and Irish accents in the persons of Fluellen and Macmorris, he was unable to draw on the institutional and discursive traditions subsequent writers exploited and consequently produced regionalisms far less convincing than Dickens's and far more reminiscent of those appearing in early modern Celtic stereotypes.[60] The effect of Fluellen and Macmorris is certainly humorous, but the humour lies more in their enactment of a stage type than in Shakespeare's manipulation of their variety and the early modern linguistic repertoire. Even less did the ecology of Middle English allow for the ironic contrast that is exploited variously by Dickens and Twain and that may produce humour of one sort or another. Writing in dialect, as opposed to dialect writing, is not comical by nature, and so while Mak's southern tooth may be funny—I certainly think he's funny, anyway—from a historical perspective there can be nothing inherently humorous in his language forms.

More generally, Norfolk or Suffolk speakers might well have considered their variety of English superior to that of London speakers, and vice versa, but the sociolinguistic factors necessary to conceptualize a coherent dialect (as modern Americans conceptualize Southern US English or African American Vernacular English) or to create a consensus about language and prestige in the ecology of a language were not present. For this very reason, in late-medieval England, unlike in many Anglophone countries today, an individual could not change social standing merely through the acquisition of another dialect or pronunciation.[61] By

---

[60] On the English cultivation of Welsh linguistic stereotypes in the early modern period, see Geraint H. Jenkins, Richard Suggett, and Eryn M. White, 'The Welsh Language in Early Modern Wales,' in Geraint H. Jenkins (ed.), *The Welsh Language before the Industrial Revolution* (Cardiff: University of Wales Press, 1997), 62–5.

[61] It should be recalled, however, that in the Middle Ages one could not socially rise through the acquisition of *any* linguistic variety: a peasant who somehow read Latin or spoke French would still be a peasant. One wonders, therefore, particularly in the discursive context of his other sociolinguistic claims for English, about the accuracy of Trevisa's assertion, that fourteenth-century 'churles,' seeing that the children of the nobles were taught French from an early age, 'willenge to be like to theyme, laborede

no means am I trying to argue that Middle English lacked social and regional variation of which at least some Middle English speakers were aware and perhaps credited with some sociolinguistic significance; even without a historical record the Uniformitarian Principle would indicate otherwise. I am maintaining that as linguistic phenomena dialects have specific—not transhistorical or transcultural—meanings within linguistic ecologies and that the ecology of Middle English was distinctively different from that of Modern English in this regard.

The two rhetorical set pieces of metalinguistic commentary can be recalled here. The one certainly demonstrates the existence and recognition of regional variation in late-medieval England, but the other intimates that the pre-eminent sociolinguistic distinction was not among varieties of English but a very general one between English and non-English languages within late-medieval England's linguistic repertoire. This distinction, which Chaucer (for example) invokes far more often than social or regional variation,[62] *was* systemic, *it* was the one that signalled what Robert L. Cooper calls communicative intent: 'intimacy versus social distance, formality versus informality, ingratiation versus insult.'[63] In a sociolinguistic environment in which anyone who read and spoke Latin was likely to speak English, too, as was nearly everyone who spoke French, it was the choice of French in the law courts (say) that signalled social distance, of Latin in education that signalled formality, and of English in casual lyrics that signalled familiarity. When late-medieval England came to cultivate linguistic varieties specifically for business writing, significantly, these varieties were not social or regional versions of English but interlanguages of English, French, and Latin—not dialects of English, then, but in a sense new languages in the repertoire—and

---

to speke French with alle theire myȝte.' See *Polychronicon Ranulphi Higden Monachi Cestrensis*, ii. 159.

[62] See *Canterbury Tales*, i. 162, 254, 4287, ii. 519, iii. 608, 1734, 1770, 1832, 1838, 1866, 1934, 2075, 2192, v. 1174, vi. 344, vii. 435, 3163, viii. 106.

[63] Robert L. Cooper, 'A Framework for the Study of Language Spread,' in Cooper (ed.), *Language Spread: Studies in Diffusion and Social Change* (Bloomington, Ind.: Indiana University Press, 1982), 8.

the macaronic language of late-medieval sermon practice points to this same pre-eminence of languages over dialects.[64]

William Labov has distinguished three developmental stages in the meaning of regional and non-standard forms within the ecology of a language.[65] At the initial stage, that of indicator, a form simply points to group membership, merely identifying the speaker with a particular social or regional community. When the form has expanded throughout the community and a particular sociolinguistic meaning has accrued to it, it has become a marker, subject to stylistic variation. And when pressure from a prestige model has thoroughly stigmatized this form, rendering it the focus of sociolinguistic comment even as correction by its users reduces its occurrence in the speech community, it has become a stereo-type, which none the less can still further language subordination of the form, its variety, and its speakers. For the nineteenth-century America of Twain, rural dialects had achieved the status of stereotype, as have Southern US English and certain foreign accents in various parts of the United States today. To early modern England, the Welshisms that Fluellen utters in *Henry V* were markers. In the late-medieval period, however, the forms underlying what linguists call social and regional dialects were not even markers; they were only indicators. Aleyn and John in Chaucer's *Reeve's Tale* and Mak in the *Second Shepherds' Play* clearly speak northern and southern English, respectively, utilizing a collection of primarily lexical, phonological, and morphological forms predominant in works known to have been produced in specific regions of England. But within the ecology of Middle English their language was not Northern or Southern.

---

[64] See Laura Wright, 'Macaronic Writing in a London Archive, 1380–1480,' in Matti Rissanen et al. (eds.), *History of Englishes: New Methods and Interpretations in Historical Linguistics* (Berlin: Mouton de Gruyter, 1992), 762–70, and *Sources of London English: Medieval Thames Vocabulary* (Oxford: Clarendon, 1996); and Siegfried Wenzel, *Macaronic Sermons: Bilingualism and Preaching in Late-Medieval England* (Ann Arbor: University of Michigan Press, 1994).

[65] Labov, 'On the Mechanism of Linguistic Change,' in John J. Gumperz and Dell Hymes (eds.), *Directions in Sociolinguistics: The Ethnography of Communication* (New York: Holt, Rinehart, & Winston, 1972), 512–38.

Synchronic variation and diachronic change

In this chapter I have examined how the late-medieval status of English took shape within in the context of the patterned, functional relations among Latin, French, and varieties of English itself. These were dynamic relations, both in the relations of the languages to one another and in their relations to social practices. Each language, each variety of that language, and each utterance in that variety performed some role in structuring late-medieval England, whether it was a Latin proclamation's maintenance of ecclesiastical hierarchies, a French myth's contribution to political action, or an English lyric's affirmation of the subordinate status of English. Collectively, the discursive practices that represented these roles constructed a relatively static status for English that changed little in the late Middle Ages. The stability of diglossia throughout this period suggests, indeed, that in this case at least discursive practice may not in fact have diverged much from sociolinguistic reality. At the same time, however, variation and change are inherent in all natural languages and their uses, and they are just the qualities that discursive conventions might well work to conceal, as Anglo-Norman historiography strove to suppress the language contact that resulted from the Conquest. By way of a conclusion to this chapter, then, I want to consider this fact: just as indications of diachronic change sometimes lie in the synchronic structural variation of a language, so glimpses of a reconfigured status of English could be identified in some of the issues I have explored. But since diachronic perspectives may transform the function and ecological significance of synchronic sociolinguistic phenomena—since post-medieval linguistic expectations can make medieval linguistic practice more modern than it was—such glimpses may truly be a change's beginning, or they may be merely a foreshadowing of it. The distinction is all-important.

A case in point is the controversial role of English in late-medieval accounts of religious dissent. The chronicler Henry Knighton, for example, voices a concern echoed by other opponents of the

Lollards—that the rendering of theological discussions in English violated social and religious as well as linguistic conventions. By translating the Bible 'from Latin into the language not of angels but of Englishmen,' Knighton observes, Wyclif

made that common and open to the laity, and to women who were able to read, which used to be for literate and perceptive clerks, and spread the Evangelists' pearls to be trampled by swine. And thus that which was dear to the clergy and the laity alike became as it were a jest common to both, and the clerks' jewels became the playthings of laymen, that the laity might enjoy now forever what had once been the clergy's talent from on high.[66]

While to their opponents the Lollards' use of English thus debased Scripture and shook the foundations of society, to the Lollards themselves the use of English to disseminate theological discussion of course became a matter of principle. To their thinking, what transpired sociolinguistically was less debasement and shaking than exposure and justice. Whatever the truth of the matter, the discursive tradition of individuals such as Knighton won out, for the Lollards first faced resistance, then restriction, and finally condemnation.[67]

Diachronically, Lollard practices and their attendant controversies could be (and have been) seen as transformative moments in English sociolinguistic history, reflecting a decisive change in the significance of English in England's linguistic repertoire. To be sure, religious thought and practice can affect the status and social functions of a variety within a linguistic repertoire, as they did in pre-modern Ireland (where Catholicism and Irish sustained one another) and Reformation England (where religious and social

[66] Knighton, *Knighton's Chronicle, 1337–1396*, 243/245.

[67] The literature on Lollardy is vast. From a strictly linguistic point of view, I have found the following particularly helpful: M. L. Samuels, 'Some Applications of Middle English Dialectology,' in Margaret Laing (ed.), *Middle English Dialectology: Essays on Some Principles and Problems* (Aberdeen: Aberdeen University Press, 1989), 64–80; Anne Hudson, *The Premature Reformation: Wyclifite Texts and Lollard History* (Oxford: Clarendon, 1988); and Margaret Aston, 'Wyclif and the Vernacular,' in Anne Hudson and Michael Wilks (eds.), *From Ockham to Wyclif, Studies in Church History*, Subsidia 5 (Oxford: Blackwell, 1987), 281–330.

initiatives coalesced). More narrowly, the King James Bible in particular could be seen as a pivotal influence on stylized English prose of the following centuries.

But it is also true that as heated as discussions surrounding the Lollards' use of the vernacular may have been and as pre-eminent as religion was in medieval culture, literary and theological works such as *Piers Plowman* or the Lollard sermons have typically had a limited role in constructing the status of English. Serving less as a means for the production of standardization and stand-ard language than as their forum, literary and religious works themselves constitute discursive traditions and not unmediated witness to sociolinguistic reality, whether of the Middle Ages or later. When in *De Triplici Vinculo Amoris* Wyclif rejects the foolishness of those who condemn writings as heretical because they are in English,[68] for instance, he expresses an intellectual and academic anxiety that responds to this theological tradition and not to the ecology of English or the linguistic practices of late-medieval England in general. The Lollard controversies, in fact, had no impact on the general fifteenth-century increase in ver-nacular manuscript production or incipient valuation of English literature. And their views were likewise absent altogether from more sociolinguistically significant areas such as business (and the interlanguages it employed) or government, where the cultiva-tion of Chancery English in fact manifested official acquiescence to the spread of the vernacular into powerful domains.

Nor did late-medieval religious heterodoxy figure in the forces that eventually did elevate, codify, and standardize English. As I suggested in the previous chapter, the institutions and practices that produce—and can therefore change—beliefs about a language and its ecology are those that broadly sustain ideology: schools, gov-ernment, law courts, business, and text-production. In the history of English, these are the institutions that have constructed a stand-ard language and have manipulated the significance of language in conceptions of ethnicity and nationality, as when the foreigner question shaped thirteenth-century sociolinguistic activity or when

---

[68] Hudson, *The Premature Reformation*, 31.

nineteenth-century phonologists cultivated identifications between character, class, and language. The modern movement to designate English the official language of the United States has arisen, similarly, from national and political myths, just as its ideology is furthered by court decisions, school policies, and stereotypes in popular entertainment. Rather than theological and belletristic works of fourteenth-century manuscript culture, it was a combination of the sixteenth- and seventeenth-century spread of English in government, business, and education, the expansion of print culture, and developments in nationalism that enabled the codification of English long after Lollardy had become a memory. And it was this codification, in turn, that ultimately has sustained the ideology of a standard that dominates more recent sociolinguistic attention to the status of English.

As clearly as retrospection might see the immanence of changes in the late-medieval conception of English, from the historicized perspective I have emphasized here these changes appear only dimly—as foreshadowings, and not as causes or indications of ongoing sociolinguistic transformation. Lollard sermons and the like may have advocated, in effect, the demise of diglossia, and Langland's rhetorical strategies certainly embodied it in ways that contribute to the special theological and literary value of *Piers Plowman*. But as these same works show, it is possible to talk about sociolinguistic concepts before those concepts play a part in the ecology of a language. The sociolinguistic world Langland represents was not in fact the one the majority of Middle English speakers inhabited, since in the overall history of English the institutions and practices that would firmly situate the vernacular in prestige domains, standardize it, and render it a medium of cultural identity were well in the post-medieval future. Even such bilingual works as the *Fasciculus Morum*, which intercalates Latin texts with English verses, sustain the traditional linguistic repertoire of medieval England, for if their use of English as well as Latin implies acceptance of the vernacular in some theological contexts, the bibliographic design of this use—when the English appears as poetic counterpoint to the Latin prose—constitutes the sort of functional distribution that is characteristic of diglossia.

Since bilingualism and diglossia can exist and evolve inde-
pendently of one other, indeed, the bilingualism of some late-
medieval preachers or some late-medieval manuscripts need not
be read as an emblem of diglossia's status in the society at large.[69]
Fourteenth- and fifteenth-century diglossia may not have been as
rigid or structured as that of the twelfth or even thirteenth century, but neither did it reflect linguistic beliefs by which, at one
extreme, languages could be used without pragmatic differentia-
tion, or, at the other, English or any of its varieties had a stable
meaning that could be used to encode social behaviour as explicitly as Latin and French could. Indeed, the discursive traditions
for representing Latin, French, and English reveal the flexibility
as well as the tenacity of medieval diglossia. These traditions
could simultaneously accommodate the traditional distribution
of languages, challenges to Latin as the language of authority, an
evolving mythology of French's significance in England, and the
continued subordination of English. It is perhaps just this kind of
accommodation, this adaptive dynamics between linguistic usage
and social practice, that most clearly reveals the ideological vital-
ity of diglossia.

Like the ongoing phonological changes on Martha's Vineyard
and in New York City that Labov charted forty years ago, so a
sociolinguistic change in progress can certainly be identified,
measured, and interpreted. But whether structural or sociolinguistic change is at issue, it is crucial to discriminate origins
from foreshadowings and genealogical development from prag-

---

[69] Fasold, *The Sociolinguistics of Society*, 40–2. Colonial societies, for instance,
with a small ruling group and a large indigenous population, can demonstrate diglossia
without much bilingualism, while a society in which diglossia has collapsed may, at
least temporarily, be bilingual without functionally distinguishing between the pertinent languages. Also see Siegfried Wenzel, *Verses in Sermons: 'Fasciculus Morum'
and Its Middle English Poems* (Cambridge, Mass.: Mediaeval Academy of America,
1978). I thus think that Thorlac Turville-Petre overstates the significance of the presence of both French and English poems in London, British Library MS Harley 2253. By
weaving the French and English verse together, Turville-Petre maintains, the compiler
implied no difference in status between the two; he likewise understands the use of
Continental forms and styles in the English lyrics as a demonstration of the growing
achievement of English verse at this time. See *England the Nation* (Oxford: Clarendon,
1996), 181–221.

matic similarity. For beliefs about a language and its social meanings, historical context and sociolinguistic principles again offer means for such discriminations. These means suggest that shifts in the status of English have happened not in a linear and irreversible direction but in fits, starts, and reversals, pointing not teleologically to the linguistic future that would be but diversely to futures that could.

4

What's a Dialect Before It's a Dialect?

Linguistic repertoires and rhetorical strategies

As a natural language in a repertoire of natural languages, Middle English acquired status and social meanings through its relation to these other languages and the sociolinguistic functions it performed. It displayed social and regional variation whose own significations, within the broad context of sociolinguistic regularities, derived from and sustained the ecology of the language. Like any conception of a language, the medieval status of English thus had a specific historical construction that in turn pointed to specific historical meanings, meanings that excluded the linguistic rationalization of English or the sociolinguistic stereotyping of individual varieties but included the functional and ideological subordination of the language and the non-systemized acknowledgement of regional variation. With this status, there was English and there were its social and regional varieties, but the latter would not seem to have been sociolinguistically well formed or coherent, either by themselves or in their relations to other varieties (of English or other languages) in the linguistic repertoire of the Middle English period. Not only did east Midlands Middle English, for example, not convey the social meaning that Estuary English or Standard American English does today; but more complexly and more fundamentally, no Middle English variety could signify or convey meaning in the same ways that such modern varieties can.

At the last chapter's conclusion I described how using modern sociolinguistic expectations to examine the late-medieval status of English for glimmers of what it would be in the centuries to follow can transform both ecology and status. I now extend my inquiry by turning back from what the significance of English would become to how it could be used in the late-medieval period. While the previous chapter's topic required a broad focus, the concerns of this chapter lead me to detailed readings of just two of the most popular works in the Middle English canon: Chaucer's *Reeve's Tale* and the anonymous *Sir Gawain and the Green Knight*. My intention in focusing on such well-known poems is to suggest that despite decades of scholarship on Middle English language and literature, much remains to be discovered about the complexities and nuances of late-medieval sociolinguistic practice. And my intent in focusing on such belletristic works is not to argue for particular literary meanings as such but, drawing upon several principles of modern sociolinguistic analysis, to lay open how the late-medieval status of English functioned, how it informed and shaped social practices such as literary composition. Although this status did not imply regional or social varieties in the way modern dialectology does, the variation underlying modern conceptions certainly did exist and, like all utterances or forms, could be used to achieve various objectives. It is the nature and potential rhetorical use of this variation within the context of the status of Middle English that especially concern me. To put the matter somewhat archly, I am here interested in what a dialect is before it's a dialect.

Chaucer, variation, and the actuation problem

I begin with a linguistic fact that characterizes Chaucer as well as almost all his contemporaries: however much variation in style and register he may use, Chaucer consistently writes in what modern linguistics would call one dialect. Indeed, whether poets or prose translators, merchants or knights, or even chickens or kings, almost all Chaucer's narrators and characters almost always speak alike. Lexical choices may sometimes suggest otherwise, for one speaker can be uniquely associated with particular words or collocations. But linguistically, such choices are very much lower-order, rooted at least as deeply in the topic or structure of a given work as in any grammatical peculiarities of individual speakers. The Canon's Yeoman, thus, uses a significant number of scientific and alchemical terms, yet these are dependent on the story he is telling, and one could well imagine that if he ever could speak of another topic, his vocabulary would change accordingly. Beyond lexicon, the language of Chaucer's speakers displays even less variation, with phonology, morphology, and syntax almost always regular, whatever the genre of the work, whatever the characters that populate it. Both Alceste in the *Legend of Good Women* and the Second Nun use [əθ] as the inflectional ending on third-person singular indicative verbs; both Theseus and Chauntecleer topicalize a redundant subject in a vocative construction; and Troilus, Pandarus, the Black Knight, and the falcon in the *Squire's Tale* all rhyme *joie* with *Troie*.[1]

In the light of the single authorship of these and other works, there is in a very limited sense nothing remarkable about their linguistic consistency: each reflects the idiolect of ultimately the same speaker, Chaucer. Beyond this sense, however, several linguistic and cultural factors come into play. Real speech does vary by regional and social groupings, and some writers—including Dickens, Twain, and Faulkner—do go to great lengths to individualize the language of particular characters. Whether fictional or real, indeed, all speakers can be described in terms of what William Labov calls the six 'major independent variables of socio-

---

[1] *Legend of Good Women*, G.327, and *Canterbury Tales*, viii. 120; *Canterbury Tales*, i. 3017–20 and vii. 3140–5; *Troilus and Criseyde*, iii. 1450/52 and ii. 139–40, *Book of the Duchess*, 1065–6, *Canterbury Tales*, v. 547–8. Throughout this chapter all quotations from Chaucer's works are from Larry D. Benson (ed.), *The Riverside Chaucer*, 3rd edn. (Boston: Houghton Mifflin, 1987). I want to stress that I am here speaking of linguistic items and not styles or usages in the senses considered in M. M. Bakhtin, *The Dialogic Imagination*, ed. Michael Holquist, trans. Caryl Emerson and Michael Holquist (Austin, Tex.: University of Texas Press, 1981). To say that most of Chaucer's writing is linguistically homogeneous is not to deny the 'heteroglossia' that Bakhtin would see present in it.

linguistics: sex, age, social class, ethnicity, race, and community size.'[2] Given the Uniformitarian Principle, and given the visible evidence of language variation in the Middle English period that the documentary record provides, one presumes that the variables Labov describes were as viable then as now, even though Chaucer and other Middle English writers seem rarely to have responded to them.

If Chaucer never linguistically distinguished speakers from one another, or if he never made metalinguistic comments about social and regional variation, the issue of his linguistic regularity would be simpler. One could then posit either that linguistic variation was of no interest to him and his contemporaries or that he had no literary resources for representing it. But the fact is that he does acknowledge and depict variation, if only sporadically, and the passages in which he does so collectively present the actuation problem: the difficulty of explaining why certain forms or changes occur—or are actualized—in some circumstances but not in others.[3] This kind of problem is separate from the one of simply recounting what happened in a particular situation. As I noted at the opening of this book, it is possible to describe both social and structural factors that might have produced the English phonological changes labelled the Great Vowel Shift. Although the explanations I there gave may adequately account for the linguistic phenomena—and some might dispute even this—they bypass the actuation problem. Why, it asks, would such social and structural forces work in the concerted way they did in the fifteenth, sixteenth, and seventeenth centuries? Why wouldn't a similar change occur at any other time, since social prestige is operative in many eras—including our own—and since a mechanistic principle such as a push-chain is theoretically operable at any time?

For Chaucer's poetry, the actuation problem takes this general

[2] William Labov, *Principles of Linguistic Change*, i. *Internal Factors* (Oxford: Blackwell, 1994), 2.

[3] Uriel Weinreich, William Labov, and Marvin I. Herzog, 'Empirical Foundations for a Theory of Language Change,' in W. P. Lehmann and Yakov Malkiel (eds.), *Directions for Historical Linguistics: A Symposium* (Austin, Tex.: University of Texas Press, 1968), 95–188.

form: why did Chaucer diverge from his ordinary linguistic usage or even simply talk about social and regional variation in the places he did? Perhaps most frequently the answer is: because such usage or variation is pointed and topical, figuring briefly with a specific rhetorical effect in a fairly narrow context. His most explicit recognition of synchronic variation in this fashion occurs at the conclusion of the *Troilus*, where invocation of 'so gret diversite | In Englissh' (v. 1786–7) appears in a metatextual constellation of references to Chaucer himself, his poem, and literary history, all of which work to champion the integrity and value of Chaucer's poetry. In the *Book of the Duchess*, Chaucer goes beyond merely noting linguistic variation by rhetorically manipulating it and correlating it with social distance. Here, the Dreamer invariably uses the honorific plural *ye* to the Black Knight, who in turn always uses the familiar *thou* to his socially inferior interlocutor. On one level the *Book of the Duchess* represents Chaucer's public acknowledgement of the love and grief that his patron and own social superior, John of Gaunt, felt for his deceased wife; such pronominal nuance could be seen to reflect this relationship, even as it serves as one of the means by which the obtuse narrator can facilitate the Black Knight's testimony both to Fair White's perfection and to the grief he feels at her loss. This is the only significant grammatical differentiation between these two speakers, however, and it may be better understood as stylistic nuance than as structural variation—as a difference in register rather than sociolect.

Other metalinguistic comments by Chaucer, some of the best-known ones in fact, are essentially not concerned with social or regional variation at all. The Manciple's rejection of *lemman* as 'a knavyssh speche' (*Canterbury Tales*, ix. 205) would seem to refer more to the referent of the word than to the sociolect in which it is used, while the Eagle's avowed decision to speak 'lewedly to a lewed man' (*House of Fame*, 866) primarily evokes register (again) and not linguistic variety. Moreover, because of the narrow context in which these metalinguistic references occur, the actuation problem in each of these cases, as in the *Troilus* or the *Book of the Duchess*, can be fairly easily resolved. The Manciple's interest in *lemman* harmonizes with a Prologue and Tale that are everywhere concerned with relations between language and reality, and the Eagle's remarks, in content as well as style, manifest the same pedantic accuracy that informs his disquisition on sound waves.

The situation differs in the *Reeve's Tale*, where the representation of language variation is sustained and where the actuation problem is concomitantly more complex. Three regional varieties are present to varying degrees in the poem: the London English that Chaucer uses in the majority of his compositions, the Norfolk dialect used by the narrator, Oswald the Reeve, and the northern variety of the Cambridge clerks Aleyn and John.[4] The second two of these are my main interest here, since they deviate from Chaucer's normal linguistic usage and since they represent the earliest extant attempt in English to use writing in dialect for a sustained literary effect, thus providing an opportune platform for examining the role of regional variation in late-medieval England's linguistic repertoire, as well as the status and meaning of English it projects. Oswald's dialect occurs only sporadically, though the regional 'So theek' (3864) as his first utterance instantly announces his linguistic individuality. While he elsewhere uses a smattering of northern forms, such as 'ik' (3867 and 3888), 'lemes' (3886), 'melle' (3923), and 'abegge' (3923), these represent but a fraction of the potentially dialectal forms in his Prologue and Tale. The very sentence that begins 'So theek,' indeed, continues 'ful wel koude *I* thee quite' (emphasis added).

It is the language of Aleyn and John, extensively studied by J. R. R. Tolkien and others,[5] that represents the tale's most sig-

---

    [4] In practical terms, Oswald's Norfolk dialect does not differ from the clerks' northern dialect, though other samples of these varieties do embody differences. See Richard Beadle, 'Prolegomena to a Literary Geography of Later Medieval Norfolk,' in Felicity Riddy (ed.), *Regionalism in Late Medieval Manuscripts and Texts: Essays Celebrating the Publication of 'A Linguistic Atlas of Late Mediaeval English'* (Woodbridge: D. S. Brewer, 1991), 89–108.

    [5] J. R. R. Tolkien, 'Chaucer as a Philologist: *The Reeve's Tale,' Transactions of the Philological Society* (1934), 1–70. The *Riverside Chaucer* briefly describes the dialect features on p. 850. Also see Norman Davis, review of J. A. W. Bennett's *Chaucer at Oxford and at Cambridge* (Toronto: University of Toronto Press, 1974), *Review of English Studies*, 27 (1976), 337; and Jeremy Smith, 'The Great Vowel Shift in the North of England and Some Forms in Chaucer's Reeve's Tale,' *Neuphilologische Mitteilungen*, 95 (1994), 433–7.

nificant dialectal achievement. More consistent than Oswald's regionalisms, the clerks' dialect is also more structurally defined, with Chaucer drawing on characteristic lexicon ('lathe', 4088), morphology ('gas', 4037), phonology ('banes', 4073), and usage ('hope', 4029). Much of the sense of the clerks' northernisms none the less derives from only two features: the graph ⟨s⟩ for the third-person singular verbal inflection and the graph ⟨a⟩ to represent the vowel derived from Old English /a:/, which is typically spelled ⟨o⟩ south of the Humber River by the beginning of the thirteenth century and which is actualized as [o] in many varieties of Modern English. The effect of Chaucer's prominent use of these limited features, like the effect of some actors' affectations of accent, is remarkably convincing. Chaucer's rendering of the clerks' dialect, Charles Muscatine judges, 'is not a complete philological transcript, but neither is it a vaudeville version, easily achieved with a few odd terms.'[6]

For the *Reeve's Tale*, the actuation problem can be put very precisely: why did Chaucer, apparently for the first time in English literature, use extended writing in dialect in this *Tale* for both the narrator and some of its characters, and why did he use it here alone? What could such use of a regional variety mean and do before that variety had been accepted as a stereotype or even a marker in a linguistic repertoire? Criticism of the *Tale* has largely answered some version of these questions by conceiving the dialect forms as rhetorical devices that build on sociolinguistic suppositions about class and language and that add to the psychological reality of the clerks and the poignancy of the situation. Seeing Chaucer as a gifted philologist whose knowledge of northern English was both literary and firsthand, Tolkien conceives the

---

[6] Charles Muscatine, *Chaucer and the French Tradition: A Study in Style and Meaning* (Berkeley and Los Angeles: University of California Press, 1957), 199. The clerks' dialect might be considered a representation of what M. L. Samuels has called a '"colourless" regional language'–a variety that transcends the most specifically localized varieties by emphasizing forms generally common throughout a wide geographic locale. See 'Spelling and Dialect in the Late and Post-Medieval Periods,' in Michael Benskin and Samuels (eds.), *So meny people longages and tonges: Philological Essays in Scots and Mediaeval English Presented to Angus McIntosh* (Edinburgh: Middle English Dialect Project, 1981), 43–54.

clerks' dialect as a 'most unusual piece of dramatic realism' that is a 'by-product of a private philological curiosity' and that panders 'to popular linguistic curiosity.'[7] He calls the poem a 'slender jest' at which only 'a philologist can laugh sincerely' but in which 'Chaucer deliberately relies on the easy laughter that is roused by "dialect" in the ignorant or the unphilological.'[8] Muscatine, similarly, maintains that the presence of dialect owes 'to some special literary demand'—specifically, the irony of having Symkyn the miller bested by clerks whose 'speech represents them to the miller as country bumpkins of no social position whatsoever.'[9] Thomas Garbáty draws on the medieval reputation of Norfolk to advance a related argument. Since many fourteenth-century residents of Norfolk emigrated to London, Garbáty maintains that

---

[7] Tolkien, 'Chaucer as a Philologist,' 3. Dorothy Everett also sees verisimilitude in the clerks' dialect, suggesting that in the *Tale* Chaucer is 'mimicking living speech' of people he actually heard. See 'Chaucer's Good Ear,' in *Essays on Middle English Literature,* ed. Patricia Kean (Oxford: Clarendon, 1955), 144–5. I want to note here that textual transmission of the *Reeve's Tale* supports the view of regional dialects that I advanced in the preceding chapter. Tolkien saw dialectal variations among manuscript copies of the *Tale* as evidence of a 'gradual whittling away of the individuality of Chaucer's text' and therefore reconstructed a hypothetical original with more northernisms than any extant manuscript ('Chaucer as a Philologist,' 12). N. F. Blake has shown, however, that during the course of transmission scribes, many of them presumably accustomed to copying northern works, actually increased the northern character of the clerks' language, primarily through changes in orthography (hence phonology) rather than lexicon. But if the scribes clearly recognized that forms associated with the north were intrinsic to the work, they give no evidence that they recognized Northern as a well-defined, internally consistent linguistic variety, for they do not change the language with any regularity. In Blake's view, furthermore, the fact that few lexical items were changed suggests that these may well have been understood as aspects less of region than of register: 'This minimal tampering with the vocabulary reinforces the point . . . that the words themselves were not important as markers of northernisms. At best they indicated a level of discourse.' See 'The Northernisms in *The Reeve's Tale,*' *Lore and Language,* 3 (1979), 5–6. Paris, Bibliothèque Nationale MS anglais 39 makes this case with particular strength. Copied by a scribe named Duxworth for Jean d'Angoulême, this manuscript everywhere manifests a northernizing tendency. Yet the language of Aleyn and John in the *Reeve's Tale* shows no more of a northern colouring than any other portion of the manuscript, a situation that implies that even a scribe who himself used northern features did not recognize the integrity of a Northern dialect. Blake's conclusions have been supported and extended in S. C. Horobin, 'J. R. R. Tolkien as a Philologist: A Reconsideration of the Northernisms in Chaucer's *Reeve's Tale,*' *English Studies,* 82 (2001), 97–105.

[8] Tolkien, 'Chaucer as a Philologist,' 2–3.

[9] Muscatine, *Chaucer and the French Tradition,* 199, 201.

Oswald's dialect would have been associated with a stock figure of provinciality whose language was 'ludicrous in polite society.' Oswald, in turn, 'took it on himself to mimic a provincial dialect in his own barbarous jargon. What hilarious nonsense and what a brilliant connotative linguistic joke!'[10]

A wholly different kind of answer to the question of why Chaucer used writing in dialect in the *Reeve's Tale* might see literary tradition as the motivation of the clerks' speech. In French fabliaux, linguistic exuberance takes many forms, including obscenity, wordplay, and solecism, with such devices and concerns so prevalent that they can be seen, Howard Bloch suggests, to be indications of the genre's central characteristic as a 'sustained reflection upon literary language writ so large across these rhymed comic tales whose subject, mimetic realism notwithstanding, is the nature of poetry itself.'[11] Further, the plots of some fabliaux, such as *Le Roy d'Angleterre et le Jongleur d'Ely*, largely turn on linguistic confusion, which is thereby a source of narrative as well as humour. Though writing in dialect is absent in all the analogues of the *Reeve's Tale*, it might be argued that a story such as Oswald's carried with it the expectation that such writing, or at least linguistic ingenuity, could be used as a stylistic feature.[12]

But all such arguments can only partially account for the presence of dialect in the *Reeve's Tale*. Like my account of the Great Vowel Shift, they interpret sociolinguistic phenomena without

---

[10] Thomas Jay Garbáty, 'Satire and Regionalism: The Reeve and His Tale,' *Chaucer Review*, 8 (1973), 6–7. For similar arguments about the realism and the putatively innate humour of dialect as the mark of an outsider, also see M. Copland, '*The Reeve's Tale*: Harlotrie or Sermonyng?' *Medium Ævum*, 31 (1962), 14–32; N. F. Blake, *Non-Standard Language in English Literature* (London: Andre Deutsch, 1981), 28–33; and Hans H. Meier, 'Past Presences of Older Scots Abroad,' in Caroline Macafee and Iseabail Macleod (eds.), *The Nuttis Schell: Essays on the Scots Language presented to A. J. Aitken* (Aberdeen: Aberdeen University Press, 1987), 118.

[11] R. Howard Bloch, *The Scandal of the Fabliaux* (Chicago: University of Chicago Press, 1986), 19. On linguistic play in the fabliaux see further Muscatine, *Chaucer and the French Tradition*, 64–5, and *The Old French Fabliaux* (New Haven: Yale University Press, 1986), 105–15; and John Hines, *The Fabliau in English* (London: Longman, 1993), 18–23.

[12] Blake, 'The Northernisms in *The Reeve's Tale*,' 7, and *Non-Standard Language in English Literature*, 29. Also see Glending Olson, '*The Reeve's Tale* as a Fabliau,' *Modern Language Quarterly*, 35 (1974), 219–30.

explaining why they may have come about in a particular situation. These responses to the *Reeve's Tale* propose readings of what the dialect does in the narrative, but they do not address the broadest implications of the actuation problem, since they do not account for why dialect should be used here and nowhere else. If a northern dialect is meant as a philological joke, it is not apparent how the *Reeve's Tale* is a more appropriate context than, say, the *Merchant's Tale* or the *House of Fame*. As I argued in Ch. 3, moreover, writing in dialect is not inherently funny; dialect writing may be, but it is a post-medieval invention contingent on social, literary, and orthographic developments of the eighteenth and nineteenth centuries in particular. And if Oswald is a boorish bumpkin, then so is the Miller, who for all his churlishness speaks a language structurally indistinguishable from that of the assorted kings and queens of Chaucer's poetry.[13] Tracing the presence of dialect to Old French fabliaux offers little more satisfaction, since Chaucer tells several other fabliaux, none of which has writing in dialect. Why should the clerks speak northern English, and not Daun John of the Shipman's fabliau, or, more tellingly, the friar and Thomas in the *Sumnour's Tale*, a work that is situated in Yorkshire? For that matter, why should Oswald use even inconsistent Norfolkisms, when the Shipman from Dartmouth gives no hint of south-west Middle English nor the Friar of his lisp? Everything positive that the writing in dialect has been seen to contribute to the *Reeve's Tale* might equally contribute in these works, and yet Chaucer made the effort only with it.

The actuation problem of the *Reeve's Tale* is thus at once literary, historical, and linguistic. Given a range of possible linguistic forms—whether varieties or specific linguistic items—and given a range of literary possibilities—including narrators, characters, settings, plots, and genres—Chaucer, a member of the court who

---

[13] Norman E. Eliason similarly notes that though the Miller is said to be a drunken churl, 'so far as we can tell from the text of his tale . . . his pronunciation is not one whit different from the Knight's. That a miller and a knight actually spoke alike is surely doubtful, but the difference apparently didn't matter' (*The Language of Chaucer's Poetry: An Appraisal of the Verse, Style, and Structure* (Copenhagen: Rosenkilde & Bagger, 1972), 36).

ordinarily wrote and presumably spoke a variety of London English, chose to produce a sporadically regional Norfolk Reeve who tells a fabliau that contains two convincingly regional clerks. In making this stylistic choice, Chaucer, like Henry III when he chose to produce his English letters, had to work with the status of Middle English and the ways regional and social variation of the vernacular figured in it; and by this status, specifically late-medieval attitudes towards language variation shaped the general conception of regional varieties (and their speakers) and their relationships with each other as well as the ways such relationships could contribute to literary works. Such a configuration—more broadly, such meaning and status for English—is therefore not the subject but the matter of the *Reeve's Tale*, some of the material that allowed Chaucer to think about and represent social concerns in the narrator, characters, and narrative of a crafted literary work.

Literary design and sociolinguistic presumption

As a reeve and a man of Norfolk, Oswald projects two well-documented satiric traditions. Because reeves collected rents for landowners, they acted as go-betweens for lords and tenants, and in the process found themselves both socially ambiguous and liable to accusations, accurate and inaccurate alike, of the abuse of power. Survival in such a position presumably required both skill and resilience, the very qualities conventionally associated with reeves and the ones Oswald displayed when, affronted, he plotted a rejoinder as the Miller told his tale.[14] The traditional reputation of Norfolk offered much the same kind of characterization. One

---

[14] On the responsibilities and reputations of reeves, see further Bennett, *Chaucer at Oxford and at Cambridge*, 87–116, and Jill Mann, *Chaucer and Medieval Estates Satire: The Literature of Social Classes and the 'General Prologue' to the 'Canterbury Tales'* (Cambridge: Cambridge University Press, 1973), 163–4. John Matthews Manly argued that Oswald's malfeasance was inspired by the fourteenth-century disrepair of contested property held by the Earl of Pembroke, some of which may have been in Norfolk. See *Some New Light on Chaucer* (1926; rpt. Gloucester, Mass.: Peter Smith, 1959), 84–94.

of the leading regions for emigration to London in the fourteenth
century, Norfolk shared in the general economic importance of
East Anglia at this time. Such a combination of expanding social
presence and economic success might well lead an observer to
resentment, and alleged avarice and greed were in fact the hallmarks of the Norfolk type. As new and frequent immigrants in
London, people from Norfolk might well further elicit reputations
of being boorish and unsophisticated, all of which would render
the description of Oswald as a reeve from Norfolk a metonymy
for cunning, avarice, and social ambition.[15]

Oswald's narrative strategies reflect these very qualities. As
several critics have argued,[16] the *Reeve's Tale* ranks as one of the
bleakest in the collection, a story vile in its plot, populated with
unregenerate characters, and told by a voice at once contemptu-
ous and hypocritical. 'Stynt thy clappe!' (3144) are the first words
Oswald utters when he perceives the Miller has insulted him, and
if the self-righteousness and hostility of this interruption portend
the rage of his *Tale*, the possessive attitude he goes on to display
towards wives and reputations also recalls the greed and social
self-interest associated with reeves throughout the period. These
same qualities appear again in the Reeve's prologue to his *Tale*.
By its very homiletic structure and sanctimony, to which Chaucer
draws attention with the word 'sermonyng' (3899), the prologue
recalls the social aspirations first imaged in Oswald's 'top . . .
dokked lyk a preest biforn' (590) and reprised when in response
Harry Bailey himself begins 'to speke as lordly as a kyng' (3900).
For all his aspirations, however, the Reeve is a dangerous, even
damned pilgrim, conflating sexuality with avarice and given to
theological despair. Financially well off, Oswald can none the
less never join the ranks of his employers, since it is implausible
that he would be able to buy his way into the gentry. Conversely,
even disregarding the ferocity of his personality, his activities

---

[15] See Mann, *Chaucer and Medieval Estates Satire*, 166; Garbáty, 'Satire and Regionalism'; and Alan J. Fletcher, 'Chaucer's Norfolk Reeve,' *Medium Ævum*, 52 (1983),
100–3.

[16] See in particular V. A. Kolve, *Chaucer and the Imagery of Narrative: The First
Five Canterbury Tales* (Stanford, Calif.: Stanford University Press, 1984), 217–56.

as a rent-collector would do little to curry sympathy and affinity among the tenants under his supervision; his job alone might lead others to fear him as 'the deeth.' Like the Sumnour, he is thus socially detached, a member of the third estate who none the less makes his living enforcing the directives of his superiors against his peers. Were he to cease being a reeve or to terminate his attachment to Norfolk, this detachment might yield a more distinct position in the hierarchy of medieval society. But because of his position as a reeve, he can have little more than a business connection with the lord for whom he works, and very few social connections—perhaps religion alone—with other members of the third estate, who are unlikely to want to share housing, recreation, or other communal activities with the man to whom they pay rent. Emblematic of the Reeve's separation from the other Canterbury pilgrims is the fact that, according to Chaucer, 'evere he rood the hyndreste of oure route' (622).

In sociolinguistic terms, Oswald is a weakly tied speaker who exists in a relatively open network—someone whose job, family, or friends provide few social connections to one another or to those who live around him.[17] Such speakers are not likely to speak the most characteristic version of any regional or social variety, for these versions statistically correlate with those who are the most well integrated into a given social group.[18] While all varieties and idiolects embody structural variation, the particular mixture of southern and Norfolk forms that Oswald speaks thus matches what sociolinguistics predicts about speakers with his socially ambiguous status. At the same time, Oswald's weak ties mark him as the kind of individual who is most likely to initiate changes in lexicon, phonology, and morphology.[19] Not firmly connected to any region or social group, weakly tied speakers have the opportunity to move among various groups and acquire various linguistic forms. Because they are weakly tied, further,

[17] Lesley Milroy, *Language and Social Networks*, 2nd edn. (Oxford: Blackwell, 1987); James Milroy, *Linguistic Variation and Change: On the Historical Sociolinguistics of English* (Oxford: Blackwell, 1992); and J. K. Chambers, *Sociolinguistic Theory: Linguistic Variation and Its Social Significance* (Oxford: Blackwell, 1995), 34–101.
[18] Milroy, *Language and Social Networks*, 30.   [19] Ibid. 197–207.

there is little consequence to their mixing the forms of different varieties, for they neither use a particular variety in their own self-definition nor risk any significant group standing through such mixing. Without attempting to resurrect Tolkien's notion that the appearance of Oswald's Norfolk language in a London poem mimics the direction from which literary English developed, a notion effectively demolished by M. L. Samuels,[20] I do want to suggest that sociolinguistically the Reeve is precisely the kind of person who would have been responsible for introducing changes to a developing London variety of English. For social more than regional reasons, figures such as the Reeve, rather than the presumptively northern-speaking but socially more integrated characters of the *Sumnour's Tale*, are the ones who probably initiated pronominal forms such as *their* and *them* and the verbal inflection [s] in southern English.

Several sociolinguistic motivations might underlie such a figure's incorporation of regional forms in his *Tale*. Most commonly, speakers use regionalisms simply due to a lack of cognizance of what constitutes a regionalism—individuals speak, that is, without any metalinguistic awareness at all. As common as it may be, however, such an explanation ill accounts for Oswald's usage, because, in so far as he employs dialect in his characterization of the clerks, he would seem to have a high degree of metalinguistic awareness. Another motivation for regionalisms, as Labov and others have shown, would be to use language as a means of identifying with a particular area whose language, for its speakers, has covert prestige. Labov's now classic study of Martha's Vineyard in fact showed that speakers can desire so strongly to dissociate themselves from a variety with overt prestige that they hypercorrect their language by speaking a regional variety containing more characteristic forms than are statistically customary. In the case of Martha's Vineyard, individuals who wished to identify with the island against the influx of summer tourists from the mainland produced an exaggerated number of the centralized

[20] Tolkien, 'Chaucer as a Philologist,' 6, and Samuels, 'Some Applications of Middle English Dialectology,' in Margaret Laing (ed.), *Middle English Dialectology: Essays on Some Principles and Problems* (Aberdeen: Aberdeen University Press, 1989), 74.

diphthongs for which the island was popularly known.[21] Such hypercorrection figures more generally in what M. A. K. Halliday calls 'the sociolinguistic play potential of one's own variety of the language.'[22] Not wishing to submerge its identity into that of a socioeconomically dominant coterie but variously pressured to do so, a particular social group may develop coded linguistic play, involving such features as syntax and lexicon as well as discursive practices, that is intended at once to define the social group, to maintain the distinctive linguistic variety of that group, and to erect barriers of intelligibility between it and other, more powerful groups.

Is this how we should understand the Reeve's regionalisms? It would indeed be tempting to read his own Norfolk forms and his projection of northern forms to the clerks as attempts to dissociate himself from the other pilgrims, for such a reading would be consistent with his character as Chaucer presents him—'thin, worn, tetchy, and uncompanionable,' in J. A. W. Bennett's memorable description.[23] Yet if Oswald's regionalisms were motivated by covert prestige, one would expect that Chaucer would have allowed the Reeve even more dialect forms, for the handful that he does use, even though they are unmistakably regional, can just barely connect him with Norfolk, and nowhere does his language become remotely obscure enough to exclude his, and Chaucer's, primarily southern Midlands audience. For the clerks as well as Oswald, in fact, language variation never impedes communication, since while we recognize the existence of language variation, we never fail to comprehend what Aleyn and John mean, and neither does Symkyn the miller nor any of his family.[24.]

---

[21] Labov, *Sociolinguistic Patterns* (Philadelphia: University of Pennsylvania Press, 1972), 1–42. For an account of similar sociolinguistic phenomena in the Ballymacarett region of Belfast, see Milroy, *Language and Social Networks*, 103–4.

[22] Halliday, *Language as Social Semiotic: The Social Interpretation of Language and Meaning* (London: Edward Arnold, 1978), 160.

[23] Bennett, *Chaucer at Oxford and at Cambridge*, 89.

[24] The one occasion on which the language of the clerks does seem to be at issue is when John tells Symkyn, 'Oure manciple, I hope he wil be deed' (4029). Here John intends *hope* to mean 'think,' a sense found in northern England, while a southerner would initially understand the word to mean 'desire.' This ambivalent usage produces humour

Regionalisms can also function as traces of a rejected variety, relict items of a language that a speaker is working to eliminate. Whether the rejected variety is an immigrant language or a regional dialect, speakers wishing assimilation can accommodate themselves to a desirable social world by approximating its language forms, much as speakers wishing separation from that world can manipulate the sociolinguistic play potential of their native variety.[25] According to this model, the Reeve, as an outsider, might use language to moderate his differences with those around him, with his primarily southern Midlands language reflecting a desire to assimilate with the rest of the Canterbury pilgrims. From a strictly literary point of view, such a model would enrich our understanding of the Reeve, for it would connect the sociolinguistic impulse of accommodation with Oswald's anger and Chaucer's manipulation of traditional stereotypes. Given the hypocrisy elsewhere associated with Oswald, the regional ambivalence of his language would mark him as someone fostering the impression of desired assimilation, even as he himself works against this impression, exposing it, willy nilly, as mere illusion. Just as the content of the prologue to the *Reeve's Tale* subverts the sermon-like qualities constructed by certain linguistic forms (e.g. lexicon and metaphor), so Oswald's character and the details of the *Tale* itself could then be seen to work against any feigned attempt at linguistic and social assimilation: Oswald's choice of a largely southern variety might gesture towards accommodation, while the content of his speech advances antagonism, contempt, and despair.

But as useful as this analysis is for approaching the regionalisms of the *Reeve's Tale*, it still leaves difficulties in terms of the

rather than confusion, however, and it is humour Symkyn and Oswald do not get or at least do not comment upon. On the quantifiability of dialect shifting, see Lesley Milroy, *Observing and Analysing Natural Language: A Critical Account of Sociolinguistic Method* (Oxford: Blackwell, 1987), 34.

[25] Gillian Sankoff points out this kind of assimilation by language is ultimately self-defeating, since it endorses a dominant group's mystification of a symbol (in this case a particular social or regional variety) of the presumptively inherent inferiority of the object (the social group itself) that it is understood to represent; once a group eliminates its troublesome linguistic behaviour, 'other symbols can always be found' (*The Social Life of Language* (Philadelphia: University of Pennsylvania Press, 1980), 14).

actuation problem and a broader understanding of what a regional variety might do before it is recognized as a regional dialect within the context of a language's social status. The Pardoner, perhaps the most hypocritical of all the Canterbury pilgrims, gives no evidence of a regional or social variety that has been suppressed through accommodation, nor does the wilful and sometimes deceitful Wife of Bath, nor the Miller, who is paired with the Reeve in the arrangement of *Tales* and in the way they frame the order of the pilgrims leaving the Tabard Inn. If Oswald's linguistic ambivalence appropriately reflects his character psychology, such ambivalence would seem equally appropriate for the Pardoner, Wife, and Miller.

The sociolinguistic principles I have been exploring treat Oswald is if he were a real person with real volition, and of course he isn't. For the sake of the argument, such treatment is safe enough and in fact affords, I think, a deepened appreciation of the *Reeve's Tale* as a work of art. It does not, however, exhaust understanding of the poem's sociolinguistic contexts or its relevance to the late-medieval status of English. Here I want to turn to the issue of how Oswald's language testifies for Chaucer's purposes rather than his own and to ask this question: granting that the Reeve is a fictional character, what do the regional forms that Oswald uses contribute to the poem in its entirety? To answer this question, I need to focus on the literary design of the *Tale*, beginning with the fact that the characters who populate it share the Reeve's distinctive mixture of social ambition and moral failure. Symkyn, the deceitful miller, is as 'any pecock . . . proud and gay' (3926), ultimately concerned not with any misery his daughter may have suffered but with his own honour:

> 'Why dorste be so boold to disparage
> My doghter, that is come of swich lynage?'   (4271–2)[26]

---

[26] Muscatine further suggests that 'disparage' here does not mean simply dishonour: 'the word has clearly a strong flavor of the older meaning, "to match unequally; to degrade or dishonour by marrying to one of inferior rank." The miller is chagrined, not at what has been done to his daughter, but that it has been done by someone of lower class!' (*Chaucer and the French Tradition*, 204).

The miller's wife matches his perverse social ambitions, for as the daughter of the parson—even if illegitimately so—she would allow 'no wight clepen hire but "dame"' (3956), and because of her lineage and education conducts herself with aloofness (3966–8). Their daughter, Malyn, projects the same false, even deluded, ambitions as her parents. Her grandfather the parson desires to bestow her into 'som worthy blood of auncetrye' (3982), while her father, as I have already remarked, regards the fact that a lineage as putatively high as Malyn's has been compromised to be a notably grievous consequence of the events in his house. Yet the Reeve records no protest when Aleyn enters her bed, and the sentiment of her farewell to him suggests that she has been a willing and experienced partner. Indeed, Oswald certainly leaves the impression that the baby of the house, referred to only as 'a child that was of half yeer age' (3971), is her son rather than brother and thereby further undermines any pretensions to innocence that Malyn may have.[27]

While the clerks' motivations of poverty and a desire to expose Symkyn's fraudulent activities might initially make them sympathetic characters, such sympathy quickly dissipates as they likewise conduct themselves with the misguided social aspiration that motivates the other characters. The miller's theft of their corn, for instance, troubles Aleyn and John less than does the fact that it represents a loss of their honour (4109–13), and when John watches Aleyn climb into Malyn's bed, his motivation to sleep with Symkyn's wife hinges not on sexual desire but on the consequences inactivity might have for his own reputation:

> 'He auntred hym, and has his nedes sped,
> And I lye as a draf-sak in my bed;
> And when this jape is tald another day,
> I sal been halde a daf, a cokenay!'   (4205–8)

[27] The infant is nearly twenty years younger than Malyn, and when his presumptive mother, Symkyn's wife, embraces John, Oswald notes, 'So myrie a fit ne hadde she nat ful yoore' (4230). In the Old French analogue *Le Meunier et Les II Clers*, by comparison, the baby is unambiguously that of the miller and his wife, just as the daughter is unambiguously a virgin who is clearly seduced, in part because the clerk assures her that he has a ring with a magic stone that can restore virginity.

In effect, social ambition constitutes a dynamic tension between the clerks and the miller, with neither side wishing to yield reputation to the other. If Aleyn and John conceive the miller as a social inferior and for that reason want compensation all the more for falling prey to his scheme at the mill, Symkyn relishes the opportunity to best the clerks as educated individuals higher up the social scale than he. He knowingly smiles at their 'nycetee' (4046) in imagining that they can prevent him from cheating them, gloats to his wife that '"Yet kan a millere make a clerkes berd"' (4096), and in apologizing for the size of his house mocks the theoretical operations of scholastic logic:

> 'Myn hous is streit, but ye han lerned art;
> Ye konne by argumentes make a place
> A myle brood of twenty foot of space.'   (4122–4)

This fundamental similarity in outlook between Symkyn and the clerks further complicates any arguments for seeing their regionalisms as satirically directed against them. They are not the fools of the *Tale*, for they spend an amorous night in the miller's house, beat him soundly, and ultimately recover the cake made from their grain. At the same time, even if their language is meant to suggest some kind of social inferiority, so that their besting of the Midlands-speaking miller is ironic,[28] they clearly elicit no sympathy from the reader. Like Symkyn, they exhibit cunning and, in particular, social ambition, while the nature of the vengeance they enact reflects a notion of self-interest that matches Symkyn's avarice and a notion of sexuality that recalls Oswald's. Miller and clerks alike conceive an open social system in which their dealings are inherently strategic, so that what they really fight over is not virtue or a cake or a bag of grain but a claim to a higher position in the social hierarchy.

With six medieval and early modern analogues in four languages, the *Reeve's Tale* provides ample contextual corroboration for the sociolinguistic qualities that I have been exploring here.[29]

---

[28] Muscatine, *Chaucer and the French Tradition*, 200–1.
[29] The two extant versions of *Le Meunier et Les II Clers* can be found in W. M. Hart,

While all versions agree on the general point of the moving of a cradle as a prelude to an amorous encounter, and while nearly every event in Chaucer's story corresponds to something similar in another version, the *Reeve's Tale* stands alone in the emphasis it gives to social pretension. The ambitions of Symkyn and his wife do not figure in the analogues, and the clerks' motivation is elsewhere plain lust, not socially motivated vengeance. Further, the characters in other versions tend not to have the moral failings of those in the *Reeve's Tale*, so that the atmosphere in general contains less social satire and more of the rambunctiousness that typically characterizes fabliaux. In the analogue *Le Meunier et Les II Clers* not only is the daughter indubitably the victim of the clerk's seduction, but the wife, far from having a 'myrie . . . fit,' admits that she has been tricked. In the *Reeve's Tale*, by contrast, Chaucer has shaped a story that everywhere satirizes social pretensions in an unsympathetic if not hostile fashion and has allowed it to be told by a figure who is himself the object of satire and who, standing outside the established social hierarchy, aspires to rise in the hierarchy none the less.

Disorder, disruption, discourse

When a variety is understood to have the integrity of a regional or social dialect as conventionally understood in modern linguistics, it occupies a clear place in a language's ecology; and with its own meanings fixed, it in turn helps to sustain the ecology in general. Even as Nynorsk is not merely the instrument but also the expression of Norwegian nativism, for example, so it contributes to the shape of Norway's linguistic repertoire and to the

'The Reeve's Tale,' in W. F. Bryan and Germaine Dempster (eds.), *Sources and Analogues of Chaucer's Canterbury Tales* (Chicago: University of Chicago Press, 1941), 124–47. Along with two German, a Latin, and a Danish ballad analogue, these two (with translations of all) appear in Larry D. Benson and Theodore M. Andersson, *The Literary Context of Chaucer's Fabliaux: Texts and Translations* (Indianapolis: Bobbs-Merrill, 1971), 79–201. For a comparative, structuralist analysis of several of these versions, see Erik Hertog, *Chaucer's Fabliaux as Analogues* (Leuven: Leuven University Press, 1991), 58–84.

social significances particular varieties can have within it. Almost perversely, this kind of contribution can include a variety's own sociolinguistic subordination to other varieties, for the identification of a variety as a subordinated dialect and the propagation of its stereotype (in Labov's terms) can occur among its speakers as well as its critics. More importantly, since language planning has as its characteristic goal extralinguistic objectives of social management, such subordination neutralizes whatever challenge the variety, its speakers, or ideas articulated in it may represent to the dominant institutions and practices of a society.[30] Thus it is in the United States today when African American Vernacular English is the punchline of racist jokes about the Oakland school board's 1996 designation of Ebonics as a genetically distinct language, and thus it was when Norman historiography effectively denied English its own discursive identity in the twelfth century; in the one case, speakers' social concerns are subverted by conceptualization of their language as inherently humorous, in the other by transformation of the linguistic repertoire in which their language existed. The very quality that makes African American Vernacular English a part of rather than simply a medium for social dissent and difference—its place in the linguistic repertoire of the United States—is thereby made to work against its sociolinguistic impact. When varieties lack the clear status of regional or social dialect in a language's ecology—as was the case with the fourteenth-century varieties of English—there will still be variation, but such varieties will not be sociolinguistically ordered with respect to each other for prestige, power, and the like. By the same token, such ordering cannot help to advance or trivialize sentiments articulated in any particular variety simply by virtue of their expression in that variety.

In this kind of ecology, the dynamics of linguistic and social variation can none the less still be volatile. With assorted monsters and angels, twelfth-century historiography graphically articulates an early medieval implication of linguistic diversity in social dis-

---

[30] As Halliday aptly notes, 'The trouble lies not in a different vowel system but in a different value system' (*Language as Social Semiotic*, 162).

ruption, and several late-medieval sociolinguistic controversies point to similar volatility. Perhaps most famously, the Lollards' translation of the Bible into English and use of the vernacular were part of a programme at once theological and social: a disruption of church hierarchies that opened up some of the sacred and powerful domains of Latin to the English-speaking masses. Inasmuch as the words of the Lollards were at issue, their books were burned as well as, and sometimes instead of, the individuals themselves.[31] As intimated by the chronicler Henry Knighton, the appearance of women preachers among the Lollards furthered this association between their divergent language practices and social disruption, since such speakers challenged gendered social attitudes towards authorized, public speech as well as traditional religious propositions. By cultivating its own written variety—what Samuels has called Central Midland Standard—and by closely supervising the production of its texts, moreover, Lollardy itself implicitly endorsed such associations between linguistic and social disruption. That is, representing itself as an advocate of genuine Christian principles and order, Lollardy utilized part of the linguistic ideology that underwrote the order it challenged: it sought discursive stability as a vehicle that would legitimate its theologically destabilizing propositions.

The disruption of language variation and the appropriation of orthodox sociolinguistic strategies also figure in the Peasants' Revolt of 1381. Discursive practices could conceive of and represent the rebels only as illiterate thugs, but though they did burn books, they also spared ecclesiastical works as well as the library of John of Gaunt. Rather than attempting to advance the cause of English orality over that of Latin textuality, the events of 1381 suggest the rebels co-opting the power of written discourse and claiming it for themselves. By propagating the six letters in which they imitated the structure of royal works, they in effect

---

[31] Reginald Pecock, for instance, was accused of Lollardy, and though his life was spared, his writings were publicly burnt in Oxford in 1457. See further Pecock, *The Repressor of Over Much Blaming of the Clergy*, ed. Churchill Babington, RS 19, 2 vols. (London: Longman, 1860), i. 128; and *The Reule of Crysten Religioun*, ed. William Cabell Greet, EETS os 171 (London: Oxford University Press, 1927), 17–22.

established their own written tradition.[32] Like Lollardy, the Peasants' Revolt thus made ambivalent use of sociolinguistic orthodoxy. On the one hand, both movements challenged and sought to replace certain traditional ideas but decidedly not to effect a complete social revolution. On the other, to do so they appropriated orthodox strategies that in the process affirmed linguistic and social disruption as concomitants of one another. In this regard at least, the neutralization of subversive language of the Middle Ages parallels modern sociolinguistic practice. Much as non-standard speakers today sustain their own linguistic subordination when they acknowledge alleged communicative deficiencies in their own variety, so, ultimately, did both the Lollards and those involved in the Peasants' Revolt by invoking associations between medieval sociolinguistic practice and acceptable social ideas.

Beyond this parallel, however, lie critical differences between the status and representation of subversive language in the ecologies of Middle and Modern English. While in the ecology of the modern period subversiveness can depend on the social status of the particular variety in which an utterance is made, in the Middle Ages, when varieties of English lacked the clear social significance of their modern counterparts, this subversion would seem to hinge on the ecology in its entirety. There, it was language variation from a traditional pattern of any sort—whether among Latin and English, men and women, or literate and illiterate—that correlated directly with social instabilities. This is essentially the same correlation, of course, that animates Norman historiography, in which variation from an imagined monoglot community evokes civil and spiritual disturbances, whatever the contact language. Unlike the practices of twelfth-century Anglo-Norman chroniclers, the proliferation of late-medieval dialect translation implies that language variation may then have been regarded as an inherently human condition that needed to be accommodated. But as the sinful outcome of Babel, it remained inherently dangerous as well, something reflecting social disruption even as it propa-

---

[32] See Steven Justice, *Writing and Rebellion: England in 1381* (Berkeley and Los Angeles: University of California Press, 1994).

gated it. All the activities I have just considered were thus socially destabilizing because of the activities themselves (such as writing subversive theology) and because they constituted a break from the inherited language ecology (such as by writing this theology in a language other than Latin). Against this broad background of medieval metalinguistic thought, I suggest, the issue was not the vernacular as such or what has increasingly been called vernacular culture but rather the disruption of a traditional distribution of varieties within the linguistic repertoire of late-medieval England. Put another way, social upheaval correlated not with the use of a particular variety (whether a language or a dialect as loosely defined) but with the violation of ecological expectations. This distinction, like that between the intentional cultivation of linguistic nationalism and Henry III's strategic use of the foreigner question, is a subtle one with profound consequences both for our view of the late-medieval status of English and for the sociolinguistic expectations we bring to it.

These issues bear directly on the question of what dialects can do before they are dialects and the actuation problem of the *Reeve's Tale*. Beginning with its teller, the *Tale* depicts a world in which social movement is everywhere possible, insistent, and reprehensible, a world of sexual and social aberration. Equally aberrant within the context of Chaucer's predominantly London variety are Oswald's few Norfolk forms and the clerks' northernisms. In effect, the poem expresses a homology of sexual, social, and linguistic deviance by means of which the significance of the clerks' language lies less in its northern associations than in the mere fact that it differs from the language Chaucer typically uses and that is used everywhere else in the *Canterbury Tales*, including the narrative of the *Reeve's Tale* itself. The irregular forms thereby index not the clerks' aspirations as such but those of a *Tale* that in its entirety represents a world of overweening social ambition. Such a sociolinguistic viewpoint also accounts for why the language of Aleyn and John, like that of Oswald, remains completely intelligible to a London audience, both fictional and real. When language varieties are structurally divergent, communication remains possible as long as context provides speakers with adequate information for interpreting what is being said.[33] Even if Trevisa's claims about the communicative difficulties between northern and southern dialects of Middle English were absolutely true, the *Reeve's Tale* demonstrates that a shared cultural background renders not only the clerks' language intelligible to Symkyn but also, perhaps more importantly, the sociolinguistic implications of the *Tale* comprehensible to a southern medieval reading audience. To exaggerate linguistic differences to the point that communication ceases, indeed, is to imply a similar break in understanding of social processes. And if what Aleyn, John, and Oswald say would have been unintelligible, then, equally, so would have been the social disruption they evoke. In effect, linguistic unintelligibility, like the trivialization of modern sociolects, neutralizes social upheaval. What makes the social ambition of the *Reeve's Tale* dangerous is the fact that it is intelligible and as such still potent.

Both directly and indirectly Chaucer's procedures in other works likewise implicate violations of medieval England's linguistic ecology in social disruption. The *Miller's Tale* doubles the plot of the *Knight's Tale* in much the same way the *Reeve's Tale* does, besides sharing with it general features of the fabliau tradition. Yet the social difference between the carpenter John and the clerks Absalon and Nicholas is never at issue, and the carpenter is duped not because of his social aspirations but because of his foolishness. The *Miller's Tale* thus lacks the qualities that I am arguing make writing in dialect appropriate to the *Reeve's Tale*, and all the characters in it in fact speak essentially the same variety of English. The *Clerk's Tale* points to this same conclusion from the opposite direction. This is a story of social differences, with the two main characters, Walter and Griselda, pointedly described as being from opposite ends of the social spectrum. But while the story may question a traditional social hierarchy, it does not undermine it in the way the *Reeve's Tale* does: at the end of the *Clerk's Tale* Walter remains marquis and is in fact able

---

[33] Trudgill, *On Dialect: Social and Geographical Perspectives* (New York: New York University Press, 1983), 29.

to pass the title to his son. As a story that ultimately maintains social stratification, the *Clerk's Tale* differs thematically from the *Reeve's Tale*; so, too, does it differ linguistically, for despite the social differences of Walter and Griselda, they speak the same variety of Middle English.

When social stability is at issue in the *Parliament of Fowls*, however, Chaucer's procedures do recall the *Reeve's Tale* by representing a stable linguistic ecology as a reflection of a stable social order and vice versa. Assembled in a parliament and speaking under the dominion of Nature and according to their 'kynde' (401), the birds in the *Parliament* constitute a hierarchical society mimetic of fourteenth-century England. Yet this society breaks down when, with the tersels unable to agree on the appropriate mate for the formel, the lower birds demand that the process be hurried along so that they, too, can choose their mates. In form as well as content, their demands openly challenge the authority of Nature and the hierarchical society that is naturalized by her. Thus, the tersel phrases his petition in elegant, courtly speech:

> 'Unto my soverayn lady, and not my fere,
> I chese, and chese with wil, and herte, and thought,
> The formel on youre hond, so wel iwrought,
> Whos I am al, and evere wol hire serve,
> Do what hire lest, to do me lyve or sterve.'   (416–20)

The lower birds, however, utilize a variety of imperatives, oaths, deprecations, and outright non-human utterances:

> The noyse of foules for to be delyvered
> So loude rong, 'have don, and lat us wende!'
> That wel wende I the wode hadde al toshyvered.
> 'Com of!' they criede, 'allas, ye wol us shende!
> Whan shal youre cursede pletynge have an ende?'
>
> The goos, the cokkow, and the doke also
> So cryed, 'Kek Kek! kokkow! quek quek!' hye,
> That thorough myne eres the noyse wente tho.
> The goos seyde, 'Al this nys not worth a flye!'
>   (491–5, 498–501)

In this way the *Parliament of Fowls* presents a situation in which rank and the maintenance of social order are topicalized: at issue is a commensurate mate for the formel, the tercels speak according to *kynde* (450), the remaining birds are similarly linked by social group, and everything transpires under the supervision of Nature. In such a situation, differing language varieties and discursive practices characterize differing social groups, with cacophony accompanying the suspension of Nature's order. As in the *Reeve's Tale*, language variation thus accompanies social disruption, a general stylistic and thematic harmony that also emerges from the way the plot unfolds after the birds' disagreement. Through the dismissive, even abusive, language of the tersels and through Nature's autocracy, order is restored and social distinctions are reinscribed. When the lower birds speak again, significantly, it is not in their distinctive earlier varieties (or registers) but as a London choir in a song that praises the harmonizing power of love.

Much the same implication emerges at the chase scene through the barnyard near the conclusion of the *Nun's Priest's Tale*, where Chaucer makes his only reference to the Peasants' Revolt:

> So hydous was the noyse—a, benedictee!
> Certes, he Jakee Straw and his meynee
> Ne made never shoutes half so shrille
> Whan that they wolden any Flemyng kille,
> As thilke day was maad upon the fox.   (vii. 3393–7)

Framed by references to the yelling fiends in hell and to the shrieking to be heard on Judgement Day, the allusion here equates the Revolt with the ultimate rebellions of Christian history, the events that constitute the alpha and omega of social upheaval.[34] At the same time, the language of the 'meynee,' despite their attempts to establish their own written traditions, appears tantamount to the cacophony of barnyard animals. Through this common late-medi-

---

[34] See further Justice's provocative reading in *Writing and Rebellion*, 207–31. Cf. Susan Crane's remark: 'Each instance of the commons' racket, silence, or misspeaking remanipulates incoherence as a depiction of social hierarchy and political tensions' ('The Writing Lesson of 1381,' in Barbara A. Hanawalt (ed.), *Chaucer's England: Literature in Historical Context* (Minneapolis: University of Minnesota Press, 1992), 214).

eval image for the rebels, the socially destabilizing character of
the ideas of the Revolt is thus linked to language whose deviance,
like that of the northern clerks in the *Reeve's Tale* and the cackling
birds in the *Parliament*, embodies the deviance it projects. For
Chaucer as for the twelfth-century chroniclers, a socially stable
world—a world in which all people know and keep their place in
the social hierarchy—is an ecologically stable one as well.

Courtly love and courtly language

 Before it constitutes a regional dialect with conventional social
significances, Chaucer's poetry shows, a linguistic variety can
indeed still figure in rhetorical strategies to produce social meanings. Beginning with Augustinian linguistics but distinctively
shaped by discursive traditions and lived sociolinguistic experience, the status of Middle English accommodated regional variation much as Norman historiography had language contact or as
other medieval discursive practices had represented violations of
diglossia: as an index of an instability that may be localized in
individuals such as Oswald, Aleyn, and the human equivalents of
assorted barnyard animals, but that ultimately points to larger and
more dangerous social disruptions. In relation to the late-medieval status of the language, Middle English regionalisms thus
had inherent sociolinguistic potential that a skilled writer such
as Chaucer might well manipulate but that none the less differed
markedly from the capacity modern non-standard forms or varieties have for rhetorical and political exploitation.
    Turning from regional to social concerns, I now focus on var-
ieties that correlate linguistic items with social categories rather
than geography but that also, like regional dialects, take their shape
and significance in sociolinguistically specific circumstances and
not by any transcendent qualities. My particular interest is with
the three conversations between Gawain and Lady Bertilak in
the third fit of *Sir Gawain and the Green Knight* and with what
these reveal about the viability of the variety that courtly society began to cultivate at a time when distinct languages—Latin

and French—served the socially individualizing and discriminatory functions typically served by sociolects. Faced with what he
understands to be a dilemma between succumbing to the Lady's
seduction and violating his obligations to his host, Lord Bertilak,
or shunning her advances in a fashion that compromises the courtliness of his behaviour, Gawain uses language to evade both horns
and arrive at his promised encounter with the Green Knight. In
the process, he is impaled by courtly language itself, showing that
sociolects, like regional varieties, can indeed have significance
and force according to the status of a language even before that
status accords them the meaning of modern dialects.

With the pentangle emblazoned on his shield, Gawain rides
from Camelot epitomizing the values to which Arthur's court and
hence chivalry aspire, and prominent among these values is the
'fyft fyue':

> . . . fraunchyse and felaȝschyp forbe al þyng,
> His clannes and his cortaysye croked were neuer,
> And pité, þat passez alle poyntez.   (652–4)[35]

If the other points of the pentangle, such as those involving perfec-
tion in the five fingers or faith in the five wounds of Christ, manifest
themselves in specific actions and individual belief, this point, in
describing the activities of a courtier, is largely realized in language. In the late Middle Ages, vassalage, oath-taking, and prom-
ise-making were all public verbal forms for declaring one's status
and allegiances, but so was what we today might call the art of
conversation, particularly in matters of the heart. In Larry Benson's
analysis, 'Courtly love . . . is especially dependent on the forms of
speech, since not only is every lover a poet, but the main characteristics of the courtly lover—his courtesy, humility, and religion
of love—are expressed in speech. To be adept at "luf talk" is therefore the first requirement of the courtly lover.'[36] Though language

---

[35] All quotations are from *Sir Gawain and the Green Knight*, ed. J. R. R. Tolkien
and E. V. Gordon, 2nd edn., Norman Davis (Oxford: Clarendon, 1967).

[36] Benson, 'Courtly Love and Chivalry in the Later Middle Ages,' in Theodore M.
Andersson and Stephen A. Barney (eds.), *Contradictions: From 'Beowulf' to Chaucer:
Selected Studies of Larry D. Benson* (Aldershot: Scolar, 1995), 302. Also see Thomas
L. Wright, '*Luf-Talkyng* in *Sir Gawain and the Green Knight*,' in Miriam Youngerman

alone does not circumscribe knightly behaviour, it thus does define the pre-eminent speech act of 'luf-talkyng,' for which Gawain's reputation precedes him to Hautdesert and to which Gawain and the Lady devote much of the third fit. In effect, successful courtly language implicates successful courtly behaviour, as in Chaucer's *Troilus and Criseyde*, where, even though she resists Pandarus's interventions on Troilus's behalf, Criseyde clearly sees conversational performance as a prominent quality of knighthood. '"Kan he wel speke of love?"' she early on asks her uncle about Troilus; '"I preye | Tel me, for I the bet me shal purveye"' (ii. 503–4). The use of language as a marker of late-medieval social status also appears in a variety of thirteenth- and fourteenth-century Old French fabliaux, which proscribe vulgarity that was linguistic rather than conceptual: courtiers might conduct themselves with a sexual promiscuity that even now can seem surprising, so long as they used the appropriate language in the process.[37]

Elsewhere Benson describes the language of love-talking as in effect the first class dialect in English,[38] and the fourteenth-century Middle English translation of the *Roman de la Rose* might well support that description. There, the Dreamer, wounded with a barb in his heart, uses an elevated register to yield to the authority of the God of Love. Delighted as much by the speech's language as by its content, the god responds by positing relations between gentility and gentle language:

> 'I love thee bothe and preise,
> Sen that thyn aunswar doth me ease,
> For thou answerid so curteisly.

Miller and Jane Chance (eds.), *Approaches to Teaching 'Sir Gawain and the Green Knight'* (New York: The Modern Language Association of America, 1986), 79–86; and David Burnley, 'Style, Meaning and Communication in *Sir Gawain and the Green Knight*,' *Poetica*, 42 (1994), 23–37.

[37] See Charles Muscatine, 'Courtly Literature and Vulgar Language,' in Glyn S. Burgess (ed.), *Court and Poet: Selected Proceedings of the Third Congress of the International Courtly Literature Society* (Liverpool: Francis Cairns, 1981), 1–19.

[38] Benson, 'The Beginnings of Chaucer's English Style,' in *Contradictions*, 243–65. Analyses of the Great Vowel Shift that involve social distance as the motivation of phonological change likewise point to the existence of in effect a medieval class dialect, though given fifteenth-century evidence such analyses presuppose rather than derive from such sociolects.

> For now I wot wel uttirly
> That thou art gentyll by thi speche.
> For though a man fer wolde seche,
> He shulde not fynden, in certeyn,
> No sich answer of no vileyn;
> For sich a word ne myghte nought
> Isse out of a vilayns thought.'   (1983–92)

Early in the fourteenth century this variety was essentially a textual phenomenon, for the courts of love described in romances were largely literary embellishments of small, casual gatherings of courtiers. But as the century passed, two sociolinguistic changes began to make aspirations to an English courtly sociolect seem attainable. First, against the backdrop of the Hundred Years War and as French speakers and domains began to contract again following the thirteenth-century increase in second-language acquisition, French was able to function less and less as a marker of the aristocracy, opening the way for the cultivation of an English variety to serve this purpose. And second, increasingly firm social stratifications began to develop from what had been a more fluid social mix in the thirteenth century, yielding more rigid distinctions between the nobility, landed gentry, and peasantry as social ranks.[39]

In this context, as a means to maintain their social identity courtiers could affect the forms of chivalric culture that they encountered in literary works (Edward III's 1344 Round Table tournament at Windsor is perhaps the best-known example), with courtly language in particular being cultivated from traditions of clerkly attention to eloquence. One sign of such cultivation was the fact that this language began to occur in other registers as well. The French poet Froissart, for example, writes enthusiastically of the refined speech of 'love *and arms*' (emphasis added) that he heard on his first visit to the English court, and John Trevisa uses courtly language in his account of birds' mating habits: 'Males drawen to the companye of females and preyen iche oþir

---

[39] Richard Firth Green, 'The *Familia Regis* and the *Familia Cupidinis*,' in V. J. Scattergood and J. W. Sherborne (eds.), *English Court Culture in the Later Middle Ages* (New York: St. Martin's Press, 1983), 87–108.

of loue and wowiþ by beckes and voys.'[40] Later, at the beginning of a 1465 letter to his wife Margaret, Sir John Paston used similar language, even though he was writing from Fleet Prison about his characteristic concerns with legal and administrative transactions: 'Myn owne dere souereyn lady, I recomaund me to yow and thank yow of the gret chere þat ye mad me here, to my gret cost and charge and labour.' Equally courtly are the syntax, lexicon, and idioms of Margaret's response: 'Ryght wourchipful husbonde, I recoumaunde me to yow, dyssyryng hertely to here of yowre wel-fare, thankyng yow of yowr grett chere that ye made me and of the coste that ye ded on me. Ye dede more cost thanne myn wylle was that ye choulde do, but that it plesyd yow to do so. God gyf me grase to do that may plese yow.'[41] This kind of language had what David Burnley calls a socio-moral as well as an aesthetic quality.[42] On the one hand, courtly speech was a medium to con-vey friendliness and graciousness; on the other, it was speech that encoded social attitudes and behaviours in its tone, pronouns of address, select lexical items, and elaborate syntactic structures. Common to all these features is the speaker's solicitude for the listener, manifested in politeness, praise, and the avoidance of confrontation.

Such solicitude is readily apparent at the opening of *Sir Gawain and the Green Knight*. As many critics have noted, the brusque-ness of the Green Knight's language compounds the boorishness of his entrance to Camelot, and the contrast between the wild-ness associated with him and the civility of Arthur's court again manifests itself in the elegance of Gawain's request—replete with subjunctives, honorifics, and semantic indirection—to assume the test for the king:

---

[40] Both examples are quoted from Benson, 'Courtly Love and Chivalry,' 300, 304. See further Richard Firth Green, *Poets and Princepleasers: Literature and the English Court in the Late Middle Ages* (Toronto: University of Toronto Press, 1980), 73–84; and Gervase Mathew, *The Court of Richard II* (London: Murray, 1968), 1–11. On the development of courtly language, see further David Burnley, *Courtliness and Literature in Medieval England* (London: Longman, 1998).

[41] Norman Davis (ed.), *Paston Letters and Papers of the Fifteenth Century*, 2 vols. (Oxford: Clarendon, 1971), i. 140, 318.

[42] Burnley, 'Courtly Speech in Chaucer,' *Poetica*, 24 (1986), 16–38. Also see his 'Style, Meaning and Communication.'

> 'Wolde ȝe, worþilych lorde,' quoþ Wawan to þe kyng,
> 'Bid me boȝe fro þis benche, and stonde by yow þere,
> Þat I wythoute vylanye myȝt voyde þis table,
> And þat my legge lady lyked not ille,
> I wolde com to your counseyl bifore your cort ryche.'
>   (342–7)[43]

Such language is what creates part of the reputation that precedes Gawain to Hautdesert, where he is welcomed as the 'fyne fader of nurture' who will instruct the court in the 'teccheles termes of talkyng noble' (919, 917), at which Bertilak and his nobles, particularly the Lady, already seem adept.[44] It is also, of course, the language that Gawain loses and the Green Knight employs in their second encounter, for at the Green Chapel it is Gawain who is given to imperatives and expletives, while the Green Knight speaks the deferential and indirect language of refinement:

> 'Gawayn,' quoþ þat grene gome, 'God þe mot loke!
> Iwysse þou art welcom, wyȝe, to my place.'   (2239–40)

Identity and courtly speech in fact figure so prominently in the poem that its examination of Gawain's character could well be seen as simultaneously an examination of the integrity of his language.[45]

---

[43] W. R. J. Barron sees 'Gawain's courtly formality' here as 'restoring the equilibrium of the Round Table in the face of the Green Knight's insults and the king's intemperance' (*'Trawthe' and Treason: The Sin of Gawain Reconsidered: A Thematic Study of 'Sir Gawain and the Green Knight'* (Manchester: Manchester University Press, 1980), 13).

[44] See lines 847, 860, 897, 1086, and 1115, as well as, of course, the whole of the Lady's speeches.

[45] See Jonathon Nicholls, *The Matter of Courtesy: Medieval Courtesy Books and the Gawain-Poet* (Woodbridge: D. S. Brewer, 1985), 131–8; and the detailed and classic account of J. A. Burrow, *A Reading of 'Sir Gawain and the Green Knight'* (London: Routledge, 1965), 71–112. I would here echo many critics by saying that linguistic skill extends to the poet of *Sir Gawain*, who is particularly adept at lexical and syntactic subtlety and who seems to have been particularly interested in language. See John Plummer, 'Signifying the Self: Language and Identity in *Sir Gawain and the Green Knight*,' in Robert J. Blanch, Miriam Youngerman Miller, and Julian N. Wasserman (eds.), *Text and Matter: New Critical Perspectives of the 'Pearl'-Poet* (Troy, NY: Whitson, 1991), 195–212; Joseph E. Gallagher, '"Trawþe" and "Luf-talkyng" in *Sir Gawain and the Green Knight*,' *Neuphilologische Mitteilungen*, 78 (1977), 362–76; John M. Hill, 'Middle English Poets and the Word: Notes toward an Appraisal of Linguistic Consciousness,' *Criticism*, 16 (1974), 153–69; A. C. Spearing, *Criticism and Medieval Poetry*, 2nd edn.

Even as largely a literary device, perhaps more register than dialect, courtly language does indeed represent the first time a particular variety of English was systematically associated with a particular social group.[46] Though the expansive court of the later English Middle Ages was neither static nor homogeneous, and though it might include a good many servants and aspiring members of the third estate as well as the nobility, typically it is the latter who are characterized as a coherent speech community by the courtly variety.[47] Like the upper-class variety of subsequent centuries, defined both by specific lexical choices (such as U vocabulary) and Received Pronunciation, courtly language could be presumed to identify its speaker as one of a category of individuals with whom particular qualities (such as honesty, courtesy, and bravery) were associated. Also like this variety, at least initially, the speakers of courtly language constituted a relatively closed social network, since the only way to acquire the variety was in a courtly setting, and the primary way to gain access to the highest echelons of this setting—excluding service—was as a member of the nobility. By the nineteenth century, of course, the exclusivity of the upper-class varieties had weakened. Middle- and working-class speakers, either on their own initiative or through educational programmes designed to propagate a standard language, became able to cultivate the variety themselves and thus blurred linguistic form as a distinguishing marker of class.[48] This sociolinguistic transformation helped to problematize what

---

(London: Edward Arnold, 1972), 45–50; Allan A. Metcalf, 'Sir Gawain and *You*,' *Chaucer Review*, 5 (1971), 165–78; William W. Evans, 'Dramatic Use of the Second-Person Singular Pronoun in *Sir Gawain and the Green Knight*,' *Studia Neophilologica*, 39 (1967), 38–45; and Cecily Clark, '*Sir Gawain and the Green Knight*: Characterisation by Syntax,' *Essays in Criticism*, 16 (1966), 361–74.

[46] The Venerable Bede tells the story of Imma, thane of Elfwin, who is captured by King Ethelred. Imma insists that he is only a poor peasant, but others recognize his noble birth 'from his appearance, clothing, and speech.' This is an isolated incident, however, and cannot be said to reflect a broad conception of a sociolect. See *A History of the English Church and People*, trans. Leo Sherley-Price (Harmondsworth: Penguin, 1955), 244.

[47] On English court culture see Maurice Keen, *English Society in the Later Middle Ages 1348–1500* (London: Penguin, 1990), 131–214; Scattergood and Sherborne (eds.), *English Court Culture in the Later Middle Ages*; and Green, *Poets and Princepleasers*.

[48] Tony Crowley, *The Politics of Discourse: The Standard Language Question in British Cultural Debates* (London: Macmillan, 1989), esp. 125–63.

had traditionally constituted the gentility of the gentle class, and, indeed, a number of nineteenth- and early twentieth-century writers concern themselves with just this phenomenon, whether seriously (as when Dickens reveals the genteel Compeyson to be a villain in *Great Expectations*) or humorously (as when Shaw's Eliza Doolittle convincingly masks her working-class background with an upper-class accent in *Pygmalion*).

Such a development did not occur with the courtly variety, spoken or written, of the later Middle Ages. The individuals who sustain this variety are exclusively courtly themselves, even if, as with the knight in Chaucer's *Wife of Bath's Tale*, they are able to switch registers and sometimes speak (and act) less formally. Lower-rank individuals may use courtly phrases such as 'by youre leve' and 'God yow see,' and, as Chaucer's *Squire's Tale* shows, an individual could employ courtly language in a practised manner.[49] But speakers who inappropriately attempt to persist in the language of a refined rank inevitably give themselves away. Such is the case with January in the *Merchant's Tale*: he may, like many a courtly lover, be able to mimic the words and sentiments of the Song of Songs, but his boorish actions with May and at the pear tree betray him for what he is. By the same token, in Malory's *Tale of Sir Gareth*, Gareth may appear at the court as an itinerant desiring food and drink rather than armour and a horse, but his refined speech implies the noble background that the events of the story inevitably reveal. Since this correlation between rank and variety is sporadic and incipient in the late Middle English period, my point is not that all nobles are represented to speak the way Gawain and the Lady do—there is nothing particularly refined in the language of Havelok or King Horn—but that only those who are nobles can genuinely speak this way.

Common ground and successful conversation

The courtly language and verbal skills of Gawain and Lady Bertilak, thus, do indeed define their status and character in a pecu-

---

[49] *Canterbury Tales*, v. 89–107.

liarly upper-rank fashion. Additionally, since the cultivation of linguistic skill figures so prominently in the court culture of *Sir Gawain*—since courtly language is a social variety largely defined by conversational skill—it comes as no surprise that the conversations between Gawain and the Lady *seem* successful for the very reasons that conversations in general succeed. Just as I used analytic tools of modern dialectology to examine regionalisms in the *Reeve's Tale*, I here approach courtly language with some concepts derived from discourse analysis. I am specifically interested in what Herbert Clark calls common ground, or conversants' mutual beliefs, mutual suppositions, and mutual knowledge, the latter of which is based on community membership and physical or linguistic co-presence. According to Clark, all successful conversation depends on this common ground, which may be communal, meaning it is shared by those belonging to a particular speech community or social group, or personal between two speakers. When speakers meet, it is common ground, in relation to the objectives of specific speech events, that circumscribes what they say to each other and how they say it—what jokes and allusions they can make, what words and syntax they use, what topics they can successfully raise. By Clark's analysis, interlocutors construct developing models of one another that they then use as the focus and inspiration of their comments: 'People have selective access to information that is pertinent to each person they talk to. They have a model of what is in the other person's mind, a model they have built up from previous contact and which they continue to update as they go on talking. It is that model that enables people to make and understand references so quickly and accurately.'[50] To understand another's comments, in short, we can limit ourselves to meanings that reasonably emerge from our common ground.

[50] Herbert H. Clark, *Arenas of Language Use* (Chicago: University of Chicago Press, 1992), 58. See the whole of his discussion on pp. 3–59 and also his *Using Language* (Cambridge: Cambridge University Press, 1996), 92–121. The use of common ground is related to what Gillian Brown and George Yule consider the Principle of Local Interpretation, which instructs a listener 'not to construct a context any larger than he needs to arrive at an interpretation' (*Discourse Analysis* (Cambridge: Cambridge University Press, 1983), 59).

This kind of analysis affords insights into not only how the bedroom conversations work but also how these conversations figure in the status of courtly language as a presumptive sociolect. Gawain and the Lady, it would seem, share common ground to an extent that should bode well for any conversation. Both are Christian, both are courtly, and both are experienced at the kinds of verbal and social games played in chivalric culture. Beyond this communal common ground is an equally extensive area of personal common ground: the Lady's sense of Gawain's reputation motivates her actions and thus defines the perimeters of their conversations, which, since they take place over the course of three days, develop a substantial body of personal mutual knowledge relating not only to their discussions but also to the hunts, dinners, and long days spent waiting for Bertilak's return. When on 30 December each 'luflych kny3t' flirts with 'þe lady bisyde' him, it is personal mutual knowledge derived from linguistic and physical co-presence that causes Gawain to recognize that the Lady's persiflage is far less innocent than others':

> Such semblaunt to þat segge semly ho made
> Wyth stille stollen countenaunce, þat stalworth to plese,
> Þat al forwondered watz þe wy3e, and wroth with hymseluen,
> Bot he nolde not for his nurture nurne hir a3aynez,
> Bot dalt with hir al in daynté, how-se-euer þe dede turned
>   towrast.   (1658–63)

If the other ladies are merely flirting, the personal mutual knowledge Gawain shares with Lady Bertilak leads him to conclude that her intentions go beyond social banter.

On a strictly formal level, Gawain and the Lady's conversations also bear the hallmarks of conversational success: textual cohesion in their specific grammatical and lexical features and discourse coherence between the larger speech acts into which these features are organized.[51] Each of their encounters begins with the kind of ritualized exchange that puts conversants at ease—'"God moroun, Sir Gawayn," sayde þat gay lady' (1208)—and each con-

---

[51] Stubbs, *Discourse Analysis: The Sociolinguistic Analysis of Natural Language* (Chicago: University of Chicago Press, 1983), 9.

cludes in a similarly explicit way.[52] Particularly in their first conversation, Gawain and Lady Bertilak also frequently use the kinds
of reciprocal vocatives and honorific titles that establish social
identity and cultivate friendship—substantives such as 'sir,' 'gay,'
'lady,' 'hende,' 'madame,' and 'kny3t.'[53] Textual cohesion likewise
emerges from the prominence of adjacency pairs in the bedroom
discussions, which contain none of the extended monologues that
characterize the poem's famous manuscript companion, *Pearl*.
Sir Gawain shows discourse coherence in the fact that *in fit three*
there seems little doubt, either among conversants or readers,
about the speech event or its illocutionary force. Comments made
by the narrator and the language and proxemics of Gawain and
the Lady all seem to point to love-talking as the speech event,
with the Lady's illocutionary force being sexual seduction. Precisely because this force seems to be more than obvious, I want to
examine some of the conversational details that point in this direction, for the fact is that the actual speech event and illocutionary
force are quite other than they appear. This disparity, in turn, has
significant implications for the viability of courtly language as a
sociolect, for the rhetorical goals towards which such a late-medieval variety could be used, and ultimately for the late-medieval
status of English.

Even before the direct conversation of Gawain and the Lady is
reported, the poet characterizes their interaction as flirtatious:

> Bot 3et I wot þat Wawen and þe wale burde
> Such comfort of her compaynye ca3ten togeder
> Þur3 her dere dalyaunce of her derne wordez,
> Wyth clene cortays carp closed fro fylþe,
> Þat hor play watz passande vche prynce gomen,
>   in vayres.   (1010–15)

From the moment Gawain peers from his bed clothes to watch
the Lady's entrance, further, the poet consistently presents him as

---

[52] Also see lines 1477 and 1759, and 1556 and 1870. On the discoursal function of
such ritualized exchanges see Ronald Wardhaugh, *How Conversation Works* (Oxford:
Blackwell, 1985), 46–7.

[53] See Hyesoon Lim Eun, 'Polite Speech: A Sociolinguistic Analysis of Chaucer
and the *Gawain*-Poet,' diss. Michigan State University, 1987.

a figure defending himself from amorous assault: 'Þe freke ferde with defence, and feted ful fayre' (1282).[54] Gawain's defensive posture suggests that it is the Lady who determines the course of the conversation, and on 30 December she is in fact the one who utilizes their linguistic co-presence to specify, from among all the subjects they presumably considered while awaiting Bertilak's return from the deer hunt, that the topic of their previous day's conversation was pre-eminently amorous:

> 'Þou hatz forȝeten ȝederly þat ȝisterday I taȝtte
> Bi alder-truest token of talk þat I cowþe.'   (1485–6)

The Lady's proxemics on the following morning, when she appears in a provocative gown and addresses Gawain with the familiar 'A! mon,' similarly suggest amorous assault, as do her proxemics on the morning of 29 December, when, uninvited, she enters Gawain's room and sits beside him on the bed. Indeed, the kisses that are exchanged by Gawain, the Lady, and Bertilak might well be regarded as currency in the erotic economy of courtly culture. In this same vein, the love tokens that Gawain and Lady Bertilak discuss on the final morning are unremarkable precisely because they seem to emblemize the general character of the conversation, which has included consideration of Gawain's reputation as a lover and his apparent reluctance to speak of affairs of the heart.[55] Thus, though the poet never explicitly declares the Lady's intentions, she clearly does conduct herself 'lyk as hym loued mych' (1281), and her unstated 'purpose' seems inescapably to be seduction:

> Bot þe lady for luf let not to slepe,
> Ne þe purpose to payre þat pyȝt in hir hert,
> Bot ros hir vp radly.   (1733–5)

In this context it is appropriate to consider one of the Lady's best-known and most discussed lines. '"Ȝe ar welcum to my cors"'

---

[54] Also see lines 1551 and 1771; the latter shows Gawain in a defensive posture whether the manuscript reading 'prynce' or the emendation 'prynces' is used in line 1770.

[55] See lines 1293–301, 1798–825, 1522–34.

(1237), she tells Gawain on the morning of the first hunt, and critics have disagreed over just how literally she intends 'cors.' In *Cleanness* God declares with respect to Abraham that He 'dyscouered to his corse' His counsel, and here 'his corse' can mean only (and simply) 'him.'[56] The Lady's 'welcum' may similarly be understood as a description rather than the blunt invitation that the line would seem to be in modern English, so that it is quite possible to read her remark as fairly innocuous. The important point, however, is that 'cors' in this construction can have an explicitly sexual connotation in Old French poetry.[57] And here, given the conversational location of the Lady's comment, her greeting, while vague for the sake of the decency inherent in courtly language, must have an unambiguously erotic illocutionary force. Her proxemics leading up to this invitation and her statements about Gawain's amorous reputation and the absence of her lord provide Gawain with the context that he must use to understand her reference or disregard the common ground that has developed between them. Indeed, following her remarks on their isolation in a locked room, her comment is purposelessly irrelevant *unless* it has a particularized implicature—an additional context-specific meaning—that supplements the superficial greeting of its locutionary force,[58] and the same is true of her command on the following day:

> 'I com hider sengel, and sitte
> To lerne at yow sum game;
> Dos, techez me of your wytte,
> Whil my lorde is fro hame.'
> (1531–4)

Such utterances present Gawain with a double bind, since his reputed skill in love-talking means that he ought to be able to understand a conversational strategy that he so clearly would like

[56] Malcolm Andrew and Ronald Waldron (eds.), *The Poems of the Pearl Manuscript: Pearl, Cleanness, Patience, Sir Gawain and the Green Knight* (Berkeley and Los Angeles: University of the California Press, 1982), line 683.

[57] For further analysis and examples see Tolkien and Gordon (eds.), *Sir Gawain and the Green Knight*, 108–9, and Burrow, *A Reading*, 81–2.

[58] On particularized implicatures see Stephen C. Levinson, *Pragmatics* (Cambridge: Cambridge University Press, 1983), 126.

to disregard if he is to avoid affronting Lord Bertilak by sleeping with his wife.

Yet despite the degree of textual cohesion and discourse coherence evident in *Sir Gawain and the Green Knight*, and despite the common ground of the Lady and Gawain, theirs are clearly not successful conversations: one of the speakers is consistently duped by the other. The pervasive speech event may be love-talking, but the Lady's illocutionary force is deception, as, in fact, is the perlocutionary effect she achieves, for Gawain does not realize until he speaks with the Green Knight at the Green Chapel that all the conversations had been staged. The 'purpose . . . pyȝt' in the Lady's heart had been to seduce not sexually but ethically, and to discover whether Gawain would conceal the allegedly magical sash from her lord. To Gawain's humiliation, the answer is 'yes.'

Co-operation, social being, and politeness

One of the most significant reasons for conversational success, discourse analysis affirms, is simply the desire of the participants to succeed. Speakers tolerate and even expect some indirection as inevitable in ordinary conversation, but they do so in the belief that they mutually want to hear and be heard. The essence of H. P. Grice's famous Co-operative Principle, indeed, is the conviction that speaker and listener alike are operating sincerely and that, in Stephen Levinson's analysis, whatever speech act one seems to be performing is, barring evidence to the contrary, the speech act that one is in fact performing:

Normally, then, in co-operative circumstances, when one asserts something one implicates that one believes it, when one asks a question, one implicates that one sincerely desires an answer and, by extension, when one promises to do *x*, one implicates that one sincerely intends to do *x*, and so on. Any other use of such utterances is likely to be a spurious or counterfeit one, and thus liable to violate the maxim of Quality.[59]

---

[59] Ibid. 105–6; also see Wardhaugh, *How Conversation Works*, 63–4; and H. Grice, 'Logic and Conversation,' in Peter Cole and Jerry L. Morgan (eds.), *Syntax and Semantics*, iii. *Speech Acts* (New York: Academic Press, 1975), 41–58.

It may, of course, be, in a given situation, that a speech act is fraudulent, yet conversation works because most people do not begin to speak or listen with this expectation; those who do are considered cynical and narcissistic, and ultimately for this reason are not conversationally successful.[60] In conversations founded on the expectation of sincerity, speakers do more than simply convey information to one another, however. Within the social semiotics of language, successful conversation also serves to enact and sustain social bonds—to perform what Sandy Petrey has called 'social being'—for if a conversation's contents constitute information, its form both reflects and mediates social cohesion.[61] As Deborah Tannen observes, 'Coherence and involvement are the goal—and, in frequent happy occurrences, the result—when discourse succeeds in creating meaning through familiar strategies. The familiarity of the strategies . . . sends a metamessage of rapport between the communicators, who thereby experience that they share communicative conventions and inhabit the same world of discourse.'[62]

This homology of successful conversation and social being throws the failure of the conversations in *Sir Gawain and the Green Knight* into striking relief. Specifically, in failing as they do, the discussions between Gawain and the Lady illuminate larger issues about the capabilities of conversation in the late Middle Ages and about the viability of language as a marker of social rank at this time—about what sociolinguistic variations can do in relation to the status of a language that lacks an established hierarchy of sociolects. As much rapport and common ground as Gawain may think himself to share with the Lady, the fact of the matter is that they do not 'inhabit the same world of discourse'— either in the topic of their conversations or in their conversational presuppositions. In the simplest terms, Lady Bertilak is not sincere, while Gawain is.

---

[60] On 'faulty interactants,' see R. A. Hudson, *Sociolinguistics*, 2nd edn. (Cambridge: Cambridge University Press, 1996), 112–16.

[61] Petrey, *Speech Acts and Literary Theory* (New York: Routledge, 1990), 20.

[62] Tannen, *Talking Voices: Repetition, Dialogue, and Imagery in Conversational Discourse* (Cambridge: Cambridge University Press, 1989), 13.

But what proves especially unsettling for the status of courtly language as a sociolect is the fact that Gawain both incorrectly presumes rapport with the Lady and fails to perceive her insincerity *precisely because* he is such a gifted conversationalist with so much communicative competence in this variety. However much he may deny it to Lady Bertilak, Gawain's reputation indicates his familiarity with love-talking—the dexterity of his denials in fact testifies as much—and, hence, with speech events of the same illocutionary force that the Lady feigns at Hautdesert. In his discussions with her, accordingly, Gawain proceeds in the fashion that best predicts coherence between his prior love-talking experience and his conversations with the Lady. Adhering to the principles of analogy with similar experiences and local interpretation of this particular experience, Gawain reasonably concludes, as his anxious thoughts on the morning of 31 December suggest, that the Lady's intention, too, must be sexual seduction.[63] The reasonableness of this conclusion is underscored by the fact that for all three conversations the topic framework—or range of topics that might be understood to be the focus of a particular discussion—seems limited to love, hunting, and courtly behaviour.[64] The first of these is in fact what the Lady herself specifies as the topic at line 1485. Although she undoubtedly is deceiving Gawain, the conversations themselves thus provide no topics that would lead a gifted conversationalist such as Gawain to assume they have a purpose other than the one local interpretation suggests.

Similarly, the structures of the conversations nowhere imply failure to meet the grounding criterion, by which speakers mutually believe that they have sufficiently understood the significance of a particular remark.[65] While the content and form of the conversation in *Pearl* (by comparison) amply indicate that neither the Dreamer nor the Maiden even adequately understands what

---

[63] Lines 1770–6. On default interpretations based on prior experience, see Brown and Yule, *Discourse Analysis*, 236; Leech, *Principles of Pragmatics* (London: Longman, 1983), 42; and Lakoff, *Women, Fire, and Dangerous Things: What Categories Reveal about the Mind* (Chicago: University of Chicago Press, 1987), 116.

[64] On topic frameworks see Brown and Yule, *Discourse Analysis*, 75–9.

[65] Clark, *Arenas of Language Use*, 148.

the other has said, in *Sir Gawain* the conversants regularly monitor the success of their conversations by attempting to clarify one another's positions. Indeed, in their attention to the grounding criterion, as in their overall design, Gawain and the Lady's conversations again have all the signs of adequate communication. After the Lady has welcomed Gawain to her 'cors,' he takes pains to acknowledge her value, while at the same time he stresses that since he is not the knight she describes, he does not deserve such favour.[66]

Politeness is another strategy in which Gawain's (and the Lady's) conversational skill ultimately undermines the success of their conversation. The character and pragmatics of politeness are culturally specific, so that its forms, frequency, and uses vary from one speech community to another. If one extreme is a popular view of American English, where politeness is often thought to be all but a lost art, the other is courtly language, in which politeness—'cortaysye' in speech—is the inalienable mark of a courtier and the ever-present enactment of social cohesion. In general terms, politeness, along with the assumption of sincerity, enables ordinary conversation by providing speakers with ways of interacting that do not threaten each other's face either overtly with insults or covertly by omitting praise. The latter kind of conversational politeness is positive, seeking to compliment listeners by indicating that the speaker shares their desires and interests, and the former, which is more frequent in ordinary conversation, is negative, seeking to avoid offending listeners by refraining from insults, comments on infirmities, and the like.

In *Sir Gawain and the Green Knight* both speakers of courtly language, not surprisingly, expend a great deal of effort on politeness. Gawain's, typically, is the negative sort, attempting to avoid insulting the Lady in turning down her requests, as when he denies that he is the proper recipient of an invitation to her 'cors.' Such polite non-compliance enables him to refuse the offer without the Lady experiencing loss of face from an open rejection, much as

---

[66] Lines 1241–4. On *Pearl*, see Machan, 'Writing the Failure of Speech in *Pearl*,' in Mark C. Amodio (ed.), *Unbinding Proteus: New Directions in Oral Theory* (Tempe, Ariz.: Medieval and Renaissance Texts and Studies, 2003).

when someone declines an invitation to a party by claiming (honestly or not) commitment to a prior engagement. Gawain uses a similarly evasive strategy of non-compliance on 30 December, when, in response to the Lady's surprise that he has not yet kissed her, he asserts, 'þat durst I not do, lest I deuayed were' (1493), and again on the following morning, when he refuses her offer of a ring because he has no gift to give in return (1823). In each of these instances, Gawain avoids insult by undermining a presupposition of the Lady's request—that Gawain would undertake an action that could be perceived as a slight, and that Gawain is able to participate in an exchange of gifts.[67] Conversely, the Lady's offer of a gift, at least in its appearance, instances positive politeness, the kind she consistently displays throughout the conversations. When she greets Gawain on the morning of 29 December, for example, she simultaneously enhances what Brown and Levinson call 'the positive self-image' that speakers normally claim for themselves:

> 'For I wene wel, iwysse, Sir Wowen ȝe are,
> Þat alle þe worlde worchipez quere-so ȝe ride;
> Your honour, your hendelayk is hendely praysed
> With lordez, wyth ladyes, with alle þat lyf bere.'
> (1226–9)[68]

She subsequently displays this same positive politeness when describing Gawain's knowledge of love-talking, calling him the 'knyȝt comlokest kyd of your elde' (1520) and 'so cortays and coynt of your hetes' (1525).

Along with the Co-operative Principle, the Politeness Principle articulates speakers' desires for conversation to proceed sincerely and non-threateningly. For Brown and Levinson, 'Normally everyone's face depends on everyone else's being maintained, and since people can be expected to defend their faces if

---

[67] On Gawain's non-compliance strategies, see further Kim Sydow Campbell, 'A Lesson in Polite Non-Compliance: Gawain's Conversational Strategies in Fitt 3 of *Sir Gawain and the Green Knight*,' *Language Quarterly*, 28 (1990), 53–62.

[68] Brown and Levinson, *Politeness: Some Universals in Language Usage*, rev. edn. (Cambridge: Cambridge University Press, 1987), 70.

threatened, and in defending their own to threaten others' faces, it is in general in every participant's best interest to maintain each others' face.'[69] Further, it is typically the case that the more effort a speaker expends on politeness, the greater claim to sincerity that speaker would seem to have.[70] What makes the situations in *Sir Gawain* odd and significant, then, is the fact that both conversants, but the Lady in particular, pervasively utilize a strategy that testifies for sincerity to further conversations that are anything but sincere. In this way, rather than avoid a face-threatening action, the Lady's politeness constitutes as much. It is certainly the case that politeness can mask the baldest kind of lies and hostility, but the politeness in *Sir Gawain* reflects a courtly sociolect that is represented as spoken only by individuals who genuinely are courtly and, hence, honest and polite. The non-courtly, such as Chaucer's Reeve or the Seven Deadly Sins in *Piers Plowman*, cannot misuse this kind of politeness because they cannot use it at all.

Given the understatement in much of the bedroom conversations, one might wonder why Gawain does not simply pursue greater clarification. Why not ask, 'Are you trying to seduce me?' The answer, again ironically, involves his communicative competence. If pressing the Lady on her general intentions or even on her use of 'welcum to my cors' would, conceivably, have compelled her to expose her own deception, it would equally have questioned her sincerity, thereby violating the Co-operative Principle and, perhaps more importantly, what Burnley calls the socio-moral expectations of courtly language. In conversation, there is often a stylistic choice between acceptance of uncertainty and temporary misunderstanding on the one hand, and, on the other, confrontation.[71] Since the poem's conversations are predicated on Gawain's reputation for love-talking, the latter is out of the question. Moreover, Gawain's ability to deflect the seduction without offending the Lady testifies to his skill in courtly language, just as his identification of seduction as the Lady's illocutionary force in effect testifies to his skill at reading the topic framework and exercising what Clark calls the Principle of Mutual Responsibil-

---

[69] Brown and Levinson, *Politeness*, 61.   [70] Ibid. 93.
[71] Wardhaugh, *How Conversation Works*, 36.

ity: 'The participants in a conversation try to establish, roughly by the initiation of each new contribution, the mutual belief that the listeners have understood what the speaker meant in the last utterance to a criterion sufficient for current purposes.'[72]

The difficulties in the conversations between Gawain and the Lady thus cannot be described in conventional ways, for their most conventional and apparently successful qualities also underlie their biggest failures and deceptions. From what the reader and Gawain see in the third fit, neither Lady Bertilak's language nor her actions are uncourtly. In fact, except at an abstract level unknown until the end of the poem, everything she says and does has the sincerity, style, and appropriateness that Gawain, with his communicative competence in the courtly sociolect, expects. If there is a specific reason for the conversations' lack of success, it is the general deception by Lady Bertilak, but strictly speaking her speech acts violate neither the Politeness Principle nor any of the maxims of the Co-operative Principle. All her utterances are relevant and in a clear manner; on any given turn she speaks neither more nor less than she should; and she cannot be said to lie in any specific, overt fashion. Gawain, bearing the pentangle and representing Camelot, genuinely does have the courtly reputation she describes, and it is in response to this that the Green Knight had initiated his Christmas game:

> 'For to assay þe surquidré, ȝif hit soth were
> Þat rennes of þe grete renoun of þe Rounde Table.'
> (2457–8)

Further, there is no indication that, had Gawain succumbed to her seduction, she would not have seen their encounter through to its logical conclusion: the Green Knight acknowledges only having sent her to 'asay' Gawain (2362).

The Lady's deception is thus at a higher level of discourse than the individual utterance or speech act, and it is this quality that gives *Sir Gawain* particular relevance for the late-medieval status of English. Everything she says may be well formed and sincere

---

[72] Clark, *Arenas of Language Use*, 139.

in the immediate local context, contributing to well-structured and coherent conversation, but she uses her local sincerity for an insincere speech act. She thereby produces an illocutionary force other than the one that seems most likely, and she achieves a homologous perlocutionary effect. And she does so, significantly, with Gawain's unwitting assistance, for his conversational skills and the common ground between himself and the Lady serve as essential means for the deception she effects. Conversation in *Sir Gawain* thereby challenges the social hierarchies that it is presumed to sustain, with courtly language undermining its own claim to mark the integrity and virtue of a social group. Spoken well, love-talking may indeed be a cultivated art that demonstrates the speaker's courtliness and that negotiates courtly social relations; it may be what Gawain presumes to speak. Or, from the opposite direction, it may be what the Green Knight does *not* speak. Thus, when the Green Knight gruffly addresses the court in the first fit, his language, like his actions, excludes him from the society of Camelot, just as when the lady speaks 'luflych' in the third fit, her language associates her with this society. If the poem ended after the third fit, with the Lady's game and the Green Knight's unconnected, there might in fact simply not be a more congenial spot—sociolinguistically speaking—than Camelot.

But the poem does not conclude with the third fit, and therein lie the difficulties for the sociolinguistic claims of a courtly sociolect. Ultimately—even counterintuitively—courtly language serves as the means for deceitful, distinctly uncourtly activities. As *Sir Gawain* plays out, Lady Bertilak in fact poses every bit the threat to court culture that her husband does and therefore stands in an ambiguous relation to it, one that simultaneously advances and undermines courtly aspirations. Her threat may even be the more serious, since it strikes at a means that court culture presumes to use to identify itself and, coming from within that culture, remains invisible to it. The real sociolinguistic problem, as Gawain perhaps never fully comprehends, is that whether courtly language is sincere or duplicitous, speakers, if they are themselves to speak this presumptive sociolect, must respond with its conversational strategies, and in articulating courtly language they construct themselves within its discourse; in so doing they yield any vantage from which the fraudulence of a particular conversation might be determined. Gawain in fact never seems to realize that love-talking itself causes his undoing, choosing instead to blame (incorrectly) cowardice, covetousness, and the temptations of women. When he arrives at the Green Chapel and there adopts the imperatives and asserations of the apparently uncourtly Green Knight,[73] Gawain further manifests what his conversations with Lady Bertilak suggest more abstractly: as a variety that speakers can adopt or abandon, a variety they can use but not evaluate, courtly language is itself a deception that cannot justify its own claim to exclusivity, integrity, and virtue.

Linguistic methods and meanings

Today, varieties such as African American Vernacular English, Geordie, Estuary English, and Standard American English are recognized by a confluence of well-defined (if still variable) linguistic forms, whether phonological, morphological, syntactic, or pragmatic. Part of this recognition, in turn, involves acknowledgement of the relative status and functions of these varieties. In the United States, Standard American English is broadly considered the variety that dominates business, government, and education—as well as their attendant sociolinguistic implications—just as African American Vernacular English variously defines group identity, intersects with economic opportunity, and focuses racial discussion. As I argued in the previous chapter, regional and social varieties of Middle English did not signify in ways that could produce such meanings, and the evidence of this chapter affirms the difficulty of mapping social rank onto varieties of Middle English.

As I also argue here, however, before it has the sociolinguistic identity of a modern dialect, a variety can still mean and perform both social being and literary work. If Dickens could use

---

[73] e.g. lines 2250, 2284, 2300, 2320.

regionalisms to convey an individual's moral character, Chaucer could use them to enact a society's instability; if in *Adventures of Huckleberry Finn* sociolects bespeak class, in *Sir Gawain and the Green Knight* they reveal their own tenuousness as well as that of late-medieval courtly culture. Without the heuristics and expect-ations of modern sociolinguistic inquiry, horizons of the medieval status of English may narrow to exclude the linguistic rationaliza-tion, nationalistic mediation, and social transformations that we have come to associate with language in the modern period. And they may likewise exclude varieties that evoke specific social significance in the way regional dialects can in the ecology of modern English. At the same time, however, even in well-known works, this status opens new vistas on how English figured in medieval social practice, vistas of which I have here offered only a glimpse.

5

After Middle English

Linguistic futures, past and present

In the often-cited Prologue to his *Troy Book*, Lydgate credits the future Henry V with a desire to see the history of Troy told in English so that the people of England, nobles and commoners alike, might have the same opportunity as those of any other country to read an account in their own tongue:

> By-cause he wolde that to hyge and lowe
> The noble story openly wer knowe
> In oure tonge, aboute in every age,
> And y-writen as wel in oure langage
> As in latyn or in frensche it is;
> That of the story the trouthe we nat mys
> No more than doth eche other nacioun:
> This was the fyn of his entencioun.[1]

Henry's subsequent career might well justify a description of him as the champion of English implied in this Prologue, for some of the events of his reign give the distinct impression of language planning on behalf of English. To his time can be traced some of the charges of a French desire to eradicate English (noted in Ch. 3), and Henry himself seems to have made a conscious decision in 1417 to shift from French to English in his correspondence. His 1416 English proclamation to marshal supplies and troops for an invasion of France, in any case, is the first extant royal proclamation in English since Henry III's letters of October

---

[1] Lydgate, *Troy Book*, ed. Henry Bergen, 4 vols., EETS ES 97, 103, 106, 126 (London: Kegan Paul, 1906, 1908, 1910, 1935), Prologue, lines 111–18.

1258. In their 1422 Latin explanation of why they are changing their record-keeping from Latin to English, further, the Brewers' Guild specifically credits Henry as someone who has consciously employed the language as a way of improving communication with his subjects, thereby setting an example for nobility and commoners to do so as well and also helping to render English 'honourably enlarged and adorned.' Henry, the notice declares, 'hath in his letters missive and divers affairs touching his own person, more willingly chosen to declare the secrets of his will, and for the better understanding of his people, hath with a diligent mind procured the common idiom (setting aside others) to be commended by the exercise of writing.'[2]

The rise of Chancery English might similarly be seen as a response to an encouraging attitude towards English by Henry. Originating in the Chancery, which was largely devoted to the production of royal correspondence, this variety spread throughout the fifteenth century to several government offices and eventually to England at large. As a variety whose lexicon, morphology, orthography, and even graphic characteristics were cultivated, Chancery had some of the qualities of a standard language. This resemblance emerges even more strongly from the fact that Chancery, like a standard language, not only functioned in powerful domains but also spread from these domains into other, less socially influential ones, such as the daily correspondence of the Pastons. While any direct connection between such later grammarians as Bishop Lowth and Chancery would be forced and improbable, the idea of a standardized English and many of the morphological and orthographic characteristics that animated Lowth have their first appearance in Henry's reign. Drawing on Chancery English and the other fifteenth-century developments I have cited, John Fisher has suggested that Henry's interest in English was in fact so strong that the king and his supporters joined it to patriotic sentiment in the Hundred Years War and a

---

[2] R. W. Chambers and Marjorie Daunt (eds.), *A Book of London English 1384–1425* (Oxford: Clarendon, 1931), 139.

burgeoning interest in Chaucer in order to cultivate the poet as a figure of English nationalism.[3]

Even as Henry and some of his contemporaries advocated and refined the use of English, however, others in the late-medieval period worked against any transformation of the status of English, imagining linguistic futures different from the one Henry evidently had or, indeed, from the one that came to be. The fifteenth-century transmission of poems from the Alliterative Revival, for example, involved manuscripts from the south and east as well as the north-west, and in this way, as Ralph Hanna has suggested, the poems 'developed as one competing form of a national, not regional, literature.'[4] French and Latin figured in other unrealized linguistic futures. Although the 1362 Statute of Pleading mandated that England's law courts should henceforth conduct their business in English, for example, French was not officially abandoned in this venue until 1731. In working to cultivate knowledge of French among aristocrats and the domains they populated, thirteenth- and fourteenth-century French grammars likewise pointed to a future in which French would remain a marker of class and education as well as the language of the law. The best-known attempts to protect the status of Latin, of course, involved the Lollards' introduction of English to new domains, which met, eventually, with vigorous and ruthless suppression, but other efforts to maintain Latin's viability into the linguistic future occurred as well. Despite the increased use of English in Parliament during the fifteenth century, two centuries later Milton could still hold the position of foreign language secretary to the

---

[3] For this argument and other important information on Chancery English, see Fisher, *The Emergence of Standard English* (Lexington, Ky.: University of Kentucky Press, 1996). Also see Fisher, Malcolm Richardson, and Jane L. Fisher (eds.), *An Anthology of Chancery English* (Knoxville, Ten.: University of Tennessee Press, 1984). Derek Pearsall has provocatively suggested that Henry's interest in English and the Lollard use of the vernacular may not be unconnected, that Henry may have seen Chancery, for instance, as an official response to the unofficial appropriation of English. See 'Hoccleve's *Regement of Princes*: The Poetics of Royal Self-Representation,' *Speculum*, 69 (1994), 386–410.

[4] Hanna, 'Alliterative Poetry,' in David Wallace (ed.), *The Cambridge History of Medieval English Literature* (Cambridge: Cambridge University Press), 509.

Council of State, for which his duties involved composition in Latin. Similarly, Latin-English sermons sustained the diglossia of medieval England and also constructed a bilingual code that, rather than English, could be used to mark religious discourse. In a similar vein, the interlanguages of French, Latin, and English that appeared in late-medieval business writing bespoke a world in which medieval multilingualism would not dissipate but rather include what were in effect new languages. Not only does the modern status of English appear but dimly in the late-medieval period, then. It also appears as only one of several widespread sociolinguistic beliefs, all of whose futures, like the future of ongoing structural change, could be neither known nor predicted by late-medieval speakers.[5]

As with any linguistic change, reconfiguration of the medieval status of English and the ecology through which it conveyed meaning happened gradually and inconsistently, not discretely and uniformly. This was, moreover, a particularly contentious reconfiguration, as Chaucer's *Reeve's Tale* well illustrates, involving an anxious response to late-medieval transformations of both English society and its linguistic repertoire. Co-existing with the advocacy of English that Lydgate attributes to Henry V, this anxiety contributes to the sociolinguistic complexity of late-medieval England. Throughout this book I have avoided resolving this complexity through a retrospective attitude towards the ecology of Middle English and the status of English that it projects, for by employing expectations of modern linguistic thinking such retrospection perhaps inevitably finds prodigies of them in the Middle Ages, just as it reduces multiple competing traditions, whose futures were unknown, to the one tradition that would prosper. Put another way, I have focused on what the status of English was, not on the indications of what it would become.

Accordingly, I have stressed the contextual factors by which this status came into being, meant, and was used. I have tried to concentrate less on what this status was not or on what socio-

---

[5] See further Machan, 'Politics and the Middle English Language,' *Studies in the Age of Chaucer*, 24 (2002), 317–24.

linguistic contexts it lacked than on what the character of the ecology of Middle English allowed. I have done this for two reasons: first, to lay open the mutually constitutive ways in which sociolinguistic institutions and practices develop; and second, to avoid arguing from the negative, a process that is theoretically limited but practically infinite. In this final chapter I take a slightly different approach. Since several of the determinants of the modern status of English are post-medieval, an emphasis on these determinants and the tardiness of their development puts many of the issues I have discussed into sharp relief and in the process suggests that if Henry V was a language planner, the institutional limitations of his plan rendered him far more similar to Henry III than to Cardinal Richelieu. In effect, I conclude my pursuit of the late-medieval status of English by leaving that status behind to consider briefly some significant early modern developments in the ecology of English and their ramifications for the status of the language.

Early modern codification, pedagogy, and sociolinguistic commentary

My point of departure is a work that brings together the medieval and the modern: Robert Crowley's 1550 edition of *Piers Plowman*. Like any edition, this one responded to several cultural impulses, but perhaps foremost of these was the increased interest in the Wyclifites and dissident theology that accompanied the Reformation. From the 1530s onwards, English printers offered many such works,[6] and Crowley's edition, even though it represented the first time *Piers* was printed, was itself issued three times in 1550, followed in 1561 by Owen Rogers's new and only slightly revised edition. In his two-page letter to the reader that prefaces the poem, Crowley gestures towards the contemporary

---

[6] See Julia Boffey and A. S. G. Edwards, 'Literary Texts,' in Lotte Hellinga and J. B. Trapp (eds.), *The Cambridge History of the Book in Britain*, iii. *1400–1557* (Cambridge: Cambridge University Press, 1999), 555–75.

utility of Langland's work by admonishing the reader not to look 'vpon this boke . . . to talke of wondres paste or to come but to emend thyne owne misse.'[7] But he also historicizes the poem with great detail, and it is this manœuvre, in which sociolinguistic assumptions are not the subject but the means of an argument, that interests me here.

Crowley begins his notice to the reader by expressing his own interest in the author and date of composition for *Piers Plowman*. To this end, he collected 'aunciente copies' and consulted 'such men as I knew to be more exercised in the studie of antiquities.' These in turn led him to a particular manuscript that contained comments indicating that the poem had been composed during the reign of Edward III: 'In whose tyme it pleased God to open the eyes of many to se his truth, geuing them boldness of herte, to open their mouthes and crye oute agaynste the workes of darckeness, as dyd John Wicklyfe, who also in those dayes translated the holye Byble into the Englishe tonge.' Here, then, is the connection between Wyclif, dissident theology, and English that I discussed in Ch. 3 and that has figured prominently in recent critical discussion of late-medieval language and society. Crowley furthers this connection between *Piers* and dissident theology by immediately describing Langland in ways that recall early modern notions of Wyclif—as a righteous, almost egalitarian voice championing God's truth to an obstinate population: 'There is no maner of vice, that reygneth in anye estate of men, whyche thys wryter hath not godly, learnedlye, and wittilye, rebuked.'

But Crowley's reference to Wyclif and English differs in several important ways from medieval references. From the connection with Wyclif he proceeds to a citation of the poem's first two couplets, which he uses to illustrate this proposition: 'He wrote altogither in miter: but not after ye maner of our rimers that wryte nowe adaies . . . but the nature of hys miter is, to haue three wordes at the leaste in euery verse which begyn with some one letter.' For a reader who knows this, 'the metre shall be very plesaunt to reade.' From the antiquity of the poem's metrics Crowley turns

---

[7] William Langland, *Piers Plowman*, ed. Robert Crowley (London, 1550), sig. ii^{r-v}.

to the antiquity of its language: 'The Englishe is according to the tyme it was written in, and the sence somewhat darcke, but not so harde, but that it maye be vnderstande of such as wyll not sticke to breake the shell of the nutte for the kernelles sake.' And after the antiquity of its language Crowley acknowledges the consequences such antiquity has had on its transmission. Noting with precision that on the thirty-sixth leaf Langland refers to a 'dearth then to come' and speculating like an editor that a subsequent passage 'is lyke to be a thynge added by some other man than the fyrste autour,' Crowley concedes the impact time can have on an author's words by observing, 'diuerse copies haue it diuerslye.' Crowley's final editorial point reprises the connection between *Piers Plowman* and Protestantism: 'Nowe for that whiche is written in the .l, leafe, concernyng the suppresson of Abbayes, the Scripture there alledged, declareth it to be gathered of the iust iudgment of God, who wyll not suffer abomination to raigne vnpunished.'

While Crowley's association of Wyclif with English may have a late-medieval familiarity, then, it has a distinctively different impact. Crowley's association is pre-eminently an act of retrospective interpretation, a reading of the past that begins with post-Reformation sentiments and that involves a series of strategies that historically situate the poem's date of composition, author, metre, language, and transmission, all of which together historically situate the editor himself as a representative of meticulous, early modern printing. In this context, Wyclif's use of English serves not as self-validating contemporary rhetoric but as a feature of early modern sociolinguistic discourse in which the present (perhaps inevitably) had appropriated the past to locate its own origins. Specifically, Wyclif had come to mean the originary moment of Protestantism, including the significance it attached to the vernacular, while the significance of English had come to assume certain qualities associated with its modern version: English as group-defining, authorizing, and ennobling, a vernacular with increasing regularity and national (but still not official) status. What for Henry Knighton was a statement of fact—Wyclif turned the 'clerks' jewels' into 'the playthings of laymen'—had become an ideologically charged event in a sociolinguistic discursive tradition that preserved some aspects of the status of English in medieval England, even as it began radically to transform others.

Institutionally, this tradition's pre-eminent feature was the slow, inconsistent fashion by which English was naturalized in the socially powerful domains that manage conceptions of language. English literary traditions had held increasingly greater social prestige since the late fourteenth century, with Chaucer in particular serving as a figure of literary origins to late-medieval and early modern poets. But while belletristic writers may initiate or popularize linguistic forms and concepts, it is bureaucracies that legitimate and institutionalize them, and in this regard it is notable that two and three hundred years after the death of Henry V (and even longer after that of Wyclif) the sociolinguistic meanings of English—its ability to mediate cultural identity— remained significantly restricted in ways still strongly reminiscent of the late-medieval status of English. Indeed, just as French and Latin persisted in some government practices into the eighteenth century, so other institutional confirmations of an elevated status for English were slow in coming. The first printed English grammar is William Bullokar's 1586 *Pamphlet for Grammar*; one more such grammar appeared before the end of the sixteenth century, and only thirty more during the course of the seventeenth. It was not until the eighteenth century, when an additional 236 English grammars appeared, that a tradition of the codification necessary for standardization was firmly established for the language. Even this slow progression conceals additional limitations on the status of English, for conceptually and methodologically, nearly all these early grammars modelled themselves on Latin grammatical categories.[8]

English dictionaries and vocabulary experienced similarly protracted growth. The earliest English dictionary in English is

---

[8] See Ian Michael, *English Grammatical Categories and the Tradition to 1800* (Cambridge: Cambridge University Press, 1970); pp. 549–87 itemize the English grammars, and pp. 588–94 arrange them chronologically. Michael also describes five English grammars that appeared only in manuscript. More generally see G. A. Padley, *Grammatical Theory in Western Europe, 1500–1700: Trends in Vernacular Grammar*, 2 vols. (Cambridge: Cambridge University Press, 1985, 1988).

Robert Cawdrey's *A Table Alphabeticall, Conteyning and Teaching the True Writing, and Vnderstanding of Hard Vsuall English Wordes*, which appeared in 1604 and which was followed by a growing number of increasingly complex dictionaries in the seventeenth and eighteenth centuries, culminating, of course, with Johnson's *A Dictionary of the English Language*, which was published in 1755. In their grammatical and lexicographical prescriptions, these grammar books and dictionaries codified English and thereby directly affirmed the status of a presumptive standard but also did so indirectly, by for the first time in the language's history proscribing non-standard or regional forms of the sort Chaucer uses for immediate rhetorical effect in the *Reeve's Tale*. In this vein, Alexander Gil's *Logonomia Anglica* of 1619 offers a remarkably detailed account of phonological variation among English regional dialects that by contrast shows the conceptual and practical limitations of the regional remarks by Trevisa, and before him Hidgen and William of Malmesbury.[9]

A crucial difference between medieval and early modern metalinguistic discussion is that the codification dependent on the latter reflects ongoing institutional change in language use and attitudes and not merely the isolated assertions of individuals, however powerful or significant they may have been. As I have noted several times, it is just this kind of broad-based institutional framework that provides the mutually constitutive contexts necessary for the evolution of linguistically precocious sentiments into prospering conceptions of language. The frequency and consistency of grammatical tools in the seventeenth and eighteenth centuries enact this sustained metalinguistic discourse, but additional, perhaps stronger (because unconnected) traditions figure as well. This is the period that witnessed the development of English literary terminology and the cultivation of explicitly English literary theory and craft in such works as George Puttenham's 1589 *The Arte of English Poesie*. It is also this period that witnessed significant changes in the structure of the language, partly as a response

---

[9] Gil, *Logonomia Anglica* (London: John Beale, 1621), 16–19; consulted in the Scolar Press edition, no. 68 (Menston, 1968).

to a perceived need not simply for the regulation of English but also for its material improvement. Syntactically, the development of periphrastic verbs enabled expression of subtle distinctions of time, mood, and aspect, while lexically, through both borrowing and new formations, the recorded vocabulary of English increased dramatically in the sixteenth and seventeenth centuries, with the years 1570 to 1630 being the period of peak growth.[10]

Early modern educational institutions also participated in the sociolinguistic traditions that transformed the status of English, but that did so only gradually. Initially, medieval grammar schools conducted their business in Latin or French, and while Trevisa's comments about John of Cornwall and Robert Pencriche indicate that English was also used as early as the late fourteenth century, the shift to it in education was no more decisive and sudden than it would be in law or government. Early modern grammar schools may have used English to teach Latin and even for rudimentary general instruction, but they also used pedagogical tools such as the *vulgaria* to inculcate students with a conception of Latin as the language of prestige, education, and social class. In his 1531 *Book of the Governour*, Sir Thomas Elyot even advocated the use of Latin 'as a familiar la*n*gage' for the son of a noble, 'hauynge none other persons to serue him or kepyng hym company / but suche as can speake latine elegantly.'[11] Thirty-seven years later Roger Ascham affirmed Latin's importance to proper education in his *Schoolmaster*, which is dedicated to the improvement of Latin pedagogy and which has as one of is presuppositions: 'Yet all men couet to haue their children speake latin.'[12] As late as 1614

---

[10] On early dictionaries, see Vivian Salmon, 'Orthography and Punctuation'; on the growth of English lexicon, see Terttu Nevalinen, 'Early Modern English Lexis and Semantics'; on standard and non-standard language in the early modern period, see Manfred Görlach, 'Regional and Social Variation'; and on English literary discussions, see Sylvia Adamson, 'Literary Language.' All four essays appear in Roger Lass (ed.), *The Cambridge History of the English Language*, iii. *1476–1776* (Cambridge: Cambridge University Press, 1999), 13–55, 332–458, 459–538, 539–653, respectively.

[11] Elyot, *The Boke Named the Gouernour* (London: Thomas Berthelette, 1531), 30; cited from the Scolar Press edition, no. 246 (Menston, 1970).

[12] Ascham, *The Scholemaster* (London: Iohn Daye, 1570), 2; cited from the Scolar Press edition, no. 20 (Menston, 1967).

Eilhardus Lubinus suggested the establishment of colleges where the entire community, scholars and servants alike, would consist only of those conversant in Latin. And until the end of the seventeenth century—though not often after that—various grammar schools still promulgated regulations that advocated the use of Latin and restricted, if not proscribed, the use of English. In 1561, for example, statutes at Guisborough Grammar School declared that the 'Scholars of the Third and Fourth Forms shall speak nothing within the School-house but Latin, saving only in the teaching of the lower Forms.' A similar 1593 regulation at King's School, Durham, required all scholars 'to use the Latin tongue in and about the School,' while a 1656 Newport statute mandated that anyone who could speak Latin must use it, rather than English, when in the company of students of comparable ability.[13] Even when such statutes were observed in the breach, their very existence points to important if inconsistent developments between the late-medieval status of English and the seventeenth-century one, developments that imply increasingly expanded roles for English even as they sustained other roles for Latin.

The status of English was transformed even more slowly at Oxford and Cambridge, where Latin remained cultivated as the language of scholarship and social rank through the eighteenth century. The 1636 Statutes of William Laud mandated the use of Latin in the Houses of Congregation and Convocation (two administrative bodies) and also in individual Halls; they further mandated that candidates for the bachelor's degree demonstrate their ability to speak in Latin and extemporaneously translate passages of English into it. The administrative counterparts at Cambridge were statutes like those at Trinity College in the sixteenth century, which prescribed Latin prayers and likewise required the use of

[13] On English grammar schools, see Nicholas Orme, *English Schools in the Middle Ages* (Oxford: Methuen, 1973) and *Education and Society in Medieval and Renaissance England* (London: Hambleton Press, 1989); Kenneth Charlton, *Education in Renaissance England* (London: Routledge, 1965); and Foster Watson, *The Old Grammar Schools* (Cambridge: Cambridge University Press, 1916) and *The English Grammar Schools to 1660: Their Curriculum and Practice* (Cambridge: Cambridge University Press, 1908). The statutes I quote are taken from Watson's *The English Grammar Schools to 1660*, 317–18.

Latin (along with Greek or Hebrew) for all conversations except-
ing those with someone not from the University. For students at
both universities, composition in Latin continued to be a central
feature of their education, with the Laudian statutes remaining at
least partly in force until the Reform Act of 1854, which among
other things allowed for the use of English in debate. If, like
grammar school regulations, both the Laudian and Trinity statutes
described a linguistic ideal rather than a linguistic reality, it was
none the less an ideal to which many aspired. In 1590 the presi-
dent of Magdalen College, Oxford, declared, 'I know myne owne
House and divers other Colleges whose scholars dare not presume
to speake any other language then Latine,' while John Potenger, a
bachelor's candidate of 1668, later noted that when he was at college it was still the custom to speak Latin at dinner. At Oxford,
sermons, orations, and the like were delivered in Latin throughout
the seventeenth century, and at Cambridge, in about 1670, John
Knightbridge founded a professorship of Moral Theology and
Casuistical Divinity that required that the professor's lectures be
delivered in Latin. Into the eighteenth century, John Randolph,
who held the Oxford professorship of poetry from 1776 to 1783,
delivered his lectures in Latin, while at Cambridge Latin continued to be used on ceremonial occasions, in the recording of University transactions, and in the disputations of students pursuing
fellowships.[14]

---

[14] See John Griffiths (ed.), *Statutes of the University of Oxford Codified in the Year
1636 under the Authority of Archbishop Laud* (Oxford: Clarendon, 1888), 140, 89;
Stanley James Curtis, *History of Education in Great Britain*, 7th edn. (London: University Tutorial Press, 1967), 138–9; John Prest (ed.), *The Illustrated History of Oxford*
(Oxford: Oxford University Press, 1993), 174; James Bass Mullinger, *The University
of Cambridge*, 3 vols. (1873–1911; rpt. New York: Johnson Reprint, 1969), i. 138; T.
H. Aston (ed.), *The History of the University of Oxford*, 8 vols. (Oxford: Clarendon,
1984–97), iv. 225, v. 517; Denys Arthur Winstanley, *Unreformed Cambridge: A Study
of Certain Aspects of the University in the Eighteenth Century* (Cambridge: Cambridge
University Press, 1935), 137; E. S. Leedham-Greene, *A Concise History of the University of Cambridge* (Cambridge: Cambridge University Press, 1996), 120. More generally, see Edward Geoffrey Watson Bill, *Education at Christ Church Oxford 1660–1800*
(Oxford: Clarendon, 1988); and Weldon T. Myers, *The Relations of Latin and English
as Living Languages during the Time of Milton* (Charlottesville, Va.: University Press
of Virginia, 1912).

The early modern sociolinguistic thinking that informed these various institutions of education, grammatical discussion, government, and law likewise bespoke protracted, sometimes inconsistent transformations in the status of English. On the one hand, continued acknowledgement of Latin's authority and prestige indicates that the linguistic controversies of the fourteenth and fifteenth centuries had indeed not been decisive, perhaps not even significant, with some of the fourteenth century's competing linguistic futures continuing to do so well into the modern period. But on the other, escalating, sustained attention to the status and characteristics of English does constitute a fundamental change from the late-medieval period.

In this vein, in his *Arte of Englishe Poesie*, which I noted above, Puttenham offered a 258-page discussion of poets, poetry, and poetics that everywhere championed and illustrated achievement in English, treating its expressive potential as comparable to that of Greek and Latin. In the process he presents a strikingly modern-sounding definition of a national language—specifically English—that in nuance and linguistic understanding transcends anything from the Middle Ages:

But after a speach is fully fashioned to the common vnderstanding, & accepted by consent of a whole countrey & nation, it is called a language, & receaueth none allowed alteration, but by extraordinary occasions by little & little, as it were insensibly bringing in of many corruptions that creepe along with the time: of all which matters, we haue more largely spoken in our bookes of the originals and pedigree of the English tong.[15]

Distancing himself even further from such generalities as those about diachronic change that Chaucer rehearses in the Prologue to Book Two of *Troilus and Criseyde* or Caxton in his Preface to the *Eneydos*, Puttenham proceeds to perhaps the earliest detailed account of true sociolects in England, advocating the supremacy of the language of court and town to that of 'marches and frontiers' or even universities,

---

[15] Puttenham, *The Arte of English Poesie* (London: Richard Field, 1589), 120; cited from the Scolar Press edition of R. C. Alston, no. 110 (Menston, 1968).

where Schollers vse much peeuish affectation of words out of the prima-
tiue languages, or finally, in any vplandish village or corner of a Realme,
where is no resort but of poore rusticall or vnciuill people; neither shall
he [the aspiring poet] follow the speach of a craftes man or carter, or
other of the inferiour sort, though he be inhabitant or bred in the best
towne and Citie in this Realme, for such persons doe abuse good speach-
es by strange accents or ill shapen soundes, and false ortographie. But he
shall follow generally the better brought vp sort, such as the Greekes call
[*charientes*] men ciuill and graciously behauoured and bred.

In its hierarchical arrangment of English varieties, its mapping of
these varieties onto social hierarchies, its equation of language and
personal character, and even its collapsing of spoken and written
language, Puttenham's analysis provides the kind of sociolinguistic thinking necessary for the several readings of the *Reeve's Tale*
that I examined at the beginning of the previous chapter. It also
conceptualizes English in a strikingly unmedieval fashion.

An even more enthusiastic instance of this newly developing
conception of English informs Richard Mulcaster's *The First Part
of the Elementarie*, a 1582 volume that promises to treat 'all those
things which young childern are to learn of right, and maie learn
at ease, if their parents will be carefull, a litle more then ordin-
arie.'[16] These 'things' fall into five categories—reading, writing,
drawing, singing, and playing—of which those relating to reading
and writing are most pertinent here. Though his volume precedes
The Art of Englishe Poesie by seven years, Mulcaster goes beyond
Puttenham to suggest not simply that English is a valuable and
expressive language in its own right but also that the English of
his own time is the best there has ever been and ever will be:

I take this present period of our English tung to be the verie height
thereof, bycause I find it so excellentlie well fined, both for the bodie of
the tung it self, and for the customarie writing thereof, as either foren
workmanship can giue it glosse, or as homewrought hanling can giue
it grace. When the age of our peple, which now vse the tung so well,
is dead and departed there will another succede, and with the peple the

---

[16] Mulcaster, *The First Part of the Elementarie* (London: Thomas Vautroullier, 1582),
5; cited from the Scolar Press edition of R. C. Alston, no. 219 (Menston, 1970).

tung will alter and change. Which change in the full haruest thereof maie proue conparable to this, but sure for this which we now vse, it semeth euen now to be at the best for substance, and the brauest for circumstance, and whatsoeuer shall becom of the English state, the English tung ca*n*not proue fairer, then it is at this daie, if it maie please our learned sort to esteme so of it, and to bestow their trauell vpon such a subiect, so capable of ornament, so proper to themselues, and the more to be honored, bycause it is their own.

Here English has achieved not simply respect but the stability that enables conceptualization of its historical development and better and worse varieties. It is all at once national language, image of change, paragon of expression, and undervalued treasure, attitudes that Mulcaster later aptly recapitulates in his justly famous declaration: 'I loue Rome, but London better, I fauor Italie, but England more, I honor the Latin, but I worship the English.' Mulcaster's arguments well summarize the conflict in the early modern status of English between a traditional subjection of English to Latin and an evolving sense of the vernacular's distinction, for the above declaration prefaces a detailed and eloquent testimony to the advantages of learning in English in an era that still prized Latin as a mark of education and prestige.[17]

Retrospection and recovery

In nuance of thought as well as in the coherence of the tradition they project, comments such as Mulcaster's and Puttenham's significantly transcend (say) Trevisa's advocacy of rendering Latin chronicles in English in his 'Dialogue between a Lord and a Clerk'; the latter is an isolated statement on a specific linguistic process—translation—while the former are institutional appeals for the transformation of the ecology of English in general. Collectively and despite the tardiness imposed by lingering traditional attitudes towards England's linguistic repertoire, the status and corpus planning and metalinguistic discursive traditions of early modern English affirm newfound roles for English, a new linguis-

---

[17] Mulcaster, *The First Part of the Elementarie*, 159, 254–6.

tic ecology, and a new status of English in relation to this ecology. What appear as random ideas, statements of fact, or controversies in the late-medieval period, or what are entirely lacking at that time, become integrated, coherent, and entrenched only during the course of the sixteenth, seventeenth, and eighteenth centuries. Rather than isolated comments or the remarks of circumscribed groups, these metalinguistic traditions, firmly situated in socially powerful domains, involve linguistic considerations of grammar, vocabulary, orthography, and dictionaries; sociolinguistic controversies over the centrality of the vernacular to the Protestant reformation and the cultural value of translating Latin and Greek masterpieces into the common language; and intellectual debates over the utility of instruction in English, the suitability of the language for learned discussion, and the character of the fledgling enterprise of comparative and historical linguistics. Lengthy early modern arguments in these areas constitute a metalinguistic discourse with naturalized opportunities for the discussion of an extensive range of sociolinguistic topics, and this institutional and conceptual ability simply to talk about so many linguistic issues, specifically those involving English, represents perhaps the most dramatic shift of all from the late-medieval period. Through this metalinguistic discourse, what was lost as the status of English evolved—that is, an elite variety represented by Latin or French—was reacquired through the sociolinguistic processes that institutionalized a standard variety of English, which ultimately came to serve the same hierarchizing and socially discriminatory roles that Latin and French had in the Middle Ages. While the origins and growth of these issues and the general shift to English are the subjects of another book about the status of a later version of English, I venture that such a book would share with this one an emphasis on the contextual factors—now including capitalism, print, and colonization—that shape such meanings and that are themselves not always specifically concerned with language.[18]

---

[18] In addition to the references I have already cited in this chapter, see Manfred Görlach, *Introduction to Early Modern English* (Cambridge: Cambridge University Press, 1978); and the dated but still valuable Richard Foster Jones, *The Triumph of the English Language* (London: Oxford University Press, 1953).

After Middle English—as an objective as well as a point of reference—is how I necessarily view the late-medieval status of English, and, as a result of my belief in the mutual and contextually specific construction of linguistic and social practices, I have done so throughout this book with what I regard as a healthy dose of scepticism. In some instances my scepticism has been directed at medieval England's representation of itself. By conceptualizing language contact as non-normative, Anglo-Norman historiography fostered discursive practices that obscured what social and settlement patterns suggest were the obvious sociolinguistic realities of daily life. Suppressing linguistic diversity in support of dominant social institutions, these practices demonstrated a disparity between what people on the street or in the meadow probably heard and what established interpretative structures told them they heard. In other instances, my scepticism concerns the application of modern sociolinguistic expectations to the ecology of Middle English and the late-medieval status of English. As naturalized as the connections between nationalism and vernacular language planning have become in the modern world, they depend on ideas, practices, and institutions that are neither linguistically universal nor endemic to the English Middle Ages. The late-medieval contexts of Henry III's extraordinary English letters did thus not allow for the use of the vernacular as a political and national statement in itself. I am similarly sceptical of the expectation that the Middle English period conceived of social or regional varieties in the way the modern period does. Like the conversations in *Sir Gawain and the Green Knight*, the use of regionalisms in the *Reeve's Tale* projects English as a language that neither conceptualizes nor realizes individual dialects as coherent, well-defined, and sociolinguistically meaningful entities.

Since linguistic practices are so contextually defined, with the same practice contributing in different ways to different language ecologies, it may well be that the status of no two languages can ever really be the same, for even speech communities that share linguistic practices and concerns can differ in their linguistic beliefs and in the contextualizations of their linguistic activities. Both seventeenth-century England and nineteenth-century

Finland sought to codify the vernacular and establish a literary tradition for it, for example, but the former did so systematically as a sovereign nation solidifying its national and religious integrity, while the latter did so in a popular and officially unsanctioned movement to define Finnish culture within the political dominion of Russia. From a diachronic perspective, the complex individuality of language ecologies becomes even more pronounced, with the institutional and social pressures that are foremost in one ecology perhaps absent altogether from another. And this can be the case whether the ecologies involve different languages (such as English and Finnish) or different synchronic moments of the same language (such as Middle and Modern English). Neither unique nor peculiar, the desultory quality of the history of the status of English is in fact indicative of sociolinguistic variation and selection across time. What limits the shape of a language's status among its users are the sociolinguistic constraints predicted by the Uniformitarian Principle, which, rather than the rhetorical approach of literary studies or the formalist approach of structural linguistics, have underwritten much of my inquiry. The many non-medieval comparisons that I have drawn both illuminate this principle and its abstract sense of what is sociolinguistically possible and also outline the distinctive characteristics of the significance of English in the late Middle Ages. If historical specifics determine the details of a language's status, general sociolinguistic principles provide the framework that organizes these details into coherent, intelligible, and learnable patterns in the domains, pragmatics, and linguistic repertoire of a speech community.

Works Cited

ADAMSON, SYLVIA, 'Literary Language,' in Lass (ed.), *The Cambridge History of the English Language*, iii. *1476–1776*, 539–633.

ANDERSON, BENEDICT, *Imagined Communities: Reflections on the Origin and Spread of Nationalism*, rev. edn. (London: Verso, 1991).

ANDREW, MALCOLM, and RONALD WALDRON (eds.), *The Poems of the Pearl Manuscript: Pearl, Cleanness, Patience, Sir Gawain and the Green Knight* (Berkeley and Los Angeles: University of California Press, 1982).

Annales Monastici, ed. Henry Richards Luard, RS 36, 5 vols. (London: Longman, 1864–9).

ASCHAM, ROGER, *The Scholemaster* (London: Iohn Daye, 1570), rpt. Scolar Press, no. 20 (Menston, 1967).

ASTON, MARGARET, 'Wyclif and the Vernacular,' in Anne Hudson and Michael Wilks (eds.), *From Ockham to Wyclif, Studies in Church History*, Subsidia 5 (Oxford: Blackwell, 1987), 281–330.

ASTON, T. H. (ed.), *The History of the University of Oxford*, 8 vols. (Oxford: Clarendon, 1984–97).

BACON, ROGER, *Opera Quædem Hactenus Inedita*, ed. J. S. Brewer (London: Longman, 1859).

BAKHTIN, M. M., *The Dialogic Imagination*, ed. Michael Holquist, trans. Caryl Emerson and Michael Holquist (Austin, Tex.: University of Texas Press, 1981).

BARBER, CHARLES, *The English Language: A Historical Introduction* (Cambridge: Cambridge University Press, 1993).

BARON, DENNIS, *The English-Only Question: An Official Language for Americans?* (New Haven: Yale University Press, 1990).

BARR, HELEN, *Socioliterary Practice in Late Medieval England* (Oxford: Oxford University Press, 2001).

BARRON, W. R. J., *'Trawthe' and Treason: The Sin of Gawain Reconsidered: A Thematic Study of 'Sir Gawain and the Green Knight'* (Manchester: Manchester University Press, 1980).

BEADLE, RICHARD, 'Prolegomena to a Literary Geography of Later Medieval Norfolk,' in Riddy (ed.), *Regionalism in Late Medieval Manuscripts*, 89–108.

BEDE, THE VENERABLE, *A History of the English Church and People*, trans. Leo Sherley-Price (Harmondsworth: Penguin, 1955).

BENNETT, J. A.W., *Chaucer at Oxford and at Cambridge* (Toronto: University of Toronto Press, 1974).

BENSKIN, MICHAEL, 'Some New Perspectives on the Origins of Standard Written English,' in J. A. Van Leuvensteijn and J. B. Berns (eds.), *Dialect and Standard Language, Dialekt und Standardsprache in the English, Dutch, German and Norwegian Language Areas* (Amsterdam: North-Holland, 1992), 71–105.

BENSON, LARRY D. (ed.), *The Riverside Chaucer*, 3rd edn. (Boston: Houghton Mifflin, 1987).

——*Contradictions: From 'Beowulf' to Chaucer: Selected Studies of Larry D. Benson*, ed. Theodore M. Andersson and Stephen A. Barney (Aldershot: Scolar, 1995).

——'The Beginnings of Chaucer's English Style,' in Andersson and Barney (eds.), *Contradictions*, 243–65.

——'Courtly Love and Chivalry in the Later Middle Ages,' in Andersson and Barney (eds.), *Contradictions*, 294–313.

——and THEODORE M. ANDERSSON, *The Literary Context of Chaucer's Fabliaux: Texts and Translations* (Indianapolis: Bobbs-Merrill, 1971).

BERNDT, ROLF, 'French and English in Thirteenth-Century England. An Investigation into the Linguistic Situation after the Loss of the Duchy of Normandy and other Continental Dominions,' in *Aspekte der Anglistischen Forschung in der DDR: Martin Lehnert zum 65. Geburtstag* (Berlin: Akademie-Verlag, 1976), 129–50.

——'The Period of the Final Decline of French in Medieval England (Fourteenth and Early Fifteenth Centuries),' *Zeitschrift für Anglistik und Amerikanstik*, 20 (1972), 341–69.

BIBER, DOUGLAS, *Variation across Speech and Writing* (Cambridge: Cambridge University Press, 1988).

BILL, EDWARD GEOFFREY WATSON, *Education at Christ Church Oxford 1660–1800* (Oxford: Clarendon, 1988).

BILLER, PETER, and ANNE HUDSON (eds.), *Heresy and Literacy 1000–1530* (Cambridge: Cambridge University Press, 1994).

BLAKE, N. F., 'The Northernisms in *The Reeve's Tale*,' *Lore and Language*, 3 (1979), 1–8.

——*Non-Standard Language in English Literature* (London: Andre Deutsch, 1981).

——(ed.), *The Cambridge History of the English Language*, ii. *1066–1476* (Cambridge: Cambridge University Press, 1992).

——*A History of the English Language* (Hong Kong: Macmillan, 1996).

BLOCH, R. HOWARD, *The Scandal of the Fabliaux* (Chicago: University of Chicago Press, 1986).

BOFFEY, JULIA, and A. S. G. EDWARDS, 'Literary Texts,' in Lotte Hellinga and J. B. Trapp (eds.), *The Cambridge History of the Book in Britain*, iii. *1400–1557* (Cambridge: Cambridge University Press, 1999), 555–75.

BOKENHAM, OSBERN, *The Reule of Crysten Religioun*, ed. William Cabell Greet, EETS os 171 (London: Oxford University Press, 1927).

——*Legendys of Hooly Wummen*, ed. Mary S. Serjeantson, EETS os 206 (London: Oxford University Press, 1938).

BOURDON, J.-P., A. COURNÉE, and Y. CHARPENTIER (eds.), *Dictionnaire normand–français* (Paris: Conseil international de la langue française, 1993).

BRAND, PAUL, 'The Languages of the Law in Later Medieval England,' in D. A. Trotter (ed.), *Multilingualism in Later Medieval Britain*, 63–76.

BRIGGS, CHARLES L., *Learning How to Ask: A Sociolinguistic Appraisal of the Role of the Interview in Social Science Research* (Cambridge: Cambridge University Press, 1986).

BROOK, G. L., *English Dialects*, 3rd. edn. (London: Andre Deutsch, 1978).

BROWN, GILLIAN, and GEORGE YULE, *Discourse Analysis* (Cambridge: Cambridge University Press, 1983).

BROWN, PENELOPE, and STEPHEN C. LEVINSON, *Politeness: Some Universals in Language Usage*, rev. edn. (Cambridge: Cambridge University Press, 1987).

BRUNNER, KARL B., *Der Mittelenglische Versroman über Richard Löwenherz*, Wiener Beiträge zur Englischen Philologie, 42 (Vienna: Wilhelm Braumüller, 1913).

BURNLEY, DAVID, 'Courtly Speech in Chaucer,' *Poetica*, 24 (1986), 16–38.

——'On the Architecture of Chaucer's Language,' in Erik Kooper (ed.), *This Noble Craft . . . Proceedings of the Xth Research Symposium of the Dutch and Belgian University Teachers of Old and Middle English and Historical Linguistics, Utrecht, 19–20 January, 1989* (Amsterdam: Rodopi, 1991), 43–57.

——'The Sheffield Chaucer Textbase: Its Compilation and Uses,' in Ian Lancashire (ed.), *Computer-Based Chaucer Studies* (Toronto: Centre for Computing in the Humanities, 1993), 123–40.

——'Style, Meaning and Communication in *Sir Gawain and the Green Knight*,' *Poetica*, 42 (1994), 23–37.

BURNLEY, DAVID, *Courtliness and Literature in Medieval England* (London: Longman, 1998).

——*The History of the English Language: A Source Book*, 2nd edn. (London: Longman, 2000).

BURROW, J. A., *A Reading of 'Sir Gawain and the Green Knight'* (London: Routledge, 1965).

CABLE, THOMAS, 'The Rise of Written Standard English,' in Scaglione (ed.), *The Emergence of National Languages*, 75–94.

Calendar of the Charter Rolls Preserved in the Public Record Office, 6 vols. (1895; rpt. Nendeln, Liechtenstein: Kraus, 1972).

Calendar of Inquisitions Miscellaneous (Chancery) Preserved in the Public Record Office (1916; rpt. Nendeln, Liechtenstein: Kraus, 1973).

Calendar of Inquisitions Post Mortem and Other Analogous Documents Preserved in the Public Record Office, 12 vols. (1904–38; rpt. Nendeln, Liechtenstein: Kraus, 1973).

Calendar of the Liberate Rolls Preserved in the Public Record Office, 6 vols. (London: Her Majesty's Stationery Office, 1916).

Calendar of the Patent Rolls Preserved in the Public Record Office, Henry III, A. D. 1216–1272, 6 vols. (1901–13; rpt. Nendeln, Liechtenstein: Kraus, 1971).

CAMPBELL, KIM SYDOW, 'A Lesson in Polite Non-Compliance: Gawain's Conversational Strategies in Fitt 3 of *Sir Gawain and the Green Knight*,' *Language Quarterly*, 28 (1990), 53–62.

CARPENTER, D. A., *The Reign of Henry III* (London: The Hambledon Press, 1996).

CAXTON, WILLIAM, *The Prologues and Epilogues of William Caxton*, ed. W. J. B. Crotch, EETS os 176 (1928; rpt. New York: Burt Franklin, 1971).

CHAMBERS, J. K., *Sociolinguistic Theory: Linguistic Variation and Its Social Significance* (Oxford: Blackwell, 1995).

CHAMBERS, R. W., and MARJORIE DAUNT (eds.), *A Book of London English 1384–1425* (Oxford: Clarendon, 1931).

CHARLTON, KENNETH, *Education in Renaissance England* (London: Routledge, 1965).

The Chronicle of Battle Abbey, ed. and trans. Eleanor Searle (Oxford: Clarendon, 1980).

The Chronicle of Bury St. Edmunds, 1212–1301, ed. and trans. Antonia Gransden (London: Nelson, 1964).

Chronicles of London, ed. Charles Lethbridge Kingsford (1905; rpt. Dursley: Alan Sutton, 1977).

Chronicles of the Reigns of Edward I and Edward II, ed. William Stubbs, RS 76, 2 vols. (London: Longman, 1882–3).

CLANCHY, M. T., *England and Its Rulers 1066–1272: Foreign Lordship and National Identity* (Oxford: Blackwell, 1983).

——*From Memory to Written Record: England, 1066–1307*, 2nd edn. (Oxford: Blackwell, 1993).

CLARK, CECILY, '*Sir Gawain and the Green Knight*: Characterisation by Syntax,' *Essays in Criticism*, 16 (1966), 361–74.

——(ed.), *The Peterborough Chronicle, 1070–1154*, 2nd edn. (Oxford: Clarendon, 1970).

——'Another Late-Fourteenth-Century Case of Dialect-Awareness,' *English Studies*, 62 (1981), 504–5.

CLARK, HERBERT H., *Arenas of Language Use* (Chicago: University of Chicago Press, 1992).

——*Using Language* (Cambridge: Cambridge University Press, 1996).

Close Rolls of the Reign of Henry III Preserved in the Public Record Office, 14 vols. (1902–38; rpt. Nendeln, Liechtenstein: Kraus, 1970).

COLVIN, HOWARD MONTAGUE (ed.), *Building Accounts of King Henry III* (Oxford: Clarendon, 1971).

COONEY, HELEN (ed.), *Nation, Court and Culture* (Dublin: Four Courts Press, 2001).

COOPER, ROBERT L. (ed.), *Language Spread: Studies in Diffusion and Social Change* (Bloomington, Ind.: Indiana University Press, 1982).

——*Language Planning and Social Change* (Cambridge: Cambridge University Press, 1989).

COPLAND, M., '*The Reeve's Tale*: Harlotrie or Sermonyng?' *Medium Ævum*, 31 (1962), 14–32.

CRANE, SUSAN, 'The Writing Lesson of 1381,' in Barbara A. Hanawalt (ed.), *Chaucer's England: Literature in Historical Context* (Minneapolis: University of Minnesota Press, 1992), 201–21.

CRAWFORD, JAMES, *Hold Your Tongue: Bilingualism and the Politics of 'English Only'* (Reading, Mass.: Addison-Wesley, 1992).

——*Language Loyalties: A Source Book on the Official English Controversy* (Chicago: University of Chicago Press, 1992).

CROWLEY, TONY, *The Politics of Discourse: The Standard Language Question in British Cultural Debates* (London: Macmillan, 1989).

Cursor Mundi, ed. Richard Morris, EETS os 57, 59, 62, 66, 68, 99, 101 (London: Trübner, 1874–93).

CURTIS, STANLEY JAMES, *History of Education in Great Britain*, 7th edn. (London: University Tutorial Press, 1967).

DARLINGTON, R. P., P. MCGURK, and JENNIFER BRAY (ed. and trans.), *The Chronicle of John of Worcester*, 3 vols. (Oxford: Clarendon, 1995, 1998).

DAVIS, LAWRENCE M., *English Dialectology: An Introduction* (University, Ala.: University of Alabama Press, 1983).

DAVIS, NORMAN (ed.), *Paston Letters and Papers of the Fifteenth Century*, 2 vols. (Oxford: Clarendon, 1971).

——Review of *Chaucer at Oxford and at Cambridge* by J. A. W. Bennett, *Review of English Studies*, 27 (1976), 336–7.

DICKINS, BRUCE, and R. M. WILSON (eds.), *Early Middle English Texts* (London: Bowes & Bowes, 1956).

DONAGHEY, B. S., 'Nicholas Trevet's Use of King Alfred's Translation of Boethius, and the Dating of His Commentary,' in A. J. Minnis (ed.), *The Medieval Boethius: Studies in the Vernacular Translations of 'De Consolatione Philosophiae'* (Cambridge: Boydell & Brewer, 1987), 1–31.

DONOGHUE, DANIEL, 'Laȝamon's Ambivalence,' *Speculum*, 65 (1990), 537–63.

DOUGLAS, DAVID C. (gen. ed.), *English Historical Documents*, iii. *1189–1327*, ed. Harry Rothwell (New York: Oxford University Press, 1975).

DOYLE, A. I., 'The Manuscripts,' in David Lawton (ed.), *Middle English Alliterative Poetry and Its Literary Background: Seven Essays* (Cambridge: D. S. Brewer, 1982), 88–100.

ELIASON, NORMAN E., *The Language of Chaucer's Poetry: An Appraisal of the Verse, Style, and Structure* (Copenhagen: Rosenkilde & Bagger, 1972).

ELLIS, ALEXANDER J., 'On the Only English Proclamation of Henry III., 18 October 1258, and Its Treatment by Former Editors and Translators,' *Transactions of the Philological Society* (1868), 1–135.

ELYOT, SIR THOMAS, *The Boke Named the Gouernour* (London: Thomas Berthelette, 1531), rpt. Scolar Press, no. 246 (Menston, 1970).

EMERSON, OLIVER FARRER, *The History of the English Language* (New York: Macmillan, 1915).

EUN, HYESOON LIM, 'Polite Speech: A Sociolinguistic Analysis of Chaucer and the *Gawain*-Poet,' Diss. Michigan State University, 1987.

EVANS, WILLIAM W., 'Dramatic Use of the Second-Person Singular Pronoun in *Sir Gawain and the Green Knight*,' *Studia Neophilologica*, 39 (1967), 38–45.

EVERETT, DOROTHY, 'Chaucer's Good Ear,' in Patricia Kean (ed.),

Essays on Middle English Literature (Oxford: Clarendon, 1955), 139–48.

FAIRCLOUGH, NORMAN, *Language and Power* (London: Longman, 1989).

FASOLD, RALPH, *The Sociolinguistics of Society* (Oxford: Blackwell, 1984).

FISHER, JOHN H., *The Emergence of Standard English* (Lexington, Ky.: University of Kentucky Press, 1996).

——MALCOLM RICHARDSON, and JANE L. FISHER, *An Anthology of Chancery English* (Knoxville, Ten.: University of Tennessee Press, 1984).

FISHMAN, JOSHUA, *Language and Nationalism: Two Integrative Essays* (Rowley, Mass.: Newbury House Publishers, 1972).

——(ed.), *Advances in Language Planning* (The Hague: Mouton, 1974).

FISIAK, JACEK, 'Sociolinguistics and Middle English: Some Socially Motivated Changes in the History of English,' *Kwartalnik Neofilologiczny*, 24 (1977), 247–59.

FITZ-THEDMAR, ARNOLD, *De antiquis legibus Liber. Cronica maiorum et vicecomitum londoniarum et quedam, que contingebant temporibus illis ab anno MCLXXVIII ad annum MCCLXXIV*, ed. Thomas Stapleton, Camden Society (1846; rpt. New York: Johnson Reprint Corp., 1968).

FLETCHER, ALAN J., 'Chaucer's Norfolk Reeve,' *Medium Ævum*, 52 (1983), 100–3.

Flores Historiarum, ed. Henry Richards Luard, RS 95, 3 vols. (London: Eyre & Spottiswoode, 1890).

FLUDERNIK, MONIKA, *The Fictions of Language and the Languages of Fiction: The Linguistic Representation of Speech and Consciousness* (London: Routledge, 1993).

FOWLER, ROGER, *Literature as Social Discourse: The Practice of Linguistic Criticism* (Bloomington, Ind.: Indiana University Press, 1981).

——*Linguistic Criticism* (Oxford: Oxford University Press, 1986).

FRAME, ROBIN, *The Political Development of the British Isles 1100–1400* (Oxford: Oxford University Press, 1990).

FRANCIS, W. N., *Dialectology: An Introduction* (London: Longman, 1983).

FRANZEN, CHRISTINE, *The Tremulous Hand of Worcester: A Study of Old English in the Thirteenth Century* (Oxford: Clarendon, 1991).

FRENCH, WALTER HOYT, and CHARLES BROCKWAY HALE (eds.), *Middle English Metrical Romances* (New York: Prentice-Hall, 1930).

GALLAGHER, JOSEPH E., ' "Trawþe" and "Luf-talkyng" in *Sir Gawain and the Green Knight*,' *Neuphilologische Mitteilungen*, 78 (1977), 362–76.

GARBÁTY, THOMAS JAY, 'Satire and Regionalism: The Reeve and His Tale,' *Chaucer Review*, 8 (1973), 1–8.

GARCÍA, BEGOÑA CRESPO, 'Historical Background of Multilingualism and Its Impact on English,' in D. A. Trotter (ed.), *Multilingualism in Later Medieval Britain*, 25–35.

GEARY, PATRICK J., *The Myth of Nations: The Medieval Origins of Europe* (Princeton: Princeton University Press, 2002).

GELLNER, ERNEST, *Nations and Nationalism* (Ithaca, NY: Cornell University Press, 1983).

GERALD OF WALES, *Expugnatio Hibernica: The Conquest of Ireland*, ed. and trans. A. B. Scott and F. X. Martin (Dublin: Royal Irish Academy, 1978).

GIL, ALEXANDER, *Logonomia Anglica* (London: John Beale, 1621), rpt. Scolar Press, no. 68 (Menston, 1968).

GILLINGHAM, JOHN, *The English in the Twelfth Century: Imperialism, National Identity and Political Values* (Woodbridge: Boydell, 2000).

GÖRLACH, MANFRED, *Introduction to Early Modern English* (Cambridge: Cambridge University Press, 1978).

——'Regional and Social Variation,' in Lass (ed.), *The Cambridge History of the English Language*, iii. *1476–1776*, 459–538.

GREEN, JUDITH A., *The Aristocracy of Norman England* (Cambridge: Cambridge University Press, 1997).

GREEN, RICHARD FIRTH, *Poets and Princepleasers: Literature and the English Court in the Late Middle Ages* (Toronto: University of Toronto Press, 1980).

——'The *Familia Regis* and the *Familia Cupidinis*,' in Scattergood and Sherborne (eds.), *English Court Culture in the Later Middle Ages*, 87–108.

GRICE, H. P., 'Logic and Conversation,' in Peter Cole and Jerry L. Morgan (eds.), *Syntax and Semantics*, iii. *Speech Acts* (New York: Academic Press, 1975), 41–58.

GRIFFITHS, JOHN (ed.), *Statutes of the University of Oxford Codified in the Year 1636 under the Authority of Archbishop Laud* (Oxford: Clarendon, 1888).

GRILLO, R. D., *Dominant Languages: Language and Hierarchy in Britain and France* (Cambridge: Cambridge University Press, 1989).

GUMPERZ, JOHN J., and DELL HYMES (eds.), *Directions in Sociolinguistics: The Ethnography of Communication* (New York: Holt, Rinehart

& Winston, Inc., 1972).

HALLIDAY, M. A. K., *Language as Social Semiotic: The Social Interpretation of Language and Meaning* (London: Edward Arnold, 1978).

HANNA III, RALPH, 'Alliterative Poetry,' in David Wallace (ed.), *The Cambridge History of Medieval English*, 488–511.

HART, W. M., 'The Reeve's Tale,' in W. F. Bryan and Germaine Dempster (eds.), *Sources and Analogues of Chaucer's Canterbury Tales* (Chicago: University of Chicago Press, 1941), 124–47.

HASTINGS, ADRIAN, *The Construction of Nationhood: Ethnicity, Religion and Nationalism* (Cambridge: Cambridge University Press, 1997).

HAUGEN, EINAR, *Language Conflict and Language Planning: The Case of Modern Norwegian* (Cambridge, Mass.: Harvard University Press, 1966).

——*The Ecology of Language*, ed. Anwar S. Dil (Stanford, Calif.: Stanford University Press, 1972).

——'Language Fragmentation in Scandinavia: Revolt of the Minorities,' in Haugen, J. Derrick McClure, and Derick S. Thomson (eds.), *Minority Languages Today* (Edinburgh: Edinburgh University Press, 1981).

HEATH, SHIRLEY BRICE, and FREDERICK MANDABACH, 'Language Status Decisions and the Law in the United States,' in Juan Cobarrubias and Joshua A. Fishman (eds.), *Progress in Language Planning: International Perspectives* (Berlin: Mouton, 1983), 87–105.

HERTOG, ERIK, *Chaucer's Fabliaux as Analogues* (Leuven: Leuven University Press, 1991).

HIGDEN, RALPH, *Polychronicon Ranulphi Higden Monachi Cestrensis together with the English Translations of John Trevisa and an unknown Writer of the Fifteenth Century*, ed. Churchill Babington and J. R. Lumbly, RS 41, 9 vols. (London: Longman, 1865–86).

HILL, JOHN M., 'Middle English Poets and the Word: Notes toward an Appraisal of Linguistic Consciousness,' *Criticism*, 16 (1974), 153–69.

HINES, JOHN, *The Fabliau in English* (London: Longman, 1993).

HODGE, ROBERT, and GUNTHER KRESS, *Language as Ideology*, 2nd edn. (London: Routledge, 1993).

HOLT, J. C., *Magna Carta*, 2nd edn. (Cambridge: Cambridge University Press, 1992).

HOROBIN, S. C. P., 'J. R. R. Tolkien as a Philologist: A Reconsideration of the Northernisms in Chaucer's *Reeve's Tale*,' *English Studies*, 82 (2001), 97–105.

HUDSON, ANNE (ed.), *The Premature Reformation: Wyclifite Texts and Lollard History* (Oxford: Clarendon, 1988).

HUDSON, R. A., *Sociolinguistics*, 2nd edn. (Cambridge: Cambridge University Press, 1996).

HYMES, DELL H., *Foundations in Sociolinguistics: An Ethnographic Approach* (Philadelphia: University of Pennsylvania Press, 1974).

——*Toward Linguistic Competence*, Texas Working Papers in Sociolinguistics, 16 (Austin, Tex.: University of Texas Press, 1982).

IGLESIAS-RÁBADE, LUIS, 'Norman England: A Historical Sociolinguistic Approach,' *Revista canaria de estudios ingleses*, 15 (1987), 101–12.

JACOB, E. F., 'What Were the "Provisions of Oxford"?' *History*, 9 (1924), 188–200.

——*Studies in the Period of Baronial Reform and Rebellion, 1258–67*, Oxford Studies in Social and Legal History, 8, ed. Sir Paul Vinogradoff (1925; rpt. New York: Octagon Books, 1974).

JENKINS, GERAINT H., RICHARD SUGGETT, and ERYN M. WHITE, 'The Welsh Language in Early Modern Wales,' in Jenkins (ed.), *The Welsh Language before the Industrial Revolution* (Cardiff: University of Wales Press, 1997), 45–122.

JOCELIN OF BRAKELOND, *The Chronicle*, ed. and trans. H. E. Butler (London: Thomas Nelson & Sons, 1949).

JOHN OF WORCESTER, *Florentii Wigorniensis Monachi Chronicon ex Chronicis*, ed. Benjamin Thorpe, 2 vols. (London: Sumptibus Societatis, 1899).

JONES, RICHARD FOSTER, *The Triumph of the English Language* (London: Oxford University Press, 1953).

JOSEPH, JOHN EARL, *Eloquence and Power: The Rise of Language Standards and Standard Languages* (New York: Blackwell, 1987).

JUSTICE, STEVEN, *Writing and Rebellion: England in 1381* (Berkeley and Los Angeles: University of California Press, 1994).

KEEN, MAURICE, *English Society in the Later Middle Ages 1348–1500* (London: Penguin, 1990).

KEMPE, MARGERY, *The Book of Margery Kempe*, ed. Sanford Brown Meech and Hope Emily Allen, EETS os 212 (London: Oxford University Press, 1940).

KIBRE, PEARL, *The Nations in the Mediaeval Universities* (Cambridge, Mass.: Mediaeval Academy of America, 1948).

KNIGHTON, HENRY, *Knighton's Chronicle, 1337–1396*, ed. and trans. G. H. Martin (Oxford: Clarendon, 1995).

KOLVE, V. A., *Chaucer and the Imagery of Narrative: The First Five*

Canterbury Tales (Stanford, Calif.: Stanford University Press, 1984).

KRISTOL, ANDRES M., 'L'intellectuel "anglo-norman" face à la pluralité des langues: le témoignage implicite du MS Oxford, Magdalen Lat. 188,' in Trotter (ed.), *Multilingualism in Later Medieval Britain*, 37–52.

LABARGE, MARGARET WADE, *A Baronial Household of the Thirteenth Century* (Totowa, NJ: Barnes & Noble, 1980).

LABOV, WILLIAM, 'On the Mechanism of Linguistic Change,' in Gumperz and Hymes (eds.), *Directions in Sociolinguistics*, 512–38.

——*Sociolinguistic Patterns* (Philadelphia: University of Pennsylvania Press, 1972).

——'The Study of Language in Its Social Context,' in J. B. Pride and Janet Holmes (eds.), *Sociolinguistics: Selected Readings* (Harmondsworth: Penguin, 1972), 180–202.

——'On the Use of the Present to Explain the Past,' in Philip Baldi and Ronald N. Werth (eds.), *Readings in Historical Phonology: Chapters in the Theory of Sound Change* (University Park, Pa.: Pennsylvania State University Press, 1978), 275–312.

——*Principles of Linguistic Change*, i. *Internal Factors* (Oxford: Blackwell, 1994).

LAING, MARGARET (ed.), *Middle English Dialectology: Essays on Some Principles and Problems* (Aberdeen: Aberdeen University Press, 1989).

——and KEITH WILLIAMSON (eds.), *Speaking in Our Tongues: Proceedings of a Colloquium on Medieval Dialectology and Related Disciplines* (Cambridge: D. S. Brewer, 1994).

LAITIN, DAVID D., *Language Repertoires and State Construction in Africa* (Cambridge: Cambridge University Press, 1992).

LAKOFF, GEORGE, *Women, Fire, and Dangerous Things: What Categories Reveal about the Mind* (Chicago: University of Chicago Press, 1987).

LANGLAND, WILLIAM, *Piers Plowman*, ed. Robert Crowley (London, 1550).

——*Piers Plowman: The B Version*, rev. edn., ed. George Kane and E. Talbot Donaldson (Berkeley and Los Angeles: University of California Press, 1988).

LASS, ROGER, *On Explaining Language Change* (Cambridge: Cambridge University Press, 1980).

——*Historical Linguistics and Language Change* (Cambridge: Cambridge University Press, 1997).

LASS, ROGER (ed.), *The Cambridge History of the English Language*, iii. *1476–1776* (Cambridge: Cambridge University Press, 1999).

——'Phonology and Morphology,' in id. (ed.), *The Cambridge History of the English Language*, iii. *1476–1776*, 56–186.

LEECH, GEOFFREY N., *Principles of Pragmatics* (London: Longman, 1983).

LEEDHAM-GREENE, E. S., *A Concise History of the University of Cambridge* (Cambridge: Cambridge University Press, 1996).

LEITH, DICK, *A Social History of English*, 2nd edn. (London: Routledge, 1997).

LERER, SETH, 'The Genre of the Grave and the Origins of the Middle English Lyric,' *Modern Language Quarterly*, 58 (1997), 127–61.

LEVINSON, STEPHEN C., *Pragmatics* (Cambridge: Cambridge University Press, 1983).

LEWIS, GEOFFREY, *The Turkish Language Reform: a Catastrophic Success* (Oxford: Oxford University Press, 1999).

LIPPI-GREEN, ROSINA, *English with an Accent: Language, Ideology, and Discrimination in the United States* (London: Routledge, 1997).

LOOBY, CHRISTOPHER, *Voicing America: Language, Literary Form, and the Origins of the United States* (Chicago: University of Chicago Press, 1996).

LYDGATE, JOHN, *Troy Book*, ed. Henry Bergen, EETS ES 97, 103, 106, 126 (London: Kegan Paul, 1906–35).

MACAULAY, RONALD, *Locating Dialect in Discourse: The Language of Honest Men and Bonnie Lasses in Ayr* (New York: Oxford University Press, 1991).

MACHAN, TIM WILLIAM, 'Language Contact and *Piers Plowman*,' *Speculum*, 69 (1994), 359–85.

——Review of *England the Nation: Language, Literature, and National Identity, 1290–1340* by Thorlac Turville-Petre, *Journal of English and Germanic Philology*, 96 (1997), 437–9.

——'Language and Society in Twelfth-Century England,' in Taavitsainen et al. (eds.), *Placing Middle English in Context*, 43–66.

——'Politics and the Middle English Language,' *Studies in the Age of Chaucer*, 24 (2002), 317–24.

——'Writing the Failure of Speech in *Pearl*,' in Mark C. Amodio (ed.), *Unbinding Proteus: New Directions in Oral Theory* (Tempe, Ariz.: Medieval and Renaissance Texts and Studies, 2003).

——and CHARLES T. SCOTT (eds.), *English in Its Social Contexts: Essays in Historical Sociolinguistics* (New York: Oxford University Press, 1992).

McCrum, Robert, William Cran, and Robert MacNeil, *The Story of English* (London: BBC Books, 1992).

Maddicott, J. R., *Simon de Montfort* (Cambridge: Cambridge University Press, 1994).

Manly, John Matthews, *Some New Light on Chaucer* (1926; rpt. Gloucester, Mass.: Peter Smith, 1959).

Mann, Jill, *Chaucer and Medieval Estates Satire: The Literature of Social Classes and the 'General Prologue' to the 'Canterbury Tales'* (Cambridge: Cambridge University Press, 1973).

Mannyng, Robert, *Handlyng Synne*, ed. Idelle Sullens (Binghamton, NY: Medieval and Renaissance Texts and Studies, 1983).

Map, Walter, *De Nugis Curialium: Courtiers' Trifles*, ed. and trans. M. R. James, rev. C. N. L. Brooke and R. A. B. Mynors (Oxford: Clarendon, 1983).

Mathew, Gervase, *The Court of Richard II* (London: John Murray, 1968).

Meier, Hans H., 'Past Presences of Older Scots Abroad,' in Caroline Macafee and Iseabail Macleod (eds.), *The Nuttis Schell: Essays on the Scots Language presented to A. J. Aitken* (Aberdeen: Aberdeen University Press, 1987).

Metcalf, Allan A., 'Sir Gawain and *You*,' *Chaucer Review*, 5 (1971), 165–78.

Michael, Ian, *English Grammatical Categories and the Tradition to 1800* (Cambridge: Cambridge University Press, 1970).

Michel, Dan, *Ayenbite of Inwyt*, ed. Richard Morris, EETS os 23 (London: Trübner, 1866).

Middle English Dictionary, ed. Hans Kurath et al. (Ann Arbor: University of Michigan, 1952–2001).

Milroy, James, '*Pearl*: The Verbal Texture and the Linguistic Theme,' *Neophilologus*, 55 (1971), 195–208.

——*Linguistic Variation and Change: On the Historical Sociolinguistics of English* (Oxford: Blackwell, 1992).

——'Middle English Dialectology,' in Blake (ed.), *The Cambridge History of the English Language*, ii. *1066–1476*, 156–206.

——and Lesley Milroy, *Authority in Language: Investigating Language Prescription and Standardisation* (London: Routledge, 1985).

Milroy, Lesley, *Language and Social Networks*, 2nd edn. (Oxford: Blackwell, 1987).

——*Observing and Analysing Natural Language: A Critical Account of Sociolinguistic Method* (Oxford: Blackwell, 1987).

MORTIMER, RICHARD, *Angevin England 1154–1258* (Oxford: Black-well, 1994).

MUFWENE, SALIKOKO S., *The Ecology of Language Evolution* (Cambridge: Cambridge University Press, 2001).

MUGGLESTONE, LYNDA, *'Talking Proper': The Rise of Accent as Social Symbol* (Oxford: Clarendon, 1995).

MULCASTER, RICHARD, *The First Part of the Elementarie* (London: Thomas Vautroullier, 1582), rpt. Scolar Press, no. 219 (Menston, 1970).

MULLINGER, JAMES BASS, *The University of Cambridge*, 3 vols. (1873–1911; rpt. New York: Johnson Reprint, 1969).

MUSCATINE, CHARLES, *Chaucer and the French Tradition: A Study in Style and Meaning* (Berkeley and Los Angeles: University of California Press, 1957).

——'Courtly Literature and Vulgar Language,' in Glyn S. Burgess (ed.), *Court and Poet: Selected Proceedings of the Third Congress of the International Courtly Literature Society* (Liverpool: Francis Cairns, 1981), 1–19.

——*The Old French Fabliaux* (New Haven: Yale University Press, 1986).

MYERS, WELDON T., *The Relations of Latin and English as Living Languages during the Time of Milton* (Charlottesville, Va.: University Press of Virginia, 1912).

The Myroure of Oure Ladye, ed. John Henry Blunt, EETS ES 19 (London: Trübner, 1873).

NEVALINEN, TERTTU, 'Early Modern English Lexis and Semantics,' in Lass (ed.), *The Cambridge History of the English Language*, iii. *1476–1776*, 332–458.

NICHOLAS, DAVID, *The Growth of the Medieval City: From Late Antiquity to the Early Fourteenth Century* (London: Longman, 1997).

NICHOLLS, JONATHAN, *The Matter of Courtesy: Medieval Courtesy Books and the Gawain-Poet* (Woodbridge: D. S. Brewer, 1985).

Of Arthour and Merlin, ed. O. D. Macrae-Gibson, EETS OS 268 and 269 (London: Oxford University Press, 1973, 1979).

OLSON, GLENDING, 'The *Reeve's Tale* as a Fabliau,' *Modern Language Quarterly*, 35 (1974), 219–30.

ORME, NICHOLAS, *English Schools in the Middle Ages* (Oxford: Methuen, 1973).

——*Education and Society in Medieval and Renaissance England* (London: Hambleton Press, 1989).

Oxford English Dictionary, 2nd. edn., ed. J. A. Simpson and E. S. C.

Weiner (Oxford: Clarendon, 1996).

The Oxford Latin Dictionary, ed. P. G. W. Glare (Oxford: Clarendon, 1982).

PADLEY, G. A., *Grammatical Theory in Western Europe, 1500–1700: Trends in Vernacular Grammar*, 2 vols. (Cambridge: Cambridge University Press, 1985, 1988).

PAGE, R. I., 'How Long Did the Scandinavian Language Survive in England? The Epigraphical Evidence,' in Peter Clemoes and Kathleen Hughes (eds.), *England Before the Conquest: Studies in Primary Sources Presented to Dorothy Whitelock* (Cambridge: Cambridge University Press, 1971), 165–81.

PARIS, MATTHEW, *Chronica Majora*, ed. Henry Richards Luard, RS 57, 7 vols. (London: Longman, 1872–83).

PARKES, MALCOLM B., and RICHARD BEADLE (eds.), *The Poetical Works of Geoffrey Chaucer: A Facsimile of Cambridge University Library MS Gg. 4.27*, 3 vols. (Norman, Okla.: Pilgrim Books, 1979–80).

PEARSALL, DEREK, 'Hoccleve's *Regement of Princes*: The Poetics of Royal Self-Representation,' *Speculum*, 69 (1994), 386–410.

——'Chaucer and Englishness,' *Publications of the British Academy*, 101 (1999), 79–99.

——'The Idea of Englishness in the Fifteenth Century,' in Cooney (ed.), *Nation, Court and Culture*, 15–27.

PECOCK, REGINALD, *The Repressor of Over Much Blaming of the Clergy*, ed. Churchill Babington, RS 19, 2 vols. (London: Longman, 1860).

PELTERET, DAVID E., *Catalogue of English Post-Conquest Vernacular Documents* (Woodbridge: Boydell, 1990).

PENNYCOOK, ALASTAIR, *The Cultural Politics of English as an International Language* (London: Longman, 1994).

PETREY, SANDY, *Speech Acts and Literary Theory* (New York: Routledge, 1990).

PHILLIPSON, ROBERT, *Linguistic Imperialism* (Oxford: Oxford University Press, 1992).

PLUMMER, JOHN, 'Signifying the Self: Language and Identity in *Sir Gawain and the Green Knight*,' in Robert J. Blanch, Miriam Youngerman Miller, and Julian N. Wasserman (eds.), *Text and Matter: New Critical Perspectives of the Pearl-Poet* (Troy, NY: Whitson, 1991), 195–212.

POLLOCK, SIR FREDERICK, and FREDERIC WILLIAM MAITLAND, *The History of English Law before the Time of Edward I*, 2nd edn., 2 vols. (Cambridge: Cambridge University Press, 1903).

POOLE, AUSTIN LANE, *From Domesday Book to Magna Carta 1087–1216*, 2nd edn. (Oxford: Clarendon, 1955).

POWICKE, SIR F. MAURICE, *King Henry III and the Lord Edward: The Community of the Realm in the Thirteenth Century*, 2 vols. (Oxford: Clarendon, 1947).

——*The Thirteenth Century 1216–1307*, 2nd edn. (Oxford: Clarendon, 1962).

PREST, JOHN (ed.), *The Illustrated History of Oxford University* (Oxford: Oxford University Press, 1993).

PRESTWICH, MICHAEL, *English Politics in the Thirteenth Century* (New York: St. Martin's Press, 1990).

The Promptorium Parvulorum, ed. A. L. Mayhew, EETS ES 102 (London: Oxford University Press, 1908).

PUTTENHAM, GEORGE, *The Arte of English Poesie* (London: Richard Field, 1589), rpt. Scolar Press, no. 110 (Menston, 1968).

RALPH OF COGGESHALL, *Radulphi de Coggeshall Chronicon anglicanum*, ed. Joseph Stevenson, RS 66 (London: Longman, 1875).

RICHARD OF DEVIZES, *The Chronicle of Richard of Devizes of the Time of King Richard the First*, ed. and trans. John T. Appleby (London: Thomas Nelson & Sons, 1963).

RICHARDSON, H. G., and G. O. SAYLES, 'The Provisions of Oxford: A Forgotten Document and Some Comments,' *Bulletin of the John Rylands Library*, 17 (1933), 291–321.

——(eds.), *Select Cases of Procedure without Writ under Henry III* (London: Bernard Quaritch, 1941).

RICHTER, MICHAEL, *Sprache und Gesellschaft im Mittelalter: Untersuchungen zur Mündlichen Kommunikation in England von der Mitte des Elften bis zum Beginn des Vierzehnten Jahrhunderts* (Stuttgart: Anton Hiersemann, 1979).

——*Studies in Medieval Language and Culture* (Dublin: Four Courts Press, 1995).

RIDDY, FELICITY (ed.), *Regionalism in Late Medieval Manuscripts and Texts: Essays Celebrating the Publication of 'A Linguistic Atlas of Late Mediaeval England'* (Woodbridge: D. S. Brewer, 1991).

RIDGEWAY, H. W., 'King Henry III and the "Aliens," 1236–1272,' in P. R. Coss and S. D. Lloyd (eds.), *Thirteenth Century England* (Woodbridge: Boydell, 1988), ii. 81–92.

——'Foreign Favourites and Henry III's Problems of Patronage, 1247–58,' *English Historical Review*, 104 (1989), 590–610.

RISHANGER, WILLIAM DE, *The Chronicle of William de Rishanger, of the The Barons' Wars, the Miracles of Simon de Montfort* (London:

The Camden Society, 1840).

RISSANEN, MATTI et al. (eds.), *History of Englishes: New Methods and Interpretations in Historical Linguistics* (Berlin: Mouton de Gruyter, 1992).

ROBERT OF GLOUCESTER, *The Metrical Chronicle*, ed. William Aldis Wright, RS 86, 2 vols. (London: Spottiswoode, 1887).

ROGER OF HOVEDEN, *Chronica Magistri Rogeri de Houedene*, ed. William Stubbs, RS 51, 4 vols. (London: Longman, 1868–71).

ROGER OF WENDOVER, *Rogeri de Wendover Chronica, sive Flores Historiarum* (London: Sumptibus Societatis, 1841).

ROMAINE, SUZANNE, *Socio-historical Linguistics: Its Status and Methodology* (Cambridge: Cambridge University Press, 1982).

——*Bilingualism*, 2nd edn. (Oxford: Blackwell, 1995).

ROSS, WILLIAM G., *Forging New Freedoms: Nativism, Education, and the Constitution, 1917–1927* (Lincoln, Nebr.: University of Nebraska Press, 1994).

ROTHWELL, W., 'The Role of French in Thirteenth-Century England,' *Bulletin of the John Rylands Library*, 58 (1976), 445–66.

——'A quelle époque a-t-on cessé de parler français en Angleterre?', in Robert Lafont et al. (eds.), *Mélanges de Philologie Romane offerts à Charles Camproux*, 2 vols. (Montpelier: Université Paul-Valéry, 1978), ii. 1075–89.

——'Language and Government in Medieval England,' *Zeitschrift für Französische Sprache und Literatur*, 93 (1983), 258–70.

——'Chaucer and Stratford atte Bowe,' *Bulletin of the John Rylands Library*, 74 (1992), 3–28.

SALMON, VIVIAN, 'Orthography and Punctuation,' in Lass (ed.), *The Cambridge History of the English Language*, iii. *1476–1776*, 13–55.

SAMUELS, M. L., 'Spelling and Dialect in the Late and Post-Medieval Periods,' in Michael Benskin and Samuels (eds.), *So meny people longages and tonges: philological essays in Scots and mediaeval English presented to Angus McIntosh* (Edinburgh: Middle English Dialect Project, 1981), 43–54.

——'The Great Scandinavian Belt,' in Laing (ed.), *Middle English Dialectology*, 106–22.

——'Some Applications of Middle English Dialectology,' in Laing (ed.), *Middle English Dialectology*, 64–80.

SANKOFF, GILLIAN, *The Social Life of Language* (Philadelphia: University of Pennsylvania Press, 1980).

SAVILLE-TROIKE, MURIEL, *The Ethnography of Communication: An Introduction*, 2nd edn. (Oxford: Blackwell, 1989).

SCAGLIONE, ALDO (ed.), *The Emergence of National Languages* (Ravenna: Longo Editore, 1984).

SCATTERGOOD, V. J., and J. W. SHERBORNE (eds.), *English Court Culture in the Later Middle Ages* (New York: St. Martin's Press, 1983).

SHIRLEY, WALTER WADDINGTON (ed.), *Royal and Other Historical Letters Illustrative of the Reign of Henry III*, RS 27, 2 vols. (London: Longman, 1862–6).

SHORT, IAN, '*Tam Angli quam Franci*: Self-Definition in Anglo-Norman England,' in Christopher Harper-Bill (ed.), *Anglo-Norman Studies*, 18 (Woodbridge: Boydell, 1996), 153–75.

SKEAT, WALTER W., 'The Oxford MS. of the Only English Proclamation of Henry III,' *Transactions of the Philological Society*, 1880–1, 169–78.

SKUTNABB-KANGAS, TOVE, and ROBERT PHILLIPSON, 'Linguistic Human Rights, Past and Present,' in eid. (eds.), *Linguistic Human Rights*, 71–110.

——(eds.), *Linguistic Human Rights: Overcoming Linguistic Discrimination* (Berlin: Mouton de Gruyter, 1994).

SMITH, JEREMY, 'The Use of English: Language Contact, Dialect Variation, and Written Standardisation During the Middle English Period,' in Machan and Scott (eds.), *English in Its Social Contexts*, 47–68.

——'The Great Vowel Shift in the North of England and Some Forms in Chaucer's Reeve's Tale,' *Neuphilologische Mitteilungen*, 95 (1994), 433–7.

——*An Historical Study of English: Function, Form and Change* (London: Routledge, 1996).

——'Standard Language in Early Middle English?', in Irma Taavitsainen et al. (eds.), *Placing Middle English in Context*, 125–39.

SMYTH, ALFRED P., 'The Emergence of English Identity, 700–1000,' in Smyth (ed.), *Medieval Europeans: Studies in Ethnic Identity and National Perspectives in Medieval Europe* (London: Macmillan, 1998), 24–52.

SPEARING, A. C., *Criticism and Medieval Poetry*, 2nd edn. (London: Edward Arnold, 1972).

STACEY, ROBERT C., *Politics, Policy, and Finance under Henry III 1216–1245* (Oxford: Clarendon, 1987).

STALEY, LYNN, *Margery Kempe's Dissenting Fictions* (University Park, Pa.: The Pennsylvania State University Press, 1994).

——*The Book of Margery Kempe* (Kalamazoo, Mich.: TEAMS, 1996).

STENTON, DORIS MARY (ed.), *Rolls of the Justices in Eyre, Being the*

Rolls of Pleas and Assizes for Yorkshire 3 Henry III (London: Bernard Quaritch, 1937).

STOCK, BRIAN, *The Implications of Literacy: Written Language and Models of Interpretation in the Eleventh and Twelfth Centuries* (Princeton: Princeton University Press, 1983).

STONES, LIONEL, and SEYMOUR PHILLIPS, 'English in the Public Records: Three Late Thirteenth-Century Examples,' *Nottingham Medieval Studies*, 32 (1988), 196–206.

STRAYER, JOSEPH R. (ed.), *Dictionary of the Middle Ages*, 10 vols. (New York: Charles Scribner's Sons, 1983).

STUBBS, MICHAEL, *Discourse Analysis: The Sociolinguistic Analysis of Natural Language* (Chicago: University of Chicago Press, 1983).

STUBBS, WILLIAM, *Select Charters and Other Illustrations of English Constitutional History from the Earliest Times to the Reign of Edward the First*, 9th edn., ed. H. W. C. Davis (Oxford: Clarendon, 1913).

SWAN, MARY, and ELAINE M. TREHARE (eds.), *Rewriting Old English in the Twelfth Century* (Cambridge: Cambridge University Press, 2000).

TAAVITSAINEN, IRMA et al. (eds.), *Placing Middle English in Context* (Berlin: Mouton, 2000).

TANNEN, DEBORAH, *Talking Voices: Repetition, Dialogue, and Imagery in Conversational Discourse* (Cambridge: Cambridge University Press, 1989).

'Tatars to Drop Cyrillic Alphabet for Roman,' *The New York Times*, 31 August 2000, A5.

TATALOVICH, RAYMOND, *Nativism Reborn? The Official English Language Movement and the American States* (Lexington, Ky.: University Press of Kentucky, 1995).

Three Middle-English Versions of the Rule of St. Benet, ed. Ernst A. Kock, EETS OS 120 (London: Kegan Paul, Trench, Trübner & Co., 1902).

TÖBLER, ADOLF, and ERHARD LOMMATZSCH, *Altfranzösisches Wörterbuch* (Berlin: Weidmann, 1925–).

TOLKIEN, J. R. R., 'Chaucer as a Philologist: *The Reeve's Tale*,' *Transactions of the Philological Society* (1934), 1–70.

——and E. V. GORDON (eds.), *Sir Gawain and the Green Knight*, 2nd edn., ed. Norman Davis (Oxford: Clarendon, 1967).

TOLLEFSON, JAMES W., *Planning Language, Planning Inequality: Language Policy in the Community* (London: Longman, 1991).

TOON, THOMAS E., 'The Social and Political Contexts of Language Change in Anglo-Saxon England,' in Machan and Scott (eds.), *English in Its Social Contexts*, 28–46.

TREHARNE, R. F., *The Baronial Plan of Reform, 1258–1263* (Manchester: Manchester University Press, 1932).

——*Simon de Montfort and Baronial Reform: Thirteenth-Century Essays*, ed. E. B. Fryde (London: The Hambledon Press, 1986).

——AND I. J. SANDERS (eds.), *Documents of the Baronial Movement of Reform and Rebellion 1258–1267* (Oxford: Clarendon, 1973).

TREVISA, JOHN, *Polychronicon Ranulphi Higden Monachi Cestrensis together with the English Translations of John Trevisa and an Unknown Writer of the Fifteenth Century*, ed. Churchill Babington and J. R. Lumbly, RS 41, 9 vols. (London: Longman, 1865–86).

TROTTER, D. A. (ed.), *Multilingualism in Later Medieval Britain* (Cambridge: D. S. Brewer, 2000).

TRUDGILL, PETER, *On Dialect: Social and Geographical Perspectives* (New York: New York University Press, 1983).

TURVILLE-PETRE, THORLAC, *England the Nation: Language, Literature, and National Identity, 1290–1340* (Oxford: Clarendon, 1996).

USK, THOMAS, *Testament of Love*, in W. W. Skeat (ed.), *Complete Works of Geoffrey Chaucer*, vii. *Chaucerian and Other Pieces* (Oxford: Oxford University Press, 1897).

VITALIS, ORDERIC, *The Ecclesiastical History of Orderic Vitalis*, ed. and trans. Marjorie Chibnall, 6 vols. (Oxford: Clarendon, 1969–80).

WALLACE, DAVID (ed.), *The Cambridge History of Medieval English Literature* (Cambridge: Cambridge University Press, 1999).

WARDHAUGH, RONALD, *How Conversation Works* (Oxford: Blackwell, 1985).

WARREN, W. L., *The Governance of Norman and Angevin England 1086–1272* (Stanford, Calif.: Stanford University Press, 1987).

WATSON, FOSTER, *The English Grammar Schools to 1660: Their Curriculum and Practice* (Cambridge: Cambridge University Press, 1908).

——*The Old Grammar Schools* (Cambridge: Cambridge University Press, 1916).

WATSON, NICHOLAS, 'Censorship and Cultural Change in Late-Medieval England: Vernacular Theology, the Oxford Translation Debate, and Arundel's Constitutions of 1409,' *Speculum*, 70 (1995), 822–64.

——'Conceptions of the Word: The Mother Tongue and the Incarnation of God,' *New Medieval Literatures*, 1 (1997), 85–124.

WEINREICH, URIEL, WILLIAM LABOV, and MARVIN I. HERZOG, 'Empirical Foundations for a Theory of Language Change,' in W. P. Lehmann and Yakov Malkiel (eds.), *Directions for Historical Linguistics: A Symposium* (Austin, Tex.: University of Texas Press), 95–188.

WENZEL, SIEGFRIED, *Verses in Sermons: 'Fasciculus Morum' and Its Middle English Poems* (Cambridge, Mass.: Mediaeval Academy of America, 1978).

——*Macaronic Sermons: Bilingualism and Preaching in Late-Medieval England* (Ann Arbor: University of Michigan Press, 1994).

WILLIAM OF MALMESBURY, *De Gestis Pontificum Anglorum*, ed. N. E. S. A. Hamilton, RS 52 (London: Longman, 1870).

——*De Gestis Regum Anglorum Libri Quinque; Historiae Novellae Libri Tres*, ed. William Stubbs, RS 90, 2 vols. (London: Eyre & Spottiswoode, 1887–9).

——*The Historia Novella*, ed. and trans. K. R. Potter (London: Thomas Nelson & Sons, 1955).

WILLIAM OF NASSYNGTON, *Speculum Vite*, in *Englische Studien*, 7 (1884).

WILLIAMS, ANN, *The English and the Norman Conquest* (Woodbridge: Boydell, 1995).

WILLIAMS, JOSEPH M., '"O! When Degree is Shak'd": Sixteenth-Century Anticipations of Some Modern Attitudes toward Usage,' in Machan and Scott (eds.), *English in Its Social Contexts*, 69–101.

WILSON, R. M., 'English and French in England 1100–1300,' *History*, 28 (1943), 37–60.

——*The Lost Literature of Medieval England* (London: Methuen, 1952).

WINSTANLEY, DENYS ARTHUR, *Unreformed Cambridge: A Study of Certain Aspects of the University in the Eighteenth Century* (Cambridge: Cambridge University Press, 1935).

WOGAN-BROWNE, JOCELYN et al. (eds.), *The Idea of the Vernacular: An Anthology of Middle English Literary Theory, 1280–1520* (University Park, Pa.: Pennsylvania State University Press, 1999).

WOODBINE, GEORGE E., 'The Language of English Law,' *Speculum*, 18 (1943), 395–436.

WRIGHT, LAURA, 'Macaronic Writing in a London Archive, 1380–1480,' in Rissanen (ed.), *History of Englishes*, 762–70.

——*Sources of London English: Medieval Thames Vocabulary* (Oxford: Clarendon, 1996).

——(ed.), *The Development of Standard English, 1300–1800* (Cambridge: Cambridge University Press, 2000).

WRIGHT, THOMAS (ed.), *Political Songs of England: From the Reign of John to that of Edward II*, rev. edn., ed. Peter Coss (Cambridge: Cambridge University Press, 1996).

WRIGHT, THOMAS L., '*Luf-Talkyng* in *Sir Gawain and the Green Knight*,' in Miriam Youngerman Miller and Jane Chance (eds.), *Approaches to Teaching 'Sir Gawain and the Green Knight'* (New York: The Modern Language Association of America, 1986), 79–86.

WYCLIF, JOHN, *The English Works of Wyclif*, ed. Frederic David Matthew, EETS os 74 (London: Trübner, 1880).

Index